A Vision
with a Task

A Vision with a Task

*Christian Schooling
for Responsive Discipleship*

Edited by
Gloria Goris Stronks
and
Doug Blomberg

With contributions from
Doug Blomberg, Peter P. DeBoer,
Robert Koole, Gloria Goris Stronks,
Harro W. Van Brummelen,
and Steven C. Vryhof

Baker Books
A Division of Baker Book House Co
Grand Rapids, Michigan 49516

© 1993 by Calvin Center for Christian Scholarship

Published by Baker Books
a division of Baker Book House Company
P.O. Box 6287, Grand Rapids, MI 49516-6287

Printed in the United States of America

Library of Congress Cataloging-in-Publication Data

A vision with a task : Christian schooling for responsive discipleship / edited by
Gloria Goris Stronks & Doug Blomberg.
      p.   cm.
   Includes bibliographical references and index.
   ISBN 0-8010-8360-5
      1. Christian education—Philosophy 2. Church schools—United States.
   3. Church schools—Canada. 4. Christian Reformed Church—Education.
   5. Reformed Church—Education. I. Stronks, Gloria Goris. II. Blomberg,
   Doug.
   BV1464.V585   1993
   377′.8′0973—dc20   93-30275

Contents

Contributors

Doug Blomberg, Editor

Lecturer, National Institute for Christian Education, Australia. Formerly teacher and vice principal, Mount Evelyn Christian School. Ph.D. University of Sydney. Author of "Curriculum Guidelines for the Christian School" and "Toward a Christian Theory of Knowledge" for No Icing on the Cake (1980). Has written many articles and presented workshops and addresses in Australia, Canada, and the United States.

Peter P. DeBoer

Professor of education, Calvin College. Ph.D. University of Chicago. Author of Shifts in Curriculum Theory for Christian Education (1983), The Wisdom of Practice: Studies of Teaching in Christian Elementary and Middle Schools (1989), and co-author of Annotated List of Chicago Tribune Editorials on Elementary and Secondary Education in the U.S., 1852–1971 (1992). Has contributed chapters to several books, published numerous articles, and made presentations in the United States and Canada on Christian education.

Robert Koole

Education coordinator for Society of Christian Schools in British Columbia. Formerly, teacher and assistant principal at Edmonton Christian High School. M.Ed. University of Alberta. Co-author of Man in Society (1980). Author of "The Social Studies" in Shaping School Curriculum (1977) and Christian Perspective for Teaching Social Studies (1990). Has presented workshops on curriculum and social studies for teachers' conventions in Alberta and British Columbia.

Gloria Goris Stronks, Coordinator

Professor of education, Calvin College. Ed.D. Northern Illinois University. Formerly on the faculty of Dordt College. Author of *The Christian Middle School: An Ethos of Caring* (1990). Has written numerous articles concerning education and made presentations in the United States, Europe, and Canada.

Harro Van Brummelen

Professor of education and assistant dean of social sciences and education, Trinity Western University. Ed.D. in curriculum studies (British Columbia). Author of *Walking with God in the Classroom* and numerous articles in books, journals, and brochures. Speaker on topics in education in Canada, United States, Australia, and South Africa.

Steven C. Vryhof

Doctoral candidate, University of Chicago. Analyzing the National Education Longitudinal Study (1988) data on CSI Schools. Former teacher at Illiana Christian High School. Coordinated the four "Chicago Conferences." Co-author of *12 Affirmations: Reformed Christian Schooling for the 21st Century* (1989).

Preface

This book is the result of a year of research sponsored by the Calvin Center for Christian Scholarship. To ensure that our study would be informed from the outset by people in the field, we chose to begin our work in the summer of 1991 with a conference of teachers, principals, board members, and parents. We invited eighteen of these conferees to address the question, "What one issue or aspect of Christian schooling is causing serious concern in your community today?"

Some of the issues they presented related to the mission of Christian schools: What is Christian education? What makes a Christian school distinctive? How can we define our identity in the context of the current discussions in education? Are we still able to provide Christian education when the cost is seemingly prohibitive?

Other topics related to curriculum: How can we organize and articulate curriculum in ways that are in keeping with our vision? Who designs and implements curricula in the Christian school? How can curricular and extracurricular programs help students develop an understanding of the need for justice in our society?

Some of the participants presented staff needs: Is the leadership we presently have adequate to the needs of a Christian school? What kind of leadership is needed? What keeps leadership from being as effective as it might be? What kinds of staff development will help us teach in ways appropriate to our vision of schooling?

Others pointed out that Christian schools should be places of community and caring: How can we help students learn to celebrate diversity in the schools we presently serve? What kind of school structure is needed for a climate of discipleship?

They brought to our attention the role of parents in Christian schooling: How can we help parents be an important part of their child's learning? When family structures have changed so much, is it still possible to speak of the church, the home, and the school working together to provide the education our children need?

Those who addressed these questions were Vern Boerman, Elaine Brouwer, Art De Jong, Tim Hoeksema, Mary Kooy, Rick Geertsma, Coni Huisman, Thelma Meyer, David Mulder, Harriet Potoka, Hilda Roukema, Tena Siebenga, Agnes Struik, Leo Van Arragon, Benita VanAndel, Judy Vos, Sheryl Wiers, and Bert Witvoet. After listening to the presentations and discussions that followed we felt ready to begin our work.

There were four full-time scholars on the team: Doug Blomberg, Peter DeBoer, Robert Koole, and Gloria Goris Stronks. The two adjunct scholars, Harro Van Brummelen and Steve Vryhof, were actively involved in all aspects of the project through their frequent visits and the intricacies of electronic mail.

Calvin College provided the team with offices that had a beautiful view of the campus, excellent computers, and a ready access to a superb library. The Calvin Center for Christian Scholarship granted funds that enabled us to visit more than fifty Christian schools in different parts of North America.

It was not easy for us to separate our study of Christian schools from the fact that each of us has given our professional lives to the service of those schools. How does one objectively examine what one loves, supports, and grieves over? We were helped to work through our biases by our school visits and the frankness with which teachers, principals, parents, board members, and students spoke to us.

Were the schools we visited communities of learning that reflected a unique vision? Many certainly were. In some schools the air was alive with learning and support. Teachers and students were actively engaged together in learning and leading each other to further learning. Other schools, however, were places where the actions of the teachers clearly implied they perceived their task to be little more than to deposit information in the heads of the students. Students who accumulated the most facts were the winners of the academic competition. Success was a matter of striving to win at different kinds of competition, whether social, athletic, musical, or academic, at the expense of a caring climate.

Most of the schools we visited fell somewhere between those two extremes. The people who spoke to us believe their own schools should continue to exist but wish they would be better, more distinctively Christian. Some expressed the concern that as a school grows older and more mature, energies go into maintaining the status quo and providing safe, comfortable environments for those who teach there. They recognized that Christian schools should be on guard against that tendency, but they weren't certain what changes were needed or how to get those changes to take place.

We also were helped to get a clear picture of Christian schools by interviews with numerous teachers, students, principals, parents, and board members. Among these were Laura Bartleson, Wayne Drost, Ron Grassmid, Adrian Guildemond, Juanita Harkema, Dirk Hart, Randell Hieres, Arthur Hill, Thomas Hoeksema, Lee Hollaar, Corrine Kass, Pieter Katerberg, Henry Kooy, Mary Kooy, Myra Kraker, Jan Lucas, Luis and Cathy Lugo, John Monsma, David M. Mulder, Rod Oosterhouse, Larry Plaisier, Jack Postma, Harriet Potoka, Richard Ravenhorst, Daniel Ribera, Jim Stapert, Joan Stob, Barry TerBeek, Steve Timmermans, Dan Vander Ark, John VanderHoek, Bob Van Wieren, Harley VerBeek, Judy Vos, David Wyngarden, and Henry Zuiderveen. There may be names we have omitted, but we trust that the ideas were remembered. Other people who provided insights, both in personal conversation and in writing, preferred to remain anonymous. All of these contributed significantly to our project.

We solicited advice from people we thought could contribute uniquely to our work. Among these were Anthony Fortosis, formerly with The Association of Christian Schools International, Sheri Haan of Christian Schools International, and Nicholas Wolterstorff of Yale University. We met and had lively conversations with the education faculties of Dordt College, Calvin College, The Institute for Christian Studies (Toronto), The King's College (Edmonton), Redeemer College, and Trinity Christian College.

Those who read and responded to our manuscript were Norma Boehm, Albert E. Greene, Joan Stob, Dan Vander Ark, and Judy Vos. Their comments were valuable and helped us make our manuscript more accessible to readers. Few projects are so indebted to other people and we are enormously grateful.

Kate Miller and Donna Romanowski greatly aided our work in the Center by recording interviews, organizing the bibliography, compiling the index, arranging meetings, and helping us with our computer problems, remaining cheerful all the while. We are thankful for the support provided by the CCCS director, Ron Wells, and by the Calvin Center Governing Board, chaired at that time by Ken Konyndyk of Calvin College's Philosophy Department. The director and board allowed us the freedom to work at our project in the way that seemed best to us. We gave the task of editing the book to Doug Blomberg and we sincerely appreciate all of his work, both during and following our period of residence. Doug in turn would like to acknowledge the assistance of Linda Triemstra at Baker Book House in bringing the book to its final form.

We tried to write a book that was informed by the realities facing Christian school communities in the 1990s. We live in a time when some school reformers are saying students in elementary and secondary schools need longer hours and more days in schools so they can do more of what they presently are doing. People who restructure schools tell us that schools need to be different because what has been done in the past has not been effective.

Because we believe Christian schools are places where teachers and students should live and learn to live as responsive disciples of Jesus Christ, Christian schools must be unique. The vision that drives these schools must affect the structure of the school, the length of the school year, the planning of the program, designing of units, instruction, and all other aspects of the school. We have attempted to describe these aspects of schools in which students will learn responsive discipleship.

This book was written primarily for teachers, but it discusses many matters that also concern parents and board members. While it specifically addresses Christian schools, we believe the ideas are important for Christians teaching in community schools. It is our hope that readers will discuss the book, challenge each other with the ideas, and come to a deeper understanding of how to make their own school the kind of school God wants it to be.

The six members of the team believe that Christian students and teachers should be engaged in collaborative endeavors creating a space for learning that allows them to share each other's joys and burdens in coming to know. Our experience with the collaboration of this study has taught us much about the personal learning that occurs when trying to clarify ideas and concepts for other team members. It took time and effort for us to understand that coming to consensus means discussing and reshaping our ideas rather than arguing and trying to force our beliefs on each other. We began the study eagerly for the sake of Christian schools. We ended it with a new regard for the importance of collaborative endeavors in learning and the importance of being responsive disciples in our own academic work.

Gloria Goris Stronks
Project Coordinator

Part **1**

Affirming the Vision

1

The Vision:

Schooling for Responsive Discipleship

Seeking God and His Kingdom

Annieville Christian Middle School is a new school. It advertises its overall goal as being "to provide a distinctive learning environment where academic, spiritual, social, and emotional needs are met . . . above all, [where students] come to understand their roles as Christ's servants in all areas of life." The school set out to integrate the curriculum around humanities and science/mathematics strands, and to use diverse teaching techniques to meet the needs of different learning types. Further, students would be involved in and responsible for their own learning, partly through exploratory electives and community-directed stewardship projects.

Annieville has attracted a multicultural clientele. Pupils with blond hair and fair skin constitute a visible minority. To the school's credit, students of different backgrounds interact as a homogeneous group. The biblical studies program is designed to meet the school's avowed aims. In the grade eight journals, for instance, students give personal interpretations and responses to various passages in the Gospel of Mark, with the teacher encouraging further thinking. A discussion of a tape on the roles people play in church leads to thoughtful responses with probing follow-up questions ("How does this relate to our school situation?"). In English, students do a great deal of journal and creative writing, some of it in collaborative settings, as they deepen their insight into what responsive discipleship entails.

Yet, little subject integration takes place, even within the strands. Long time blocks with a particular teacher are still arbitrarily divided into forty-five-minute slots. One lesson is dragged out to make it fit the time slot, even though the same teacher teaches the next subject. Subject organization still seems strictly according to traditional subject lines, and subject content prepares students more for future subject content than for life outside the school setting. Nothing is said about an important election held the day before. A Christian perspective is evident mainly in the opening devotions and Bible study. Two months into the school year, the school had done little to bind the student body together into a compassionate learning community where students pray and study and serve and rejoice together. Students sparkle with enthusiasm and creativity in some classes, but display mostly docile compliance in others.[1]

The Annieville Christian Middle School community did many things right when founding its new school. It prayerfully considered what types of school experiences would foster personal and communal discipleship enabling graduates to contribute redemptively to society. It concluded that it wanted its students to come to know God and learn to serve him in all areas of life. It explored the implications of biblical views of learning and of the person for learning-teaching situations for twelve-to-fifteen-year-olds. It developed a mission statement and a set of objectives. It explored how learning could be structured so that all students would feel they had a special role in the community of learning. It gave the principal and staff ample time for painstakingly planning the program prior to the start of the school. Annieville set out with high ideals.

The ideals that Annieville Christian School espouse may be summed up in one phrase: schooling for responsive discipleship. We share these ideals. In this introductory chapter, we want to give some substance to "responsive discipleship" by expanding on three of its essential aspects: unwrapping students' gifts, sharing each other's joys and burdens, and seeking *shalom*, that dynamic harmony of right relationships restored by God's grace. These dimensions are focused in our commitment to seek first God's kingdom and his righteousness and justice. We educate for a life of worshipful kingdom service, for a life of God-imaging love,

---

1. The school situations described in this chapter were observed by the authors, except for the one on ecology, which was described by a teacher during the conference with which our study began. All names in this chapter are fictitious.

truth, and justice. Our aim is that our students are made new in their attitudes and transformed by the renewing of their minds (Eph. 4:23; Rom. 12:2). We want Christian schools to claim and exercise the fruit of the Spirit. Like Christ, we seek to walk in love and make ourselves poor in order to enrich others (2 Cor. 8:9). None of this is possible, of course, without the sanctifying renewal of the Holy Spirit, but that does not detract from our responsibility to be instruments of the Spirit in our educational tasks.

These three dimensions do not encompass all that can be said about discipleship, but the letters of Paul in general and Philippians 2 in particular make their importance clear. In a secular age in which self-centered, individualistic autonomy and materialism prevail, we believe that the focused learning experiences that schools provide ought to contribute to each of these three. Christian schools help students to unfold their gifts so that they "shine like stars in the universe as [they] hold out the word of life" (Phil. 2:15–16). They encourage teachers and students to be willing sharers of joy and bearers of burdens, looking to the interests of others (Phil. 2:4). And schools as learning communities seek and celebrate shalom as the participants are called to continue to work out their salvation with fear and trembling in and through their learning and teaching (Phil. 2:13).

Despite their best intentions, schools (like Annieville) will fall short of these ideals. No matter what schools do, they will not always touch their students in ways that they intend and hope. At Annieville, the school community asked the right questions and the staff planned painstakingly—yet teachers wrestled with daily failings. Here we have to remember Christ's promises that if we continue to seek his kingdom and righteousness and justice, in and through our educational program as elsewhere, we need not be anxious. God will grant our students what they need. The power of Christ's Spirit is mightier than the forces of darkness, and his grace is perfected in the shortcomings of teachers and students. God's gift is that every day we again have the possibility of being God's work of art, created in Jesus Christ to do good works.

As responsive disciples of Jesus Christ, Christians live between memory and vision. Our lives in the present occupy that thin slice of time between the past and the future, between the establishment of God's kingdom (with Christ's atoning sacrifice) and its completion (with his imminent return). Through God's grace we may erect signposts for that kingdom. The Christian school does so by seeking to conserve, discern, and reform, and in turn encourages its students to become conservers, discerners, and reformers within the kingdom contours of the Bible.

First, the Christian school community conserves and passes on the story and world view of its tradition: its meaning, purpose, roots, cultural anchorpoints, and accumulated wisdom. In a society driven by change and wild swings in values, the Christian school emphasizes the nonnegotiables for a meaningful life: faith in God, trust in his Word, personal salvation in Christ, reliance on his Spirit, commitment to family and community, a calling of service and self-sacrifice. It combats the rootlessness and loss of meaning so prevalent in modern life. Telling the Christian story, it conserves the truths of the gospel and uses them to answer questions for the child such as, "Who am I? Why am I here? What is life for?"

Second, as discerner, the Christian school discerns the spirits of our time. It encourages critical analysis of the world and human experience. It never fears inquiry; it promotes different ways of knowing and new insights. It tests all things and holds fast to the good. It combats the anti-intellectualism and fuzzy thinking of the day.

Third, the Christian school inquires how the tradition it is conserving leads to reforming society. It is guided by a vision of a new and better world: the kingdom of God. It models and teaches a life of reforming discipleship that is responsive to God as it works in creation and in the structures of society. It seeks to reform injustice and unrighteousness and strife.

In the Christian school, the roles of conserver, discerner, and reformer—practiced institutionally and individually—come together in a full-orbed life or responsive discipleship, characterized by unwrapping God's gifts, sharing each others' burdens, and working for shalom.

Unwrapping Gifts

What is it like to be part of a grade nine high school class? Julie puts down some sheets of paper but pays no attention as the teacher opens with prayer to start the day. She looks bored as the class discusses, with animation, the trade of a hockey player and, with less animation, an upcoming election. Her teacher has the class use the first period to complete a social studies research report.

Julie plays with her hair and talks to a friend. After a few minutes, she starts working on a science assignment. When the teacher approaches her desk, she quickly takes the draft of her social studies project and asks him a question, successfully diverting his attention from her unauthorized science assignment.

Five minutes later, after discussing the merits of various perfumes with her friends, she distracts her teacher once again.

Julie finishes her science assignment, due the next period, and then counts and discovers that she doesn't have enough words in her social studies project. She immediately waves her hand to attract the teacher's attention, maneuvering him into giving her ideas so she won't have to do more research. The teacher, in the meantime, first tells one friend and two minutes later another to move away from Julie: their chatter distracts the rest of the class. Julie smirks as she randomly finishes highlighting the "main points" of an article of a student in the desk behind her who went to the washroom.

Ten minutes of banter and scrutiny of a neighbor's physical education equipment ends with the defense, "But I don't understand any of this!" to her teacher. But fifteen minutes later, after more chatter and a quick glance at a relevant article, Julie is able to give her teacher an astute albeit black-and-white analysis of her topic: she knows far more about her topic than she wants to let on. At the end of the period, when the teacher tells the class that next period he expects much more effort, Julie and her two friends apologize as they line up with the others near the door, waiting for the bell.

During the next period Julie reacts very differently to the science teacher, whose objectives are clearly stated and carried out. Julie volunteers and answers a question right away, and works well in a collaborative small group setting. When stuck for an answer, however, she again tries to get the teacher to do her work for her. A few minutes later her group becomes dysfunctional because of a disagreement. The teacher points them to one of the group rules: "everyone contributes equally; all cooperate," and appoints person B in each group as a noise monitor. Julie chews gum, looks out the window once in a while, but remains on-task and interested in the activity.

After a ten-minute break, Julie enters her French class. She looks bored but pays attention throughout. The class is fast-paced and the teacher calls on her fairly frequently. When working for a few minutes with a classmate, she cooperates quietly even if not energetically. In her Bible class, she again listens passively and unenthusiastically, but participates when required to do so. Is this the same student who relished manipulating her teacher and disturbing the class during the first period? Do different teachers affect her attitude and work that differently? Or did she run out of steam?

After lunch, Julie goes to art. I ask her whether she likes school. "I don't like art." "But do you like school?" "Yeah, I do, really." Four minutes into the class, she smuggles the bare beginnings of her drawing to someone she considers a good artist. The teacher is oblivious. "I can't draw," she says to me inconspicuously, hoping I'll be a silent partner in her crime. "I'm just getting him to fix it up . . . honestly."

19

A little later, the teacher notices Julie with another friend: "What's going on here?" "I'm just getting some help." Julie works intermittently on her drawing, talking frequently to her friend. Twenty minutes into the period, the teacher talks to Julie and her friend about their lack of progress, and they settle down for a while. During the last quarter hour, however, Julie once again alternates her work with talking with friends and looking at her school photographs distributed at noon. During the last period, physical education, Julie is initially more interested in her shoe than in warming up, but then becomes fully involved in volleyball skill development and practice.

What does Julie's day add up to? For Julie it was first of all a social event, a time to be with friends. Interruptions for learning are tolerated when teachers set and enforce high expectations. Julie enjoys school because she is with her friends. But she is too wrapped up in herself and her friends to be at all concerned about responsive discipleship in general or about unwrapping her own gifts in particular. Nevertheless, although the only overtly Christian aspects of her day were devotions and a Bible class, the school does, as we shall see, make concerted efforts to promote the development of students' talents within a positive Christian framework. While the school needs to ask how it can better reach Julie, it does have a number of integral units in place that touch the minds and hearts of its students.

The first essential ingredient of responsive discipleship is that students unwrap their gifts as they learn. Think of a boy who finds it difficult to unwrap a long-expected birthday parcel received in the mail from his grandparents. The package has lots of knotted string and tough strapping tape. But he tries his best and opens it full of anticipation even when he finds it hard. And once he has opened the package and pushed aside the inside wrapping papers, he experiences the tingling of surprise and wonder and thankfulness. He then sets about to make what he has uncovered a meaningful part of his life, using it to enrich not only himself but also others around him in his family.

Whether easy or difficult, learning leads to responsive discipleship when students use their unique God-given talents to increase their gifts (Matt. 25:14–30). There is a spectrum of gifts that students use and extend through learning, including imagination and creativity, language competence, mathematical and spatial reasoning and ability, social perception and interaction, spiritual and moral discernment, and physical proficiency. In the process, students experience the awe and wonder of God and his world. They see the power of sin in their lives and in the world but also marvel at the potential and actuality of God's grace in Jesus Christ. This learning enriches their lives and those around them as they respond with deepened insight and commitment.

Julie's school works hard at unwrapping the gifts of its students in such a way. Recently, for instance, all grade eight, nine, and ten students explored in an integrated, week-long unit, what it is like to live as a First Nations Canadian or Native American today. Some preliminary activities resulted in the students indicating what questions they had about native people. Their questions were categorized into social problems, arts and culture, education, land claims, prejudice, family life, and native spirituality. Groups of about sixteen students each focused on one of these categories and then met to set their own agendas, which included field trips, speakers, projects, and reports back to the whole student body. Despite some inevitable logistical glitches (and exhausted teachers!) the students unwrapped many gifts. They became more aware of and sensitive to the moral and cultural ideals of other peoples. They learned to take initiatives and develop social contacts with people outside of their usual community groups. They extended their oral and written language skills, and applied their creative gifts in their presentations. They learned, above all, that they could successfully take hold of their own learning, and that their decisions determined to what extent they would respond as disciples during and beyond this unit.

Still, despite these promising efforts, we ask questions. Julie was part of the native peoples unit and yet seemed little changed a few months later. Even if during the unit she used her abilities responsively and responsibly, how much long-term effect did it have? Did she understand the implications of the content and process of learning? Does the influence of our individualistic, materialistic, and hedonistic society, also evident within the school, undo what the school tried to accomplish, especially during the difficult adolescent years? Does *Seventeen* magazine tell Julie each month that her looks are much more important than developing her gifts? Does the lifestyle of her peers—and perhaps her own family—negate the discipleship focus of what she learns in school? Does her preoccupation with herself as well as her conviction that only "our" way is right inhibit her from analyzing the motives of others and prevent her from unwrapping her learning gifts? Does the school itself minimize the impact of such a unit by so often emphasizing regurgitation of information or narrowly-focused academic abilities?

Or do we perhaps sometimes expect too much of the school? Do teachers forget that some students, after a discussion of Hopkins' "Pied

Beauty," may still answer in all seriousness that in this poem Hopkins "praises God for the ingredients of a pie"? Do we forget that despite our best efforts, some students learn—and suffer—a great deal more by being ostracized by the rest of the class than they gain from all our teaching? Or that the discussions the students arrange with a band of native people are much less glamorous—and therefore less significant to them—than being on the school basketball team? Or that the constant emphasis on good grades weighs as a heavy burden on those whose gifts are in areas that do not receive the same recognition?

Contradictions as well as constraints appear to be an unavoidable part of school life. A school drops students from an oversubscribed Spanish class or its student council solely on the basis of poor marks, even though these opportunities might be the best way for those students to unwrap their gifts and respond as disciples. A high school that talks about meaningful learning nonetheless tells a professor of Old Testament taking his son on a three-week trip of the Holy Land that it will lower his son's grades for the days absent. Some schools still indicate nothing more than grades on report cards, even though such an approach inhibits the growth of all but the top quartile. At the same time, the often difficult societal milieu underscores that teachers frequently lack the resources or supportive context for helping students optimize their gifts. Adolescents like Julie may find their search for identity so consuming that no matter what teachers do, their response is limited. Abused children or ones who are emotionally unstable may sap a teacher's time or energy. The chemistry among the class leaders may undermine a teacher's best efforts.

Nevertheless, we believe that often schools can do more to unwrap their students' gifts, and part 2 of this book provides many examples. The school, like the sower in the parable, scatters seed that will take root only when the ground is ready to receive it. But that, of course, still leaves the question of what quality seed we use and how we help prepare the soil.

Though some seed will fall on rocky ground and other seed will sprout but be crushed by weeds, Christian schools can do a great deal to cultivate students' gifts. We help them experience and explore and ponder the awe and wonder and mystery of God's great creation. We nourish them in becoming life-long playful and thoughtful learners. We help them sense how we all are products of a culture that is burdened by the results of sin, but in which, by God's grace, we may work at recreating small corners into more God-glorifying ones. We help students tell stories: in their journals, in their creative writing, in their presentations, in their art, in their music. These stories, when taken together, unravel and reweave their inner beings, deepen and enrich their identities, uncover and recover the meaning of their lives. We encourage students to appropriate the biblical story and vision as their own, deepening and extending their responsive discipleship day by day, week by week, year by year.

We help students analyze moral and religious norms and develop commitments, enabling and encouraging them to act on the basis of what they profess. Socially, we assist them to learn to interact respectfully and trustworthily with others. We give them historical, political, and social insights that help them to understand our culture—and that impel them to responsible action. We teach them the basics thoroughly so that they understand and can cope with their environment. We help them become critical thinkers who can detect the idols of our times and ask questions that enable the Christian community to be light and salt in our culture. We help them exercise and improve their physical skills to enrich and fulfill their lives. School learning is not limited to unwrapping intellectual gifts alone!

Students' gifts are not unwrapped unless we tap into their creativity and imagination. God has put these qualities close to the root of our being, made as we are in his image, yet schools often stifle rather than nourish them. Students' playfulness and power of expression are intended to lead to joyful response to God's call. In the face of the powerful cultural images that would divert us to sinful ends, schools that are Christian help students to critique these images and to develop their gifts for the re-creation of their own lives and the redirection of our culture back to God.

It is inspiring when a small Christian high school encourages its grade twelve students to publish a pamphlet, "Aspects of a Worldview," which is worthwhile reading for all Christians (Gesch 1991). The same class has also written publishable essays about the place of science in our world from a Christian perspective. The school's grade nines vigorously discuss Christian responsibility with respect to social inequality, and, within the perspective of Romans 12:2, analyze current events in the school newsletter. At another small school, a multigrade high school class creates a museum with "artifacts" showing what the Middle Ages were like religiously, politically, culturally, and physically. Clearly, students unwrap their gifts responsively. As part of their discipleship of the mind they critique and identify basic values and beliefs, beginning also to articulate their own and to communicate them to others.

23

Sharing Each Other's Joys and Burdens

Craigsville Christian High is, by almost any measure, a good school. It maintains an accepting, caring, responsive atmosphere that engenders positive self-awareness. The student lounge, directly in front of the school office, is a place of informal camaraderie and good humor, a place where even an adult visitor is readily included in the relaxed discussion and banter. Craigsville's students and teachers go out of their way to make classmates with disabilities feel part of the learning community, whether these disabilities be physical, mental, or emotional. Participation in community service projects is an integral part of the senior biblical studies courses. Many students are involved in a valuable peer counseling program. Staff members model what they preach, whether that be picking up litter in the hall or making decisions on the basis of biblical norms. An ethos of caring permeates the school. Each person entering Craigsville's doors is made to feel special.

"The reality of school is not the reality of life in society, but let's make it as life-like as possible and then use our Christian principles to guide us," the principal says. "While our school community is too diverse—religiously and educationally—for radical change," he continues, "there are lots of things we *can* do in our current system."

The school assesses prospective teachers especially on their personal relationship with Jesus Christ, their eagerness to share this with their students, and their ability to foster a mutually respectful and compassionate learning environment. The school emphasizes that these characteristics are the foundation that the school uses to deepen everyone's insight into how the lordship of Jesus Christ affects all of life. What excites the principal is the growth in both personal faith and in world view perspectives among students, teachers, and parents from diverse evangelical backgrounds.

Craigsville Christian High, in other words, tries to make responsive discipleship part of its ambience. And yet Craigsville also exemplifies that, perhaps inevitably, schools are contradictory institutions. In an effort to provide meaningful learning experiences for all students, for example, the grade nines are divided into four separate levels in mathematics. In the honors section, taught by an experienced specialist, the students work in groups, use a range of sources, learn through a variety of creative large and small group teaching methods, and successfully tackle higher-order questions. In the third level, the "modified" section, on the other hand, while the teacher is just as caring, though not a math specialist, students work individually on drill sheets that reinforce basic skills. Little teaching takes place except during individual explanations. The students look at mathematics as a necessary chore that might as well be gotten out of the way as quickly as possible. While both math programs are quite traditional, the honors section deals with interpretations (and misinterpretations) of statistics in everyday life, with all students using scientific calculators. The modified section, on the other hand, is practicing pencil-and-paper grade-six-level fraction calculations, something of little relevance in an age of calculators.

The teachers mention that they feel this grouping has proven so successful that next year the English classes may be similarly divided. Apparently they are not aware that research shows that such grouping is self-fulfilling, harms learners of average and below-average abilities, and undermines the unity of the community of Christ that the school deliberately nurtures. While grouping may have made teaching the higher levels more enjoyable, the modified section showed some disturbing characteristics. Their work was not very relevant or interesting. They learned routines and algorithms but were not challenged to do any higher-order thinking. Because of the nature of the class, the teacher had to enforce strict discipline, with students having no opportunity for interaction or group work. In short, responsive discipleship was fostered much more in the honors than in the modified section.

That consequence is not Craigsville's intent. The school offers, for instance, a grade eleven activity-based science and technology course for students who are not college-bound. The course evaluates the use of technology from the standpoints of Christian lifestyle and stewardship. Students are faced with the question, "Does our use of technology reflect our desire to be imitators of God?" They investigate technology and leisure time, energy and environmental trade-offs, and military and defense technology. Teachers recognize the importance of this type of course and would like to offer it to a much larger, heterogeneous group of students. The school, however, feels it cannot deviate from the much less meaningful and abstract "official" courses for university-bound students.

In sum, Craigsville Christian High is a school whose graduates will have experienced what it means to have lived in a caring, empathic Christian community. And yet, it also is a school that needs to consider how its class and course structures in some ways detract from this goal.

Schools help students unwrap their God-given gifts not primarily for their personal growth and advantage. Rather, they develop their individuality in order that they may offer their unique gifts to the body of Christ and to society (Rom. 12:3–8). Our culture has lamentably and dangerously privatized most of life and lost sight of its communal nature. We have lost the sense that people must mutually care for each other and commit themselves to being responsible for the effects of their actions on others (Benne 1990, 88). Instead, people seek individual gratification and self-fulfillment. Arrogant autonomy has displaced daily self-denial and compassion. The high incidence of dishonesty, violence, divorce, and poverty in North America speaks poignantly of self-centeredness and a lack of commitment to love others as ourselves.

God calls us to live in and contribute to community. Our gifts have been apportioned to us by God's grace for building the body of Christ and doing works of service (Eph. 4:7, 12–13). God asks us to live interdependently, in schools and classrooms as well, as covenant communities that promote the common enterprise of responsive discipleship. In such communities, teachers and students pledge to respond voluntarily and lovingly to the needs of each other on the basis of common vision and values. Teachers accept students as having intrinsic worth as images of God who are able to fulfill meaningful roles in the classroom community. That implies that teachers search out and, when necessary, allocate mutually helpful tasks and responsibilities to all their students.

Within schools that are covenant communities, teachers and students show heartfelt respect, compassion, and support for each other. They are receptive and open to dialogue, fresh insights, and innovative experiences, avoiding cliquishness. They include all members in both formal and informal class activities, downplaying exclusivistic competition. They foster cohesiveness, implementing peer support systems and collaborative learning. They appreciate and value others and their work, sharing tasks and products. They contribute to the learning success of others. They reach out to others in the community, especially those who are disadvantaged. In this way an ethos of caring and an atmosphere of encouragement and trust pervade the school.

Classrooms and schools will, of course, experience strains in the attempt to foster such an atmosphere. Students and teachers and organizational behavior are always contaminated by sin. One principal said that his diligent faculty teamwork to provide a caring community with Christ-centered learning seemed to be thwarted daily by the blatant disrespect of a minority of students. A teacher described the heartache of a Christian school student who told her, "I hate high school. I'm not a jock, I can't sing, and . . . I'm a Christian." In such cases we must not only pray that the school will accept the student's grief as its own, but also as a community take steps to work at turning around its own plight.

Caring covenant communities are not soft. They are forceful and demanding when necessary, yet resilient. They provide settings where personal feelings and fears as well as shortcomings are addressed forthrightly (Palmer 1989, 15). Teachers as authoritative servant-leaders and intercessors try to resolve the underlying causes of unacceptable behavior in ways that place the responsibility to restore the learning community on the persons concerned. Personal failures, while endured, are used as new learning opportunities.

Structures imposed by logistical considerations, such as rigid timetables or streaming and tracking, may also detract from community. With God's help, teachers, students, and parents face community fractures caused by individual failings or systemic deficiencies squarely, dealing openly with the resulting brokenness and pledging themselves anew each day to communal discipleship.

A grade ten biblical studies teacher who wanted to forge his class into much more of a covenant community began a voluntary community service group, "Shining Our Lights." The group found that the desire to serve God in service projects was implemented most effectively communally, with team members supporting each other. The students reached out to urban street kids and inmates of a detention center, reporting their experiences to the whole class. A subgroup became involved with church-planting efforts during the summer.

The next year, in grade eleven, the class reached a consensus that everyone would participate. The students who admitted uncertainty about their faith chose activities in which they would not need to proclaim their beliefs openly. The learning taking place inside the class was now complemented for everyone by outside response. The students were exposed to diverse service possibilities and were encouraged to become long-term participants. Meanwhile, they learned to appreciate each other in new ways as they worked together on projects they could or would not do alone. In-class response also improved, with the classroom climate becoming more mutually supportive.

Forging a learning community does not require "outside" service work at some grade levels. What is most important in any case is what takes place within the school walls. In one school, a great amount of collaborative work takes place on days when integrated themes are studied. Many projects become class projects, with each student contributing something that enhances the whole. Each person in the school is assigned a special task that is needed for the school to function well. Also, a "buddy" system allows older and younger students to do things together and learn from each other through planned activities. Better students help weaker ones with their math as a matter of course. Students in the higher grades volunteer and are assigned to tutor students in lower grades. Within an atmosphere of supportive informality, the students appreciate that the teachers have high expectations and maintain a high level of learning.

In short, we need to address how our classroom structures can help foster care and concern, justice and mercy, understanding and mutual support. Individual competition, such as that engendered by posting only the work of the best students on the bulletin board, does not lead to a sharing of the joy of learning nor to the bearing of each other's burdens. A true learning community is not characterized, however, by romantic indulgence. It is caring and sustaining but also challenging and rigorous. It is rooted in the knowledge that God, our faithful Father, is our ultimate burden bearer to whom we respond in gratitude by giving of our all.

Seeking Shalom

A thematic unit on ecosystems in Paulton Christian Elementary School provides students with opportunities to marvel at God's faithful handiwork in his creation. As they investigate, discuss, and write about forest, meadow, swamp, and pond ecosystems, they also begin to grasp how humans have distorted God's perfect and beautiful patterns, often for selfish short-term economic gain and with devastating long-term implications.

In the unit, teacher Christine Parker helps and propels her students to plan concrete ways of being informed healers of our broken environment in just, responsible, and self-sacrificing ways, both individually and as a group. The students invite experts to discuss with them environmental disasters such as oil spills, drift netting, and clear-cutting. They explore how governments deal with environmental issues. Christ-centeredness is emphasized not only through caring and forgiving relationships within the class, but also through community involvement outside of school.

Christine Parker's structure provides her students with ongoing opportunities to share their insights, understandings, and experiences. They write and share what they already know about ecosystems. Their own questions provide a large part of the unit's agenda. Christine allows her students certain choices about which topics to explore, what activities to complete, how to represent the knowledge they gain in products, and whether to work alone or in small groups. They become part of the decision-making process, taking ownership of their own learning and how their learning community functions. Moreover, the students regularly evaluate themselves, sometimes on the basis of criteria established by the class. She gives students many responsibilities within a framework of mutual respect and high expectations, holding them fully accountable for their learning decisions, their implementation, and the resulting products.

Throughout the unit, Christine invites and re-invites the students to look through the window of faith. She plans devotions that point her students to biblical norms and mandates, and asks them to discuss particular issues from a biblical perspective of stewardship. She directs her students to resources, shares personal experiences and thoughts, and reads stories aloud. All of these activities become avenues for further discussion, exploration, and response. She knows that ecological issues challenge our whole society as well as each of her students to live with more integrity, seeking to reestablish biblical shalom. She therefore keeps the glasses of faith perched steadily on her nose in order to help her students claim a biblical vision of what it means to be responsive disciples.

Christian schools seek shalom, the biblical peace and justice that heals brokenness and restores creation to what God intended it to be. Shalom rests in and brings about restored relationships between humans and God, among persons in community, and between humans and their world. Shalom brings freedom from the self-centered excesses of North American society. It embraces religious and moral harmony as well as true piety. A shalom-filled classroom is one where pedagogy reflects tactfulness and trust, where curriculum fosters justice and harmony, where discipline redirects to discipleship, and where evaluation sensitively fosters self-reflective growth. In such a classroom we celebrate God's majesty and goodness and lament the power of sin within and beyond the learning community (Wolterstorff 1985).

Our planet faces the possibility of extinction because of our unstewardly use of God's gifts. The prevalent (if weakening) pride that we can solve our problems through economic growth flies in the face of increasing ecological decay, indiscriminate violence and crime, disabling poverty and unemployment, and excruciating personal abuse. All of us are touched to some extent by these tragedies; some of our students' lives have been devastated by one or more of them.

Yet God promises his shalom: he lifts up the humble and fills the hungry with good things (Luke 1:51–53). If we are to promote shalom in and through our schools, then, can we do any less? In our schools, do we feed the hungry, welcome the stranger, and visit the sick and those in prison? Do we reach out to the needy, the elderly, the emotionally wounded, the disadvantaged minorities? Do our students become alert to the needs of others, and disposed to do something about those needs? Are our graduates socially aware and concerned and active in issues ranging from the sanctity of life to the preservation of God's earth to opposition to discrimination against minority groups

29

in society? Since discipleship involves justice and holiness (Eph. 4:24), do we address issues of personal and social justice in every course, at every level? Where there is no vision of biblical shalom, meaningful learning will perish.

Paulo Freire accuses Christians in the Western world of speaking and writing about Easter, but not *doing* Easter in our educational institutions (Evans et al. 1987, 229). Doing Easter, for Freire, means becoming completely committed to the power of Christ's gospel to cut through the injustice of this world. He means that the industrialized nations, with only a minor proportion of the world's population, would take steps to ensure that they no longer consume the major part of the world's resources. He argues that our renewal in Christ's resurrection would spur us to genuinely improve the lot of those living below the poverty line, of the homeless and famished, and of those who cannot afford or have no access to proper medical care.

Do our schools merely celebrate Easter or do we *do* Easter? Do we question the dominant underlying values of our culture? the way in which our governments use power? how labor unions often consider only their own self-interest? that we Christians also get caught in materialism? Do we analyze the roots of the evils embedded in our social systems? Do we help our students consider issues from a global perspective, so that they can contribute locally to justice and responsible stewardship?

Some Christian schools, to be sure, do a great deal to promote such Christian understanding and dispositions. One teacher told us enthusiastically about a unit called "Choices" in his grade ten English class. He used a mixture of short stories, poems, news articles, teenage-oriented comics, and rock music to discuss how people make choices about what to do with their lives. He dealt head-on with decisions teenagers make about such issues as sexuality, drugs, suicide, how to spend time and money. The video *The Man Who Planted Trees* was followed by a discussion on what it means that each of us is called by God to bring about shalom in our own lives and those of others through "planting trees."

After the in-class activities, the students chose a "tree planting" organization such as the Red Cross, the Salvation Army, Hope International Development, the Mennonite Central Committee, or Citizens for Public Justice. They made contact and took a school day to visit its offices and interview key personnel. They made reports to the class as well as posters promoting the organization. The unit helped the students, according to the teacher, to become respectful of the people involved. They began to appreciate how these individuals had made choices about their lives. They considered how they themselves can and must make choices that would affect their lives but also those of others. They experienced how it is possible to bring about biblical shalom, even if in only a limited way, in situations crying out for justice and compassion.

We strive to make our classrooms into communities characterized by mutual service and renunciation of power and prestige (Segovia 1985, 7). This is often difficult in classrooms where, today, some students are unwanted at home, some have been abused, some are caught up in their parents' materialistic lifestyle, and some are part of the drug scene. Yet even in such circumstances—*particularly* in such circumstances—teachers and students together must strive to learn together, to look not only to their own interests, but also to the interests of others. Like Christ, we keep before us the need to humble ourselves to serve others (Phil. 2:4–8). To the extent that we do, our schools will be places where, despite recurring shortcomings, we can celebrate God's shalom.

Schooling for Responsive Discipleship

At 12:30 on a sunny afternoon early in October, nineteen children come into the colorful, learning-inviting kindergarten room. Teacher Susan Wright sings a song that acknowledges them all by name as they leave the coat area near the outside door. They find their places in a circle on the floor behind laminated placemats on which they had printed their names and painted a picture during the first week of school.

Ken, on Susan's right, sits on a tree stump: he is the special person of the day. Michael, on her left, waits with an expectant smile: it's his sixth birthday today. Susan takes her guitar and everyone joins in singing "Happy Birthday." "Use your hands to show me six," Susan says. She reads a poem on her chart about turning six and asks some "thinking questions" about it. She discusses how our lungs function as she blows up a balloon. She is careful to explain that all children have a special place in kindergarten, whether they're four, five, or six: Ken had decided, the week before, that being four made him too young to do any of the "work."

After only four weeks of school, the children anticipate and already cherish the well-established routines. They clap along as they sing five or six songs, several with signings and body movements. They act out three choral poems, each teaching them something about fall, the theme they are studying, or about counting. Four children participate in communal prayer and a dozen in "show-and-tell." Susan uses these as opportunities for imaging God through building confidence, instilling community, and developing language skills. Susan works hard at her students being and becoming responsive disciples of Jesus Christ. They blossom as she helps them nurture their gifts. They learn to reach out to and help each other, and to take delight in celebrating God's goodness and faithfulness.

Susan encourages all children to volunteer their involvement. She checks off their participation on an evaluation sheet on her knee. The students "write" and "erase" numbers with their fingers in the air, and playfully learn some basic phonics as they discuss the calendar and the weather. They proudly "read" a big book without Susan's help. "You're just too smart!" Susan exclaims. The children excitedly identify author Robert Munsch and join Susan in telling the story and chanting the repetitive patterns. Susan asks many open-ended questions as she uses the story of Abraham to emphasize God's challenging call and faithfulness. When some children's attention wanders, a quick double clap refocuses their attention.

Susan emphasizes personal responsibility. The children choose their own learning center during activity time. They know that for some centers such as the water table, they must set the timer if there are more than four of them so that others will get a chance, too. After completing a painting at one of the easels, they put their painting in the drying rack and then allow others their turn. Susan deliberately asks a shy but bright child to help another one having difficulty with a task. Ken, the "special person," uses a small rechargeable vacuum cleaner as the children routinely clean up before going out for recess. Susan asks two arguing children to decide how they can resolve their problems peacefully. When, as happens occasionally, she sends children to the "time-out chair," they themselves decide when they are ready to rejoin the class.

Susan keeps close track of which children visit each learning center. She attracts some to those where she wants more participation by sitting there for a few minutes. Each day, she closes and opens some centers as specific learning needs become clear. Each center, Susan asserts, teaches the students at least three different educationally worthwhile things in the six developmental areas that she uses to design and evaluate her program: the spiritual and moral, social and emotional, social responsibility, intellectual, aesthetic, and physical dimensions. Susan organizes her program so that children learn to express and exercise their faith, to joyfully help and support each other, to take responsibility for their own learning and behavior, to take risks as they expand their learning horizons, to delight in the beauty of God's creation, and to marvel in newly uncovered motor skills.

But, Susan wonders, what is going to happen to each of her students as they move on through school? Will they advance in their understanding and practice of responsive discipleship—or will their child-like wonder and faith and joy in learning gradually fade? What about Ken, whose culturally limiting home background and slow development already make it painfully clear that he will be frustrated in any "standard" classroom situation? What about Teresa, whose aggressiveness has already made her "boss" in classroom and playground situations—and who loudly insists she will "do Ken's work for him: he can't do it anyway"? What about Peter, whose lurid imagination makes him fantasize cutting off limbs from dolls with make-believe knives? What about Esther, who constantly craves attention because her overwhelmed single mother can't find any time for her? What about Quentin, an emotionally withdrawn child who seldom wants to join in with the others? What about perfectionistic Michelle, who is already sounding out words but is afraid to take risks as she begins to write words and stories? To what extent can the school continue to foster responsive discipleship in each of these children, especially when they often encounter many conflicting influences?

Susan tries to lay a sound foundation. The structure of her classroom, with its unobtrusive but well-established routines, allows for a great deal of freedom, encouraging responsiveness and responsibility. Her themes—such as creation, God made me special, transportation, and Japan—all embed the beginnings of a Christian world view in simple but not simplistic ways. Above all, she helps each child feel special and nurtures their attitudes and abilities at their level of development:

> I can tell a lot of work went into that. Tell me more about it.
> It's okay to make mistakes. What do you think you have learned about . . .
> I have confidence in you. You'll make the right choice.
> Since you don't seem to be happy with that, what will you do differently next time?
> I like the way you handled that.
> What do you think you can do now?

In describing Susan's class one volunteer mother paraphrases what God said to Joshua: "Very soon the children realize that the Lord their God has given them the land for a possession, and that therefore they don't have to be afraid but can be strong and courageous."

Indeed, encouraging children to take possession of God's marvelous creation in perceptive and creative, sensitive and warmhearted, trusting and trustworthy ways: that is not only what Susan's classroom but what all Christian schooling tries to attain.

God calls each believer to a life of discipleship. The church summons us to such discipleship by proclaiming the redemptive and

33

enabling work of Jesus Christ. It points us to the Way, the Truth, and the Light, setting forth the guidelines and norms of God's Word. The Christian family nurtures children in everyday discipleship, providing an environment where the bond of faith and love with God and with other family members may be experienced and extended.

Like the church and the family, the Christian school has a responsibility to foster discipleship. Its way of encouraging discipleship as well as the scope and depth of topics it considers differ, however, from those of the other settings. In school, students distance themselves from situations and phenomena in order to focus on particular aspects in structured ways. The school's educational setting enables children and young people to respond to God's call in all aspects of life, by broadening and deepening their experience of his creation in more formal ways.

School experiences reinforce, extend, remake, and apply students' gifts. Those gifts are not limited to intellectual ones but also include spiritual, ethical, interpersonal, intrapersonal, aesthetic, spatial, and physical gifts. Christian schools reinforce that living as a Christ-confessing community means sharing such gifts as well as sharing each others' joys and burdens. Further, Christian schools help students become committed to seeking and proclaiming God's shalom—his mercy, peace, and justice—throughout our society. The school's task lies in promoting understandings, abilities, tendencies, and practices that enable students to be discerning participants in our culture and that help them take on a strategic discipleship role in society. Christian schools endow the cultural mandate of Genesis 1:28 and the Great Commission of Matthew 28 with special significance as they help students respond to God's call everywhere in life. All this is what Susan tries to do in her kindergarten class in simple but not simplistic ways.

Disciples of Jesus Christ follow him in obedience. They acknowledge and trust Christ's trailblazing, using his power and directives to nurture the potential in themselves, in others, and in the rest of God's creation. Discipleship, as often pointed out, includes responsibility or accountability.

What has been noted less often is that discipleship also encompasses *responsiveness*. In their school encounters with the dynamics of life in God's creation, students are called to *respond* with wisdom and knowledge, with discernment and creativity, with playfulness and perseverance, and, above all, with love and compassion. We want such student response to be freely given and authentic, but, at the same time, we wish the response to reflect the fruit of the Spirit (Gal. 5; Eph. 4–5). Teachers encourage honest response, thus discouraging hypocrisy. At the same time, they cannot tolerate response that, while genuine, undermines shalom in the classroom learning community.

The personal, freely-given response that schools foster goes much beyond memorization or slavish imitation. All truth is God's truth, and knowledge of truth is an essential ingredient of discipleship. But knowledge is never something static: it always demands obedient response. A lack of knowledge, God indicates in Hosea 4, does not mean not understanding concepts or not recognizing truth; rather, it means not acting faithfully on our "head knowledge." This has important implications for the way we structure learning situations and the methods we use to evaluate student progress, for instance. Students (and teachers) who are responsive disciples respond personally and wholeheartedly to the learning and teaching situation they face as they develop their gifts in God-glorifying ways. They learn to believe fervently, care compassionately, love unconditionally, discover breathlessly, evaluate discerningly, create imaginatively—and also grieve profoundly when the power of sin prevents Christ's shalom from breaking through.

Such responsive discipleship is much more encompassing than what we evangelicals have often assigned to the "spiritual" dimension of life. It embraces any situation where we use our learning encounters to find joy in God's creation and to seek God's kingdom of justice. A kindergartner excitedly discovers that 3+2 always equals 2+3—and begins to apply that in everyday situations. A student festively paints the stunning beauty of an alpine meadow, or draws the anguish of a person whose life is racked by years of pain and suffering. A boy finds satisfaction in reading a story to a younger student, and the younger one delights in listening. A group of students together complete a science project that illustrates God's laws for gravity. A girl ponders in her journal about coping with her broken home situation. A class researches and debates how to respond to today's popular music. A high school class organizes weekly social events in a home for juvenile delinquents. A school basketball team plays in a caring, honest, and truly playful way. A student finds a creative way to solve an algebra problem, while another is pleased to have mastered a basic algorithm.

All these situations exemplify responsive discipleship if the participants use God's gifts to celebrate the lordship of Christ over every nook and cranny of life. Even horse bells and cooking pots can be holy to the Lord (Zech. 14:20) and therefore instruments of our discipleship, but this depends on how we use them, in what context, and to what end.

Telling others the Good News of Christ is one crucial aspect of responsive discipleship. But we also proclaim the Good News by bursting into bloom like a crocus (Isa. 35:1), proffering Christ the gifts he first gave us with the added vibrancy and color realized through responsive learning and teaching. The numbers we multiply, the chemicals we mix, the volleyballs we spike, the poems we write, the maps we draw, the textbooks we read, the critical analyses we develop, the procedures we learn, the attitudes and dispositions we develop—all these are gifts of God to be used as offerings to him. Everything we do in school can be part of responsive discipleship if we light candles within our own and each other's lives and within our cultural darkness. God through his grace then uses our learning activities in service of his kingdom and accepts both students and teachers as co-workers who strive for excellence in whatever they do (1 Cor. 3:9).

In Christian school classrooms, teachers both model and foster responsive discipleship. They lead their students as they themselves follow their Lord and Savior. To do so, they search Scripture for the significance of its teachings, building on the richness of our tradition while allowing the Holy Spirit to lead them into new insights. Today, that often is not an easy task. It involves overcoming the religious and moral numbness that characterizes our culture. It means reclaiming those largely inoperative virtues that form part of the fruit of the Spirit: love, self-sacrifice, integrity, humility, righteousness, and justice. It cannot happen without countering the prevailing attitudes of autonomous individualism, self-centered consumerism, and moral relativism. Yet, by God's grace and through the power of Christ's Spirit, we may work at developing structures and programs in which responsive discipleship becomes a way of life.

Christian teachers, then, are called to empower students to follow Jesus in a school setting. Schools set out deliberately to nurture personal, nonprogrammed response by broadening and deepening students' experiences and insights. Schools help their students respond to carefully chosen, significant aspects of human life, respond normatively and authentically, reflectively and actively. In the Gospels, Jesus required his disciples to respond by driving out evil spirits and curing illness very soon after he called them, despite their glaringly incomplete understanding. In school, teachers similarly foster purposive knowing and doing in order to encourage response, right from the day students enter kindergarten. At the same time, they celebrate the diversity of responses that God's spectrum of gifts in the students make possible, always emphasizing that God calls us to respond within his norms of love, truth, and justice.

Teachers stimulate students to be reflective, to consider the meaning and implications of their actions and products. They help them be compassionate, creative, and responsible agents of change within and without the school. They help them experience that in God's kingdom the wolf and the lamb can feed together, that swords can be beaten into plowshares, that nations can blossom like lilies. Righteousness and justice, love and compassion, peace and joy—those are the foundations for the pedagogy, curriculum, and administration of a Christian school that models and nurtures responsive discipleship.

On the one hand, students and teachers can never exhaust these dimensions of responsive discipleship. Christ's mission and direction evoke unceasing and ever-deepening response. On the other hand, no school ever attains these aims completely. The consequences of human sinfulness touch all teachers and students each day. They face disappointments and frustrations and stresses. But they can always rest in God's promise that he will sustain them when in the classroom they respond obediently as committed disciples. Unwrapping our gifts in a supportive community in order to seek and celebrate shalom is something that gives purpose and meaning to the learning and teaching in Christian schools.

> Do not grieve what talents God did not give you, but recognize and rejoice in the worth of others. Discover your particular gifts and develop your unique potential. . . . When you find joy and laughter in your life, give others your joy, 'The gift you have received give as a gift.' (Dunn 1985, 14–15)

Questions for Discussion

1. The chapter develops these dimensions of responsive discipleship in a school setting: unwrapping gifts, sharing joys and bearing burdens, and seeking shalom. Think of examples of how each of these aspects of responsive discipleship is developed in your classroom. Can you think of other dimensions of responsive discipleship that are not developed in the chapter? Are there any that you would consider at least as important as these three? If so, what would be the classroom implications?

2. The chapter claims that responsive discipleship is an important aim in nurturing children in the home, in church, and in school.

Can you distinguish the different emphasis that would be present in each case? In what ways can the home, church, and school complement rather than duplicate each other?

3. The emphasis on sharing each other's joys and bearing each other's burdens is not intended to deemphasize academic rigor or the striving for excellence in learning. Can you give examples where sharing joys and bearing burdens within a classroom enhances the quality of learning? On the other hand, are there ways in which academic rigor can undermine a sense of Christian community? How can Christian schools promote both as they help all students unwrap their gifts?

4. Seeking shalom is a demand of God that is not often related to the aims of schooling. If this is an important aspect of fostering responsive discipleship, what implications does teaching shalom have for the content and structure of learning at various grade levels?

2

Challenges to the Vision:
Cultural Constraints in the Nineties

The Public School Monopoly vs. the Family's Right to Educate

John eased his van into his driveway, carefully, so that the paint ladders attached to the roof wouldn't hit the overhanging tree branch. It was 9:45 P.M., a typical end to a typical day. After nine hours of painting and wallpapering for a local contractor, John had eaten a quick supper before heading out for his moonlighting jobs. Gathering his lunch pail and records, he climbed the steps to his door. Once inside, he saw his wife, Judy, sitting at the empty kitchen table. John knew that if she was sitting there not doing anything she probably wanted to talk.

"This isn't working, hon," Judy said, not unkindly.

"What's not working?" said John, with a quick kiss to her cheek.

"Your working nights like this. The kids and I hardly see you. Half the time you're stressed out and exhausted. There's got to be a better way."

"Like what?" John replied. "You know we depend on this income. Without it, we couldn't pay tuition."

"Well, I'm wondering," said Judy, somewhat hesitantly, "if Christian schooling is worth it."

"You're kidding," said John. "I'm working night and day like this and you're not even convinced it's worth it?"

"Not if we never see you," said Judy, warming to her side of the debate. "What's more important: the kids getting a Christian education or the kids spending some time with their father?"

"Judy, we've been through this before. The public schools aren't very safe. There are all kinds of lousy influences on the kids there." He settled into a chair and searched under the newspaper for the remote control.

"Bev sends her kids to the public school, since Nick left her, and she says the place is fine. The teachers care. There aren't any big problems with drugs and stuff."

John shook his head. "Besides, Christian education is more than a school without drugs," he said, clicking the remote to get the evening news. "In a Christian school, we parents get to determine what gets taught and how. Not the district office or some textbook publisher."

"What about the family?" said Judy, sensing she wasn't making progress.

"I'll make more of an effort," said John, getting absorbed in the newscast.

Judy sighed. "Well, I'm getting ready for bed." She held up a light green sheet of paper. "By the way, the school newsletter came today. Tuition is going up again next year."

One cannot understand Christian schooling unless one understands the social and educational milieu in which Christian schools operate. This chapter analyzes some of the political, cultural, and social constraints that undermine, or at least inhibit, the Christian school effort, and suggests that Christian schooling, if understood as educating for responsive discipleship, can be a powerful institutional response to a troubled society.

The broadest political and legal constraint under which Christian schools labor is the public school monopoly. Public schools in the United States collect no tuition but receive 220 billion dollars in public monies. Christian schools in the U.S. receive little in government assistance and must depend on parents' tuition payments usually for 80 percent or more of their budgets. The situation in Canada is somewhat more just, but it varies from province to province. The result is that Christian schools almost always lack the financial and human resources provided to public schools.

Although some might argue that the conditions of sponsorship for Christian schools (often a parent-controlled society) can result in better fiscal accountability, a clearer sense of mission, and the closeness of community, the essential financial inequity remains: Christian school supporters are taxed twice for education, once for the community's children, and once for their own. Many Christian parents, usually young, usually at the lower-paying beginning of their careers, and faced with all the other financial demands of raising a child, often find paying Christian school tuition a challenge requiring tremendous sacrifice. In addition, although some parents sacrifice greatly, tuition and school contributions in many areas fail to meet the financial needs of teachers. Many Christian school educators receive between two-thirds and three-quarters of a public school salary, a hardship and an injustice not sufficiently addressed by the school's supporters.

The public school monopoly depends on a modern cultural understanding that certain areas of life, such as religion, are private, and other areas of life, such as business and education, are public or secular in nature. For this reason, North Americans generally embrace the notion that some schools are public because they do not espouse any particular religious or moral viewpoint beyond a general civic-mindedness and are thereby worthy of public funding. Other schools are private and should be prevented from receiving tax monies.

As Rockne McCarthy and his colleagues (1982) have carefully documented, the history of education in America has been one of the spread and growth of this publicly supported, bureaucratically centralized, "religiously neutral" public school system. The family's right to educate has been subsumed by the government's need for control. State or provincial legislatures empower schools, but they also control schools with a wide variety of requirements: mandatory attendance until a certain age, a set number of school days per year, a set number of hours per day, curriculum requirements (e.g., X number of years of social studies), teacher certification requirements, school building requirements, financing structures, and so on. Although some government influence (such as safety minimums) has no doubt improved schooling, the essential absurdity, that schooling can be morally and religiously neutral, and the essential injustice, that the state, not the parents, should have the greater say, remain as the twin pillars of the public school monopoly.

If the monopoly is both absurd and unjust, why does it persist? Why can't the monopoly be broken up? Charles L. Glenn, Jr., in *The Myth of the Common School* (1988), examines the power of the *idea* of the common school. He uses "myth" not in the sense of false reality or imaginary vision but as *compelling cultural idea*. For him, the myth of the common school is a powerful component of the sustaining ideology of modern democracy. The public school has come to symbolize the Ameri-

41

can experiment: all are together; all are learning to respect and get along with each other; all are given equal opportunity. Glenn suggests that the crisis in confidence in public schools today draws much of its irrational quality from the exaggerated hopes that we have cherished over the past century and a half. "It is no wonder that suggestions that the common school be diversified, that the 'public school monopoly' be broken up, that our society's secular church be disestablished arouse the deepest anxiety and confusion today" (Glenn 1988, 84–85).

The public school monopoly makes up the larger context, the "background noise," of Christian schooling. Because of the monopoly's cultural power, the Christian school has two strikes against it before it even comes to the plate: the disadvantage of no public funding, and the suspicion of the wider culture. Any genuine renewal of Christian schooling with respect to the wider political culture unavoidably will have to take into account this "myth of the common school."

But in addition to the public school monopoly, Christian school educators labor under a variety of cultural and philosophical expectations regarding the way children are "schooled." Almost everyone in North American society has learned that schooling occurs in a certain way, accompanied by certain methods, certain sequences, and certain expectations. Variation from these norms is suspect. Innovations often meet heavy resistance, this time not by legislative decree, but by the expectations of all those involved in the educational process.

The Subculture of Schooling vs. the Unwrapping of Gifts

Glennis and Nate will normally begin their schooling experience in preschool or nursery school, a setting designed more for social interaction and guided play than for serious academic work. Preschool is followed by kindergarten and elementary school. In North America, the school year begins in late August or early September and ends in late May or early June, a relic from a predominantly agricultural past. (Today, such a school calendar remains entrenched by vacation time preferences.) Glennis and Nate are assigned to a "class" with children of the same age. The school commits itself to a new class only when economies of scale permit, when a certain number of similar-age students requires a new class to be organized. The class begins a lock-step progression through the "grades." The emphasis during the early years is on reading and arithmetic; the sciences and social studies are explored somewhat; and music, physical education, art, and (in very few schools) a foreign language, are "extras," the first programs cut when funds become tight.

In first grade, the class is divided into reading groups according to aptitude. Glennis is with the best readers. Nate is with the slowest. Because the class-room is small and filled with twenty-eight individual desks arranged in rows, the possibilities for learning activities are limited. Worksheets and "seat time" activities make up much of their day. By age twelve, Glennis and Nate may enter a middle school or junior high school. They shift from having essentially one teacher responsible for all the subjects to having several teachers, each responsible for a certain subject area. Glennis and Nate receive doses of each subject, often in prepackaged curricula, often in textbook form, often in time periods of forty-five minutes. They move from class to class, switching orientations as needed to accommodate a science class on aquatic ecosystems, a history class on ancient Greece, a music class on American jazz, a geography class on South America, and so on.

After the prescribed number of "periods," the normal school day ends for Glennis and Nate. Most of their classmates return home; many stay for "extra-curricular" activities. The school offers several sports throughout the school year, such as soccer, volleyball, and track, but, in America especially, the tri-umvirate is football, basketball, and baseball. Glennis and Nate must "try out" to secure a place on the team. Glennis makes the volleyball team. Nate is "cut" from the basketball team. In addition to the sports teams, a few clubs meet after school, pursuing activities such as photography, theater, or skiing. Nate, who likes to make models, decides to go home when school is out.

The methods of instruction in high school classes are quite similar. A teacher usually lectures or supervises a learning situation. Assignments, usually the reading of a text, are given and often done in class. A "quiz," often a set of multiple-choice questions, is a short evaluation given about once a week. A "test," which covers more material and might include an essay question, is given every two or three weeks. Class discussion is encouraged on occasion but normally not required. Some teachers "grade on the curve," which assures that the bottom 15 percent, regardless of their scores, will get the F grades. While such a method builds failure into the system, some teachers defend it because it "motivates" the children. After the grades are given, the students quite often are "ranked," resulting in a "valedictorian," the student with the best grades in the class.

Glennis enjoys school and participates vigorously, both academically and socially. Nate would rather be working but he has learned that if he shows up, makes no trouble, and does a modicum of work, he will pass the course and receive the credit necessary for graduation. Powell, Farrar, and Cohen (1985) called these arrangements "treaties"; though they are an unspoken agreement between the two parties, both teacher and student have clear expectations. Essentially, the student promises to go along with the system—to show up,

give a degree of cooperation, and refrain from disrupting the whole arrangement—and in return, the teacher will "pass" the student into the next grade.

Glennis excels at volleyball and enjoys it, but this year, she will miss her family's vacation because of the required conditioning practice. The interscholastic
sports program is important to the life of the school. The administrator says it
promotes "school spirit." Parents say it keeps their children active and "off the
streets." The school has "school colors," white and blue, and a nickname, "the
Wildcats." The boys' games are well-attended by vocal fans. A cheerleading
squad made up of girls encourages fans to cheer by performing various gym-
nastic-like routines. A "pep band" adds to the energy. The game itself is intense;
the purpose, as one father commented, is clear: "We like a winner." Last year
parents petitioned for and achieved the removal of the coach because of the
team's losing record.

By age fourteen, Glennis and Nate and their same-age classmates are ready
for high school. The social dimension of schooling now thoroughly overshadows
the academic endeavor; for most students, popularity is their high school priority. In classes, they continue to receive instruction in the various subjects, but
now they choose one of three high school "programs"—general, vocational,
or college preparatory. The programs differ according to the types of classes
offered, the degree of difficulty, and the vocational and educational opportunities that follow upon graduation. Glennis chooses college prep. She also has
been accepted into honors classes and will be taking the advanced placement
tests, enabling her to gain college credits while still in high school. Nate chooses
the vocational program. He senses that his program is somehow not as worthy as that taken by the college-bound students.

One highlight of Glennis's and Nate's senior year, and one of the rites of
passage in the subculture of schooling, is the senior banquet or prom night, a
dinner for the senior class usually followed by an evening of late-night celebrating. In recent years, the banquet has become, for some parents and their
children, a financial black hole. Another rite of passage is the graduation exercise itself. The diploma is granted because the student has gained the proper
number of "credits" in the proper subject areas. The treaty arrangement has
come to its proper conclusion. Teachers, parents, and even the students themselves may have no idea what they have actually accomplished, what it is they
know and can usefully apply, but the diplomas they receive "mean something"
in North American society. They are credentials for moving into the world of
work or further education.

While variations undoubtedly occur, much of North American
schooling, including Christian schooling, looks like what Glennis and
Nate experienced. Do Glennis and Nate attend a Christian or a public

school? It's hard to tell. Christian schooling too often looks exactly like its public school counterpart: fragmented, superficial, and deeply antithetical to Christian presuppositions and purposes.

As the narrative suggests, schooling in North America has developed a highly refined model resembling factory production. Building design, teachers as technicians, scheduling, prepackaged curriculums, the ringing of bells, assignments, grouping of students, accumulation of credits, testing/grading/ranking of students—all such practices assume that a product is being manufactured in some way. Mass production assumes similarity of treatment and conformity of outcome; it hardly provides the best model for the unwrapping of gifts, the sharing of burdens, or the seeking of shalom.

A consistent theme that runs through Glennis's and Nate's schooling experience is the primary role of competition. They learn and achieve almost always in comparison with others. Glennis and Nate quickly learned that getting As (as Glennis did) or Ds (as Nate did) doesn't simply mean one got an A or a D on a report card; it means one is an A person or a D person (Kohn 1986). Such messages are sent, consciously or unconsciously, throughout the schooling years. As David Purpel (1989, 35) observed, "Students learn very quickly that the rewards that the schools provide—grades, honors, recognitions, affection—are conditioned upon achievement and certain behaviors of respect, obedience, and docility."

Grading, however, is not the only form of competition in the schools. This is because spelling bees, science fairs, and the state band competition are used as a form of control: "The class that sells the most magazine subscriptions will get a pizza party!" Even group efforts such as the athletic team end the year by appointing a Most Valuable Player. The system needs winners; just as important, the system needs losers. We give dignity only to those who achieve. In fact, as Purpel (1989, 36) suggests, "the schools' job includes, however unintended, that of identifying those who are of little or no worth."

The questions surrounding competition and the subculture of schooling go straight to the heart of schooling in general and Christian schooling in particular: "*Is there no other way to control and motivate students?*" Competition, along with other bureaucratic structures, is an institutional tool that promotes conformity rather than the unwrapping of individual gifts. When the definition of winning is narrowed to grades, athletics, and popularity, only a few can win. When "excellence" comes to mean only high scores on standardized tests, schools bypass, as Purpel (1989, 18) put it, "the serious and perplexing questions of what should be taught, for what reason, and for which model of humanity and community." When our schooling procedures are so prescribed and so self-serving, it is difficult to teach children to be "responsive" to anything but the system and the ways of working it to their advantage.

Individualism vs. the Sharing of Burdens

"I send Glennis to this school to learn something, so she knows what she's supposed to know for college. I don't send her here to learn how to get along with other kids or serve others. That can come later. This is a school, for crying out loud."

Bill Mathers hadn't intended to raise his voice but his conference with the school's principal was proving frustrating.

"Look," he continued, "I know this is a Christian school. I know we want the kids to be nice to each other and so on, but I am frankly worried about the academic excellence of this place. Glennis has enjoyed attending here but she's now in a position to get a college scholarship. She's even thinking about being a doctor. She needs accelerated math and history and science, not projects to increase her sensitivity to the world's problems."

"I understand what you're saying, Mr. Mathers," said Claire Brown, "but here we don't think academic excellence, as you call it, and social involvement are mutually exclusive. We've collaborated with Habitat for Humanity to build this house because we believe the project teaches things that can't be learned from books alone."

Although Bill Mathers sensed some merit in Mrs. Brown's ideas, he persisted. "But it seems so inefficient, such a waste of time. You don't see the Academy kids building houses. They're taking AP courses. Ninety-eight percent of their kids go on to college. They become doctors and lawyers and engineers."

"I'm all for that!" cried Claire, enthusiastically. "Doctors and lawyers and engineers are important for society's work and for God's work. All I'm saying is that besides being trained as a doctor, Glennis should be educated to be a healer, a peacemaker, an agent of shalom. Our school not only holds up the ideal of social involvement, it gives the whole life philosophy—a Christian world view—that gives meaning and motivation for a lifetime."

"OK," said Mathers, thinking of a new tack. "But why not just let the slow kids who have trouble with academics build a house? That would be great for them—give them a sense of accomplishment and so on. And let the bright kids do real schoolwork."

Claire swung her chair around in order to look out the window a moment. Although she appreciated this parent's concern, she rejected the implications of his perspective.

"Mr. Mathers, do you know Nate Simpson?" Mathers nodded, so she continued. "Nate is someone many consider slow. He finds schoolwork a constant source of failure. For too many years already, he's been like Robert Frost's 'Hired Man'—nothing to look back on with pride, nothing to look forward to with hope, so now, and never any different. The Housing Project is for Glennis and those who enjoy school—I hope I've already explained why that's so. But it's also for the Nates of the world. Nate is a wonder with tools and materials. He and others could be separated in order to develop their gifts, but that's not how we do things in the Christian community. We try to share each other's burdens and celebrate each other's successes. It's hard for students to do that when they're tracked academically and socially. We're trying to build structures here that send a different message."

Mathers seemed to be listening, so she continued. "For example, we want students to know that academics—areas such as math and physics and social studies and Bible, in this case—can be directly connected to real life and real needs. One can't build a house without knowledge of how certain materials save or waste energy, or without the ability to measure and compute correctly. One wouldn't want to build such a house unless one had a sense of the housing problem in this country, its social and economic causes and its effects. One wouldn't feel impelled to build such a house unless one had examined and prayed over our obligation as Christians to care for others. One wouldn't build an ugly house because we are called to create beauty in form and function. See, we're trying to integrate all these dimensions into one single project, a whole. Academics aren't being shortchanged; they're being enhanced and embedded in students' minds and bodies. Besides, we want students to recover the idea of craftsmanship. We want them to know that using their minds to fashion something with their hands is a fine ideal worthy of their best effort."

Mathers thought for a moment, nodded slowly, and said, "OK, I'll give it a try, see how it goes." Rising to leave, he winked, and added, "How about teaming up Glennis with your plumbing supervisor. I've got this persistent drip from our upstairs bathroom faucet . . ."

What is the essence of the schooling experience in North America at the end of the twentieth century? Purpel (1989, 33) would reply, "When we go to school, we are taught mostly to learn to be alone, to compete, to achieve, to succeed." This analysis of schooling may sound glum, but it summarizes our culture as well, for the two are inextricably related. We have what he (1989, 36) calls "an ethic of conditioned love: we will love you if you achieve." This deeply rooted cultural orientation towards achieving in competition, along with its expression in our schooling structures, is an outgrowth of the individualism of our day. Our cultural hero is the individual who accomplishes despite great odds; we are less enthusiastic about the suffering servant who bears the burdens of others. The essence of schooling in contemporary society is that it is a vehicle for getting ahead, and "ahead" has meaning only in relationship to others.

The best-known documentation of our cultural individualism is Robert Bellah and associates' *Habits of the Heart* (1985), in which they trace two kinds of individualism, *utilitarian* and *expressive*. The former suggests a Ben Franklin, "whatever-works-for-me" approach and is best represented by the rational, self-interested individual who has replaced traditional loyalties with market motives. Expressive individualism, on the other hand, celebrates a life free of all constraints and conventions, a life rich in experience, a life that luxuriates in the sensual as well as the intellectual, a life of strong feeling. This Walt Whitman approach to life allows for human flourishing, but gives priority to *my* flourishing. Both strands of individualism are starkly obvious in our schooling methods. On one level, we attend school to get ahead, to make our way, to prepare for the career. But we also attend for personal fulfillment, for "self-actualization," and for personal flourishing.

Neither kind of individualism has much to do with bearing others' burdens and sharing their joys. Bellah's greatest concern is with the loss of community in our society. Because traditional social ties have been crippled by the new economic relations, people must find meaning, purpose, and closeness in community elsewhere. Bellah calls the new social network that develops the "lifestyle enclave" and suggests that "whereas a community attempts to be an inclusive whole, celebrating the interdependence of public and private life and of the different callings of all, lifestyle is fundamentally segmental and celebrates the narcissism of similarity" (Bellah et al. 1985, 72). He notes that people seek out and join up only with those of similar economic success and social status. Together they pursue leisure and consumption according to a similar standard—and *lifestyle* becomes the all-important term for describing all of life not connected directly to one's work. Why should we do one thing rather than another, especially when we don't feel like it or don't find it profitable? Historically, the question "Who requires this of me?" could be answered "God" or "church" or "community." But now the answer can only be "self."

What about the Christian school community? Is it simply another lifestyle enclave, a group that shares similar economic and social status, but with the added glue of similar religious beliefs? Do we teach a religious and moral code but keep it on a personal, Sunday-only plane? Is it possible to be a disciple and not reach out to others different from us? Who decides? To modern ears, a "life of discipleship" sounds extremely odd or at least quaint, and "bearing each other's burdens" is understood not as a biblical command, but as a psychic reward for "those who are into that." Where, we should ask, does unwrapping one's gifts, sharing each other's burdens, and seeking shalom, come in?

Robert Coles, the eminent child psychiatrist, has observed this individualism and the resulting moral relativity in his study of young children. Coles and his colleagues interviewed more than five thousand children in grades four through twelve, asking questions such as "Do you believe in God?" "How do you decide what is right and wrong?" "What system of values informs your moral decisions?" The answers reveal a fairly complicated belief system among children but one that often runs counter to traditional values. "I saw an awful lot of kids who are bright," says Coles, "but whose conscience is not all that muscular. . . . What I think we are seeing here is a conflict. On the one side, kids with a strong belief in the Judeo-Christian religious ethic, and on the other side, [kids] paying very close attention to that 'get ahead at any cost' attitude that they've picked up in their family lives" (Coles and Genevie 1990, 40).

Although me-first and winning-is-everything were common themes among the children, Coles believes that the important finding of his study is that many children have no firm religious or moral code to guide them. They may do the "right" thing, but they do it because it makes them happy, gets them ahead, keeps them out of trouble, or seems best for everyone. The children to a large extent merely reflect the values of their society. "Given their membership in a highly competitive, SAT-conscious culture, some children can very easily entertain the notion of cheating. . . . They're so fiercely committed to using the schools to achieve their own ends. Sadly, as so-called 'cultural literacy' grows, what should be called 'moral literacy' declines" (Meade 1990, 49).

Christian schools, too, may teach "love your neighbor" in Bible class, but it does little good if other school structures teach "make sure you win." Our modern Western individualism may have provided us with a "freedom" of sorts but we have a poor understanding of our place in the universe, of how we relate to each other, and of how we ought to be living.

Social and Ecological Decline vs. Shalom

"Are you going to talk about the drug problem at school?" asked a Christian high school student we were interviewing. It seems an undercover policeman had recently been on campus, though his "cover had been blown." We were somewhat taken aback: we don't like to think of Christian schools as places with these sorts of problems. Teen pregnancy, alcohol abuse, intimidation of people who are different, theft, obscenity, and blasphemy—unfortunately, we have to acknowledge that these are common problems, in some places more than others, certainly, but problems that need to be faced.

There are Christian school students who never sit down with their families for an evening meal; teenagers who are frightened to go home because they might be beaten by an alcoholic parent; children who cannot take their friends home because their parents don't want to be bothered with the noise and distraction; adolescents who have no curfew, or if they do, need only be home by the set time without advising their parents of their whereabouts. Christian school students do not come from perfect homes.

Then there are the very young children—and the not so young—traumatized by the break-up of their parents' marriage, not sleeping adequately, estranged from a loved one, or not remembering whose house they will be staying at the coming weekend, or not able to arrange to have friends over because they are spending it with one parent in a suburb far away.

When we look at the social problems faced by the community at large, we can no longer pretend that we are immune from them. Nor of course should we expect to be. Sin clings closely to us, even in our communities of faith.

Marc Miringoff (1992, 18) had this to say about our social plight: "It's like the movie 'Jaws.' We can't keep denying there's a shark out there. There are people bloodied on the beach. We can't leave the beach open and let everybody swim. We better take action." The Index of Social Health, published by Miringoff's Institute for Innovation in Social Policy, tracks such social problems as infant mortality, child abuse, teen suicide, drug abuse, unemployment, poverty, homicide, and the gap between rich and poor.[1] The 1991 report documented the worsening of social problems over the last twenty years. In 1970 the index stood

1. The "Gap Between Rich and Poor" refers to the difference in the proportion of the total aggregate family income received by the richest fifth and poorest fifth of the country's families.

50

at 68 (on a scale of 100); by 1989 (the last year for which complete data are available) it had fallen to 33, the worst rating in twenty years. The report notes, among other trends, that child abuse, teen suicide, and the gap between the rich and the poor have grown worse nearly every year since 1970; that, of the six problems relating to children and youth, four—child abuse, children in poverty, teen suicide, and high school dropouts—grew worse.

Andrew L. Shapiro (Marty 1991, 3) recently observed that among Western industrialized nations, the U.S. is:

> Number One in percentage of children living below the poverty line, Number One in teen pregnancy, Number One in murders of males between 15 and 24, Number One in murder by handguns for all ages, Number One in percentage of population incarcerated, Number One in percentage of commuter trips made by private auto rather than public transport, Number One in per capita energy consumption and Number One in emissions of air pollutants.

Martin E. Marty (1991, 3), in whose *Context* newsletter Shapiro was quoted, wryly adds, "It'd be nice to be Number Two in some of these. We have to try harder."

What does this mean for Christian schools in a society aching for shalom? Increasingly, Christian school communities are directly affected; but even if they have been to this point spared, Christians who take the Bible and culture seriously must feel their responsibility to address these problems. To simply isolate ourselves and our children from social ills and to ignore the biblical call to seek shalom is to fail in our calling as responsive disciples of Christ. Christian school communities must lead children to see the assaults on shalom evident in specific areas of modern life and then equip them with the skills and disposition to do something. Three areas in particular deserve attention.

Economic Overconsumption and Environmental Degradation

Economic exchanges—day-in, day-out, large-scale, small-scale, city-wide, world-wide—do much to shape people's lives. Economic activity, while not the only factor, determines to a large extent a person's present well-being and future potential. Because business contributes much to the health of a society, it is essential that it be carried out in a way that glorifies the Creator. Material well-being (not to be confused with raw prosperity or unrestrained consumption) is a legitimate human pursuit, an authentic dimension of shalom. But stewardship of God's gifts is the key: biblical mandates on the well-being of other people and the created world are clear and plentiful (Tiemstra 1990).

We must not pursue the enjoyment of God's created wealth at the expense of shalom. David Korten (1990), an international relief and development expert, divides the world's five billion people into three segments: marginals, sustainers, and over-consumers. This table shows the challenge facing Christian educators: How do we teach students who have material wealth as their main goal, when so many in God's world have so little? Are we simply equipping our students to be the next generation of over-consumers?

TABLE 1					
	Number	Food	Water	Shelter	Transportation
Marginals	1 Billion	Inadequate	Contaminated	Primitive	Foot
Sustainers	3 Billion	Healthful	Clean	Modest	Bus/Bike
Over-consumers	1 Billion	Meat-Based	Clean	Conspicuous	Car/Plane

From the Christian Reformed World Relief Committee's *Partner* letter (1 April 1992). Based on material in David C. Korten, *Getting to the 21st Century* (West Hartfield, Conn.: Kumarian, 1990).

Some fear that the teaching of economic justice or the economic implications of shalom "politicizes" Christian schools; however, teaching an economic status quo is just as "political" an act, usually more self-serving, and contrary to the biblical call. Glenn Tinder (1989, 69) writes, "The notion that we can be related to God and not to the world— that we can practice a spirituality that is not political—is in conflict with the Christian understanding of God." He points out that the extremes of ostentatious wealth on the one hand and Calcuttan poverty on the other testify to our weak moral and spiritual grounding. While we celebrate the global downfall of authoritarian communism and the establishment of free market economies, we need to remind ourselves that the principles of capitalism are dangerously anticommunal. As Tinder (1989, 84) concludes, "A system that enables an industrial society to achieve a degree of order and efficiency without depending on either goodness or governmental coercion cannot be entirely despised. Nevertheless, even if capitalism worked as well as its supporters claim, it would by Christian standards fail morally and spiritually."

This failure is evident in its impact upon the world which God has entrusted to our care. Calvin DeWitt (1991, 14–22) describes seven degradations of the creation: land conversion and habitat destruction, species extinction, land degradation, resource conversion and wastes and hazards production, global toxification, alteration of planetary exchange, and human and cultural degradation. These degradations, suggests DeWitt, form an "arrogant assault on the fabric of the biosphere," a crisis beyond what the world has ever known, a crisis rooted in a profound *religious* misunderstanding of how we should relate to each other and to the created world. The problem is that in the last several centuries, "we have chosen to redefine the long-recognized vices of avarice and greed as virtues. We have come to believe that 'looking out for number one' means getting more and more for *self*" (DeWitt 1991, 22).

Our schools cannot pretend that these economic pressures and their environmental consequences do not exist. The question is whether we have the will to confront them.

Media Domination

According to the authors of *Dancing in the Dark*, most children today are immersed in an independent youth culture that is transferred and communicated through electronic media (Schultze et al. 1991). The traditional triangle of influence—church, home, and school—has become a rectangle that includes the electronic media. A nightmare world seems close to reality: children's social and sexual expectations shaped by thousands of hours of TV shows, their values and life goals determined by advertising, their leisure time spent with video games, VCRs, and headset radios (Clark 1989). Reading and reflective, principled thought takes too much effort (Postman 1985). Children (like some adults) want only speed, toys, and sugar.

At the same time that we may resent how the media dominate our lives, we also realize they have great potential for informing us of the condition of our global world. With such information we are better equipped to make responsible decisions that could move our world closer to shalom. Because media "savviness" will become more and more essential if we are to be discerning, responsive disciples of Christ, the Christian school must serve up an antidote to the media-driven superficiality and violence and sex-as-commodity orientation that surrounds us.

Too often teaching such media discernment is neglected. Media courses might include filming technique or anti-advertising units, but they fall short of analyzing the full range of the media industry's economic, social, and cultural effects.

On the positive side, the Christian school should teach children to claim the cultural good available in media culture. Children would learn to forego those TV shows, movies, music, or magazines that are sensationalist and superficial in favor of the deep and abiding. Students would also learn to find reliable sources of information from the various media and to use that information wisely. In sum, as Vern Boerman (1975) put it, the Christian school joins with the church and parents to hammer the rectangle back into a triangle.

The mass media are but one facet of a life dominated by the trappings of technology, the myriad of devices—fax machines, cellular phones, computers, pagers—designed to make our life easier, which can in fact accelerate it to a pace seemingly beyond our control. We live "in an era so seduced by the instantaneous that we're in grave danger of losing our ability to wait. Life moves at a staggering pace" (Kidd 1990, 17). The "ability to wait," to pause and reflect, suggests Kidd, is a key to spiritual growth that we have misplaced, or more accurately, hurried past, in an age of rapid change. Perhaps Christian educators, when considering the latest educational technology, should go beyond discussing its educational effectiveness to ask, "What does this technology do to our souls?" (Monsma 1986).

Family Mobility and Social Disintegration

In the last half of the nineteenth century, as social mobility and economic opportunities increased, fathers left the home for the workplace, leaving mothers to assume more of the child-rearing duties. One hundred years later, mothers made the same move from home to workplace. Janice Castro (1992, 41) writes, "With both parents typically holding down jobs, home life has been reduced to a mad scramble at the end of the day to cram in shopping, laundry, cooking, mending—and, oh, yes, communication." The school was the only logical institution to assume the responsibilities abdicated by the parents—from serving breakfast to handing out birth control aids to teaching students how to drive.

We lament not simply the problems faced by the nuclear family, which, improperly understood, can lead to further privatization, isolation, and loss of genuine community. We also lament the social mobility and disruption in contemporary society that seems to be accelerating. Broken homes, substance abuse, runaway consumerism, gangs, alcoholism, teen suicide, poverty, free-floating anxiety about the future and the meaning of life—what are the implications for educators of such a deterioration in the fabric of North American society? What can the school as school do? What is the relationship between the way our schools are structured (often impersonally) and oriented (usually competitively) and our felt loss of community? For example, how much of the substance abuse among young people is actually self-medication? How often are problem peer groups (in their worst form, gangs) simply the way kids obtain the feelings of belonging and acceptance that they crave?

All of our concerns—economic injustice and environmental break-down, media domination, family and social disruption—are only examples of areas needing attention by Christian schools. These are areas where the world is hurting. These are jumping-off points for mission. These are some of the best places to work as responsive disciples of Christ.

Christian schools have an institutional role in bringing about shalom, human and creational flourishing. An eloquent explanation of what shalom is comes from Cornelius Plantinga (1990, 24–25). "We call it peace, but [shalom] means so much more than just peace of mind, or cease-fire among enemies. In the Bible shalom means *universal wholeness and delight*, each created thing a wonder, each created person a source of joy, and the Creator and Savior opening doors and speaking welcome to his children." Our calling in education, says Plantinga (1990), is to equip ourselves with the knowledge, skills, and attitudes "that can be thrown into the struggle for shalom." The question now before us is how to build places where such education takes place.

The Challenge Facing Christian Schooling

Charles Glenn (1988) describes the "myth of the common school" and its power over our cultural life. Robert Coles (1987) claims we are neglecting the moral and spiritual lives of children. Robert Bellah (1985) has described our loss of a common moral vision and the language of moral discourse. Dozens of educational scholars have described the subculture of schooling and its emphasis on competition and individual enhancement. What do we as Christian school educators and parents make of all this as we seek to shape our schools for the twenty-first century?

Because "schooling" is a subculture, its structures and procedures and programs—the take-it-for-granted givens—are deeply entrenched in the expectations of everyone. Everything from the agricultural year to cheerleaders to diplomas awarded for "seat time" are a part of the subculture. There is little questioning of the status quo. There is little discernment. Those involved shrug, "We've always done it this way. It seems to work pretty well. Why fix it if it isn't broken?"

Of course, whenever one brings a large number of people together, there have to be routines and organization. Time and space and other resources have to be allocated. This will be done fairly and efficiently. But an organization can unfortunately take on a life of its own, and the living, growing communal purposes that were originally meant to be served can suffer as a consequence. Any subculture's resistance to change is partly psychological (we are creatures of habit) and partly institutional (schools are very conservative organizations). But in addition, the schooling subculture provides benefits to society that are not specifically educational. Schools provide a warehousing or baby-sitting function for children until society is ready for them in the workplace. They are a sorting mechanism, providing credentials for moving into economic and social positions. Employers and colleges embrace the credentialing system as a means of ascertaining the quality of applicants. Various tests (ACT, SAT, etc.) are a part of the processing and sorting structure. Thus, much depends on the school fulfilling its assigned function in society.

The entrenched nature of the schooling subculture and the inability of those involved to reconsider aims and methods led Jeannie Oakes (1985, 27) in *Keeping Track* to complain:

> We seldom think very much about where practices came from originally and to what problems in schools they were first seen as solutions. We rarely question the view of the world on which practices are based—what humans are like, what society is like, or even what schools are for. We almost never reflect critically about the beliefs we hold about them or about the manifest and latent consequences that result from them. And I think this uncritical, unreflective attitude gets us into trouble. It permits us to act in ways contrary to our intentions. In short, it can lead us and, more important, our students down a disastrous road despite our best purposes.

Christian schools need the institutional self-examination suggested by Oakes as much as public schools because Christian schools often have an unsettling resemblance to their public counterparts. Critics would say that the schools are tainted, that they are "both in the world and of it," that they are simply private schools staffed and populated by people who go to church. In their methods, curricula, structures, and ethos, Christian schools have followed too closely the public school's

56

lead. They have not taken advantage of their unique position to be an alternative; they have not fully worked out the specifics of practice that arise out of their vision of life.

Christian schools, like most schools, are conservative institutions. They have been more reactive to red herrings originating from the church or parents than proactive on the basis of a sound reading of research, the culture, and their guiding faith. Far from advocating change that is based on research, Christian educators have often been strongly skeptical of such research, choosing to neither fund it nor trust it. As a result, the problems of Christian schooling go undetected, and the successes go unexplained.

For example, if Christian schools enjoy high academic scores (and often they do), is such achievement due to the conditions of sponsorship—usually parent-controlled societies? Or is it simply because most Christian school students are from white, two-parent, $40,000-plus, English-speaking households? Only empirical research can enable us to answer these questions (Vryhof 1992).

Besides attending to serious research and its recommendations, Christian educators must help Christian communities see how their individual Christian schools have become what they presently are. They need to narrate—to tell the story, to identify the social and cultural influences, to put up the mirror of self-recognition, to acknowledge both successes and sins—in order to show how institutions have both stood against and accommodated themselves to the surrounding culture.

For example, many Christian schools were originally intended to isolate and insulate their children from the surrounding culture, preserving an ethnic and a denominational purity. Some schools have matured greatly from such beginnings but many remain limited to a particular ethnic and denominational group. Why is that? What social and cultural expectations have shaped us and continue to shape us in such directions?

Christian school people need to realize that the *context* of Christian schooling—in this case the secularized and fragmented subculture of schooling in North America—might not fit the mission of the Christian school as understood today. We may be trying to put new wine into old wineskins. Our children—new creatures in Christ—do not belong in the traditional schooling structures. We should not expect nor should we *want* Christian schooling to match the surrounding cultural context.

Profoundly important questions result: What is the mission of the Christian school in twenty-first century society? Indeed, what is the nature and task of the Christian life in today's pluralistic world? How are we to think of our institutional mission? What is it we ought to be about? Then educational specifics must be explored: What ethos should characterize a Christian school? What curricula should be offered? What structures and relationships should be put in place? How do we assess? And finally, when, if ever, do we say we have succeeded?

A Vision with a Task

A vision without a task is but a dream;
a task without a vision is drudgery;
a vision with a task is the hope of the world.

Inscription in a church in Sussex, England, 1730

The current educational scene *seems* alive with ferment and innovation ranging from philosophy for children to video-disk science instruction to cooperative learning to writing-across-the-curriculum to whole language. How many of these innovations are really taking hold in Christian schools? How many *should,* given the task of Christian schooling? What is the best new wineskin for the new wine? As Christian school people consider the dozens of educational ideas around them, what elements of a Christian vision of education can help them make their decisions?

The answers to such questions will move us beyond the ordinary picking and choosing among educational specifics (or worse, following the whims of today's most powerful subset of parents) to a fundamental restructuring and reorientation of the school's mission and purpose in which educating for responsive discipleship—the free and willing commitment to be faithful to all that Christ has taught us—becomes the highest priority.

Education, David Purpel (1989, 12) insists, requires not only knowledge and skills, but also "a commitment to a vision of who we are and what we ought to be." Such a vision is unavoidably religious. In the public school, the espoused vision is unmitigatingly secular, though many communities and teachers work to subvert this. But, as John Alexander (Marty 1991b, 1) affirms,

Kids need to be nurtured in an environment sensitive to spirituality. Where the wonders and horrors of the universe are considered at least as often as are the names of the state capitals. Where the adults lead lives of grace and truth, and where justice is as important as grades. Where the study of poetry does not focus on meter but on finding ways to express depths unknown to scientific formulas.

And, we would add, where service of God in a loving relationship with him is the pervasive theme.

But a vision is not only a way of seeing: it is also a way of going. The vision comes with a task wrapped up in it. Being God's people in the world here and now, with all the weight of sin that constrains us, requires our energy and our effort, with God's wisdom guiding us in our weakness.

Such a vision with a task should not be triumphalistic, in the sense of assuming that we can proudly and brazenly transform the world after our own image. We cannot transform a world marred by sin; this task belongs only to the Lord and Ruler of this world. He will one day return to establish the new heavens and the new earth. Our task is to be a "presence," to live in the world with integrity, to witness to the light of Christ, and to follow him as faithful disciples.

Refusal to take on this hands-dirty-in-the-world dimension of the Christian life must not be considered an option. Our culture, with its extreme of wealth and poverty, is aching for shalom. Christians may not simply wait for the rescue of their souls while working for the American dream. Glenn Tinder (1989) calls for a "hesitant radicalism," an approach to political and social change that is both cautious and far-reaching. No negotiator of compromise, he claims attitudes toward the kingdom of God have to be acted on. This is a matter of spiritual integrity.

> To anticipate the coming of the kingdom is merely sentimental, a private frivolity, unless one tries to reshape society according to the form of the imminent community, a form defined by equality and universality and requiring particular attention to the disinherited and oppressed. . . . From a Christian standpoint, a frightened refusal of all social change would be highly inappropriate. (Tinder 1989, 84).

Understanding both the reality of evil and the reality of grace, then, the Christian community seeks to be a Christ-like presence, salt and light in a needy world. And its schools educate each young person to be just such a presence.

As John sat in front of the television, his mind began to wander. Why did they send their kids to a Christian school? In one sense, he had never given it much thought. He had been to a Christian school and so had Judy. He had always just expected that when their children were old enough, they would follow in their parents' footsteps.

John thought about what Judy had said. "Is it mainly for safety's sake that we made that choice? Of course, I want the best for my kids. I want them to have strong moral values, to be able to get good jobs. I want them to know that God is important in everything they do. But I'm just not sure anymore. It takes such an incredible toll on me and my family. Is Bev right—are caring teachers and a safe environment enough?"

Picking up the newsletter, John got up and went to the kitchen to get himself a juice. Coupon drives, band nights, sports teams—what else was happening at the school? "What do I really know about the curriculum? How different is it from what happens in public schools? Are Judith and Michael any different than they would be in another school? What do I really want from the school anyway?"

Questions for Discussion

1. In what ways does the "myth of the common school" or the public school monopoly affect the establishment and renewal of Christian schools? What can be done to effect a system that better acknowledges parents' rights and the explicitly religious nature of schooling?

2. It has been said that the one word that best describes North American culture is "competitive." Discuss the advantages and disadvantages of a culture that values competition so highly. What types of school structures could provide personal and institutional motivation to become what God wants us to be without paying the price of competition?

3. To what degree is your school community a "lifestyle enclave" as described by Robert Bellah? What could be done in your school to increase diversity, social involvement, and the sharing of burdens?

4. This chapter suggested three contemporary challenges to shalom: economic overconsumption and environmental degradation, media domination, and family mobility and social disintegration. Discuss the validity of each of these three and offer any others which you think are just as, perhaps more, urgent. How should Christian schooling adapt its structures and emphases to address such challenges?

Part **2**

Realizing the Vision

Prelude

Mountain City Christian School stands on the corner of Park Avenue and Mountain Street in Forest, a suburb of Mountain City. The school was founded in 1912 and for its first fifty-one years was located in the city. By the early 1960s it became clear that most of the supporting school community would soon have moved to Forest and other surrounding suburbs so in 1963 the school relocated.

Presently there are approximately six hundred students in kindergarten through grade twelve. Kindergarten and the first five grades are housed in the lower level of the original building that stands along Park Avenue. On the second floor are grades six through nine, which have recently come to be called "middle school." During the 1970s, the original building became crowded and a building for the high school was constructed facing Mountain Street.

In the late 1970s there was a decline in school enrollment because people were having smaller families. In addition, in the mid-1980s a number of younger parents had moved back into the downtown area of Mountain City and after a few years had started a middle school campus, to the relief of those board members who had become weary of their push for change. To offset this decline in enrollment the school was making an effort to attract students from backgrounds other than that of the traditional supporters of the school. Enrollment is up again with 60 percent of the students being from four churches of the denomination that had originally started the school and the other 40 percent from a variety of denominational backgrounds.

These people of diverse backgrounds bring with them different ideas and expectations concerning Christian education and the school association meetings reflect those differences. Some of the board members remember with nostalgia the times when there seemed not to be so much turmoil; others see this as a new opportunity to examine and clarify the mission of the school and how it applies to the present day.

Central Station Christian School is in the heart of Mountain City in the old railroad station that was recently renovated. The parents who had moved back into the city quickly became aware of a need for Christian schooling not only for their children but also as a service to the inner city, where the children came from a wide range of socioeconomic and cultural backgrounds. With some help from grants from businesses and at great personal expense they worked to implement their dream for what a Christian school should be. They decided to begin with a middle school partly because that was where most of their own children were; mostly, however, it was because they realized the strong influence school and peer relationships have on children as they move through their middle and high school years and are no longer quite so strongly influenced by their families' values. Presently in its fourth year of operation, the school has seventy-five students in grades six through nine and the parents are hoping to add the high school grades year by year. The business community of the central city has contributed to the endowment fund that allows children of lower socioeconomic families to attend. They view the school as an important way of bringing life back into the center of the city of 150,000 inhabitants.

As Ken Heard pulled away from the curb in front of Central Station, his face wore a puzzled frown. Were the teachers in that small middle school correct when they claimed that the attitudes of students toward each other, toward school life, and toward their own calling as students are influenced as strongly by the structure and curriculum of the school as they are by relationships with the teachers and with each other? School structure and curriculum were pretty much the same in most of the schools with which he was familiar. If you changed either of them, would that really change student attitudes and behavior?

The board had gone along with the teachers' request that the renovation of the old railroad station include a large open activity area surrounded by small individual work cubicles just off the learning center, and he could see that the renovation provided an unusual and attractive educational setting. Rob Boonstra, the architect who served on the Central Station school board, had really caught the vision of the teachers when he designed the school. But arranging the curriculum so heavily around integral units and keeping the students actively involved with the museums and libraries of the city created a completely different learning environment than the one Ken was used to. He had been relieved that their design included a few classrooms such as those he was familiar with at Mountain City Christian, the larger suburban school for which he was also responsible.

As he drove through the tree-lined streets, past the old firehouse with its attractive boutiques and the gabled Warehouse Condominiums, Ken remembered how this area of the city had looked five years ago. The younger professional people who had moved back into the old city at the beginning of the restoration argued that Christian education was needed for their children as well as for the children of the lower-income families in the area adjacent to Station Park, across the street from the front entrance of the school. They decided to begin small, with a school for grades six through nine. The Mountain City board thought the plan was a good one and Ken was enjoying the experience of being involved in the development of a new school in spite of the time it took to travel between the two campuses.

In all fairness Ken had to admit that he had learned more about the possibilities of what Christian education could be during the four years of Central Station's existence than during all of the rest of the twenty-five years he had been involved with schools. Head teacher Karla Hubbard and the other three teachers on the staff were constantly discussing (rather heatedly at times) issues concerning how the structure and curriculum of the school related to their beliefs about schooling as expressed in their mission statement. All of them seemed convinced that the way instruction and learning took place was central to the task of the school but could not be separated from the larger structural issues.

Ken thought Central Station's staff was interesting. Ted Pakula, with his background in science, math, and computers, seemed to serve as the team conscience concerning ecology. Emmy Perez, although only in her second year of teaching, contributed much from a social studies perspective. Sam Freeland's expertise in music, art, and communications brought the community together in wonderful ways. And Karla Hubbard, as well as teaching herself, provided instructional leadership in addition to keeping the school running smoothly.

Since the beginning of his teaching career Ken had thought of a Christian school as being an orderly place where students were taught to have a Christian point of view, to act like Christians, and to be successful in the work that was assigned to them. He knew that was what the parents expected and he saw his task as principal of a parent-controlled school as one of making certain the parents were pleased with their children's schooling. He really believed that in a Christian school the teachers should teach from a Christian perspective and he made sure that at least once a year he had someone, usually a minister or a professor from a Christian college or a coordinator from a Christian school organization, talk to them about what that meant. Some of the teachers got a little tired of such philosophical speeches but he thought it was good for them. Still, Ken wondered whether more than this was needed. Simply talking about a Christian perspective didn't really seem to change anything unless the structures were in place to allow change to occur.

Ken recognized that in some respects the teachers at Central Station had a more difficult task when it came to pleasing parents because the students were from such diverse backgrounds. On the other hand, Karla and the others had insisted from the beginning that the school must be one where the emphasis was on parental involvement and direction rather than parental control. The constitution was clear that teachers were hired to exercise their professional judgment within the guidelines established by the purpose of the school. Parents who chose to enroll their children in the school were required, with their school-age children, to be interviewed by a committee that consisted of a teacher and a board member. They had to attend sessions in which they discussed the meaning of the mission statement and were encouraged to ask questions about the purpose of the school. Prior to enrollment the students were expected to sign a statement describing the expectations the school had concerning their participation in the school community. All of these expectations had to be met by every school family, whether they paid the regular tuition or qualified for the reduced fees for lower-income families.

The idea of reduced tuition for lower-income families was important to Ken because he was concerned that Mountain City Christian was excluding families who could not pay for it. Christian schooling should be available for every family who wanted it rather than just for those who could afford it. A school that provided education for only middle- and higher-income families would have great difficulty teaching for responsive discipleship.

This engagement of parents in understanding the purposes of the school seemed to make a difference in the expectations the parents had of the school. Ken had attended the association meetings of Central Station and couldn't help noticing that the atmosphere there was rather different from his own school where some of the parents interpreted "parent control" to mean that the parents could tell the teachers and principal what to do whenever they felt like it. In certain ways, the parents at Central Station seemed to view their teachers with greater respect than the parents at Mountain City Christian did.

Just last Wednesday Ken had listened to Karla and her staff explain to the parents why, to as great an extent as possible, the curriculum should be integrative and why efforts must be made to have the students interact with each other while they learned. Karla said that the integral curriculum begins with the belief that life is already full of meaning before we separate it into subject areas and that this fullness of meaning can only be found in Jesus Christ. An integral curriculum does not reject the academic disciplines; rather, it gives them a less dominant role in the content and structure of curriculum. The explanation had helped him as well as the parents see schooling in a new light.

Privately, Ken was surprised by the large turnout for the meeting and suspected it was because of the requirement that parents with children enrolled in the school must participate in specified activities, which included attendance at school goal-setting meetings. He wondered how such a requirement would work at Mountain City Christian with its eighty-year tradition of being the school where most people of his denomination sent their children. Parent-teacher conferences were very well attended but the school association meetings drew a poor crowd. The P.T.A. had disbanded because of lack of interest, although there still was a fund-raising committee that planned the Harvest Festival held every September. Some parents never darkened the door of the school and others came only when they had something to complain about. To require such parents to attend school meetings and to suggest that they would want to be actively involved with their children's learning, as Central Station did, would not meet with widespread approval, Ken was certain. Too many of them thought they had fulfilled their responsibility when they had paid the tuition.

At an earlier meeting Ted Pakula and Emmy Perez had described the concept of responsive discipleship. They said that the Christian school has the particular responsibility of fostering discipleship in greater depth and breadth and with more encompassing response than either the church or the home. The school provides a social-educational setting whose structures enable children and young people to respond to God's call in all aspects of life.

Responsive discipleship, as Ted and Emmy had explained it, covered every aspect of schooling. It is extremely important to a Christian school because the tendencies students develop during their school years to think and act in certain ways, to a great extent, determine how they will think and act as adults. Ted and Emmy described the goals of Central Station School as being to help students and teachers learn to unwrap their gifts, share each other's burdens, and seek God's shalom. The students would respond to their calling as students by developing the knowledge, skills, attitudes, and willingness to take responsibility for their own learning as far as it was possible for them to do so.

They explained that students would learn to respond as disciples of Jesus Christ living and working in community by learning to unwrap the gifts God has given them. Students would learn to willingly take responsibility for each other's learning, care, and nurture and, together with the teachers, would try to build a community in which they rejoiced over each other's successes and carried each other's burdens, showing respect, compassion, and concern for one another. They would learn to respond as disciples who are obedient to the cultural mandate to care for all aspects of God's world, and the calling to seek God's justice and peace in all areas of life.

Emmy had explained that the students would be expected to live as responsive disciples while they are in school as well as learn what discipleship means for the future. She described the school as a place where students and teachers would build a community for seeking God's shalom. But she made it clear that an important part of the students' learning these aspects of responsive discipleship was in the way the parents and teachers would work together to reinforce these ideas and activities in the home and in the school.

She said that many parents think being involved in their childrens' education meant going to school to help in the classrooms or on the playground. The staff at Central Station School understood that, given present-day society, such involvement could no longer be expected. However, she pointed out that whether or not both parents are employed outside the home, they know they have a role in their children's education. School learning is only one part of the great amount of learning children are constantly engaged in. Parents will want to provide a learning environment which will enrich and reinforce school-related learnings and will provide opportunities for new experiences.

That will mean knowing which themes and topics are being studied in school so they may at times be talked about around the dinner table. That will mean making certain the television set and radios are off so that the family will be engaged in reading for enjoyment and talking about what they have read. Sometimes it will mean doing service activities together as a family and talking about those who are in need. It will mean reinforcing the school's teachings concerning environmental issues by living in ways that protect the physical world. Sometimes it might mean helping their children with a particular subject-related activity. Emmy said the staff recognized that parents of students enrolled at Central Station School wanted to be involved in their children's learning and the teachers would make certain to keep them informed about the school so that such involvement could occur.

Ken had to admit that the staff at Central Station presented their ideas well but he was a realist and wondered to what extent the Central Station teachers could pull the whole thing off. It bothered him that Karla and the others seemed to think that their goals for Christian schooling ought to be the goals for every Christian school. It was all so much more difficult when the school was larger and had a long-standing tradition in the community. How would the Mountain City School teachers and education committee react to such ideas? Well, they would find out when they discussed the mission of the school at the staff orientation sessions which would start on August 15.

He turned onto the expressway and could see the empty building that had housed Barker Shoe Manufacturing Company before its move to the suburb of Forest. The parents of the six hundred students in the K-I2 school in Forest owed Tom Barker a debt of gratitude for his years of financial support. In fact, Barker Shoes had provided a good-sized grant for the renovation of Central Station as well. As he entered Forest and headed for Mountain City Christian, he noticed with relief that the trip had taken only thirty minutes. He pulled into the school parking lot and looked around at the neat buildings that architect Rob Boonstra had called "billowing bland boxes of beige bricks." The elementary and high school buildings with the recently completed connecting gym might not please Rob's aesthetic sense but Ken felt a sense of pride about it all. He entered his office to get ready for the first orientation session.

Mountain City Christian School and Central Station Christian School do not actually exist, of course. But we have visited their counterparts in many different places in North America and talked with hundreds of teachers, administrators, parents, and students. Rather than explicitly describing practices in schools we have visited, we are using these two schools to show what is happening and what can happen in Christian schools. Mountain City and Central Station are not perfect schools, nor is either of them a place where change cannot occur. But change will occur differently in the two schools because each works in a different social context and is at a different stage in its development.

Mountain City has the advantage of a large supporting community but the disadvantage of some traditions that are not in keeping with a school in which students will learn to be responsive disciples. Central Station has the advantage of being young and open to developing its own stories and traditions reflective of its purpose for schooling today. However, it has the disadvantage of a narrow base of financial support and a small teaching staff that could easily become overburdened. We will show what happens as each school community and staff tries to understand what it means to educate for responsive discipleship.

3

How Do We Get from Vision to Mission?

What should be the purpose of a Christian school? Who decides that purpose? How should the purpose be carried out? For what learnings should the school be held accountable? The way these questions are answered will provide a direction for the school. Without an answer to these questions the school is open to every wind of change that blows through the community.

Each interest group will have its own idea of how to answer these questions. Some parents and teachers will say that the chief purpose of the Christian school is that students will be as successful as possible in intellectual pursuits in a good moral environment. Others will see the school as a socializing agency where students are sheltered from worldly influences. Some will feel that the Christian school should be a place in which students are opened to new ideas and new ways of thinking. Others will think that Christian schooling is accomplished when students work their way through textbooks in a disciplined and orderly manner. There will also be people in the community who believe that the school should be a place where students are called to personal commitment to Christ and learn to witness to their faith. Consequently, each time there is a change in board members there may be changes in expectations concerning what a school ought to be.

Why Should a Christian School Have a Mission Statement?

Defining the purpose of a Christian school is not merely a matter of coming to consensus concerning what a particular group of people want as the direction for the school, nor is it a matter of negotiating a compromise between competing interest groups. The purpose of a Christian school has to be based on a scriptural vision of Christian education. Its purpose should be an affirmation in response to scriptural revelation, with its central themes of creation, the fall into sin, redemption in Christ, and the fulfillment of God's kingdom when Christ returns. A school cannot be everything to everyone. The people who support the school must understand where the school is going, why it is going there, and how it intends to get there. No two Christian schools, no matter how good, will be exactly alike; nor will either of them be all things to all people. Each should reflect the needs and vision of the people in its own supporting community and each should have its own statement of mission.

Most Christian schools started with a vision, a response to biblical revelation that included particular beliefs about the purpose, direction, and practice of schooling. However, the vision with which schools started has not always been written down. When that happens the vision is in danger of becoming clouded.

A school should have a statement that clearly reflects its vision. Without such a statement, serious misunderstandings can arise over school board decisions.

Pastor: The deacons in our church agreed to sponsor some Southeast Asians. They went to the school board with the money to enroll the children in our local Christian school but they were turned down. The argument of the board was that these people were Buddhists and so were unacceptable. The fact is that the Asians practiced no religion. The school refused to help minister to the needs that only schools are equipped to meet.

A statement is needed to explain clearly what the school is for and what vision will guide its actions. Lee Hollaar (1991, 3) suggests that such a statement may serve as a map:

One must check the map regularly to see if one is still on course or to see if the map is still current, supported by the latest reliable information. This map provides direction and informs the development of curriculum materials such as course and unit outlines. It implies pedagogy, the how of teaching. It suggests ways of evaluating classroom and school practices and policies. It suggests appropriate governance models and practices. It suggests appropriate leadership styles.

A *mission statement* encapsulates the core of that vision in two or three key points. A well-written statement ought to describe what the parents and teachers of that school community believe about learning and teaching. It should tell what the students will experience in the school and why they will have those experiences. It should state what kind of community and environment will be established in that school and why.

If an important purpose of the school is that students and teachers will live and learn to live in community as responsive disciples of Jesus Christ, experiencing what it is to respond personally and communally in all areas of life, then that must be clearly stated in the mission statement. If an important purpose is that students will experience taking responsibility for their own learning and for each other's learning, care, and nurture, that must be stated. If an important purpose is that students learn to be servants of Jesus Christ, helping those who are in need, that must be a part of the mission statement. The school will then be committed to identifying ways of thinking about curriculum, instruction, discipline, evaluation, and even the structure of the school day and year, that are in conformity with this statement.

Mission Statement of Central Station Christian School

Central Station Christian Middle School, a denominationally and culturally diverse educational community, seeks to provide a secure learning environment in which students and teachers can explore and evaluate all of life under God. Recognizing a variety of student abilities, it aims to uncover and develop the unique giftedness of each student so that he or she may become a follower of Jesus Christ who is a faithful and creative servant of God and neighbor and steward of His world.

"One of the things we have tried to do at Central Station School," said Karla Hubbard in her presentation of Station's mission statement, "is to keep the statement before the teachers, the students, and the parents. We are trying to live in the spirit of Deuteronomy 6 in which we are told that we are to impress God's commandments on our children and write them on the door frames of our houses and on our gates.

"In that spirit we are trying to keep our mission in constant focus in the school. We have commissioned a sculpture representing our mission for the entrance of the building. Our students have made wonderful posters and banners representing phrases from the statement. You will find it on our report cards and on our newsletters. We use it for a focus for all that we do."

There is research evidence that effective schools have principals and teachers who understand the mission of the school and are able to articulate that mission because it is such an important part of their thinking (Rutherford 1985). The ethos of the school is created, in part, by leaders who state in a variety of ways that at this school we stand for these ideas, we are these kinds of people, and we will accomplish these things. The mission statement is our way of thinking about and talking about ourselves.

Principal: I think we have a serious add-on problem in our school. There are all sorts of interesting courses people would like to have us teach. For example, we should really teach an interdisciplinary course like "Living in Hope." And some parents are asking us to have advanced placement courses. It would be worthwhile to have all students know a good deal about computers. Yet, we only have time and resources for some of these. How do we decide how to use the resources that we have?

A well-written mission statement that is kept before the school community can protect the school from the "add-on" problem. Very often a group of parents will bring to the principal an idea for the curriculum or a way of doing things that seems interesting but will take instructional time to accomplish. Or an individual teacher will be impressed by a method or a practice described at a conference and will propose that all the teachers at that level of schooling try out the idea. The mission statement can help the principal and teachers determine whether including that idea in the curriculum merits excluding some other aspect.

Process for Developing a Mission Statement

In thinking about how a mission statement might be written for a Christian school, it is necessary to identify guiding principles that are in keeping with biblical norms. Some organizations have developed such principles which schools might consider when writing their mission statement (Van Dyk 1985; Van Brummelen and Vriend 1981; Vryhof et al. 1989).

The Potter's House Christian Middle School has identified the following principles:

1. *Responsive disciples:* Each student is encouraged to enter into a personal relationship with a loving God who will help the student learn how to respond to him and to all aspects of his creation.
2. *Interrelatedness of all aspects of God's creation:* Each student is encouraged to understand how every element of God's creation is interrelated. The world in which a student lives is intricately connected with his or her personal development (spiritual, intellectual, social, physical, and emotional). Students are encouraged to see how, as Christians, their beliefs will help them establish life-long biblical principles in every area.
3. *Living in community:* Students are encouraged to develop relationships built upon trust, respect, and appreciation. We value the uniqueness, ethnic diversity, and cultural background of each student. We are a "family" at The Potter's House. Students learn to work together in cooperation, assuming responsibility not only for their own learning, but also for the accomplishments of others. Our family extends beyond peer relationships to loving relationships with staff, school families, and our local community.

Involving the Parents in Articulating the Mission Statement

Teacher: I'll tell you what happened at our school. The board decided that we had to have a mission statement. The principal was supposed to write it but he was really dreading the task. So he asked me if I would be willing to help. Together we came up with what we thought was a pretty good statement.

Interviewer: What happened to the statement after you wrote it? Did the board adopt it?

Teacher: I know the principal gave it to the school board but from what I heard, there wasn't much discussion about it. They must have adopted it, though, because last year I saw it in a handbook for new parents. But we never discussed it as a staff and, as far as I can tell, most of the staff doesn't know it exists unless they saw it in the handout.

What happens in cases like this is that those who have been assigned the task of writing the mission statement for a school often simply look around and ask, "What have we been doing in the past and what are we doing now?" The result of that exercise finds its way into the document and the past and present activities provide information concerning how the school will be guided in the future. This hardly provides the visionary direction needed for a Christian school.

It is essential that parents become actively involved in creating the mission statement if it is going to have an important place in the life of the school. God has given parents the ultimate responsibility for the nurture of their children. Christian schools came into being and continue to exist because of the deep commitment of parents to schooling that honors the lordship of Christ. Recognizing that parents share with teachers the task of educating students, it follows that parents must have a primary role in stating the mission and direction of the school.

How the involvement of parents will occur will vary because each school community is different. If a school has existed for a long time the community will need to rethink the vision. A new school community will want to set about articulating a vision. Either way, the board should appoint a committee consisting of two or three members of each group: parents, teachers, and board members. One process for accomplishing this work has been outlined at the end of this chapter (question 3).

The mission statement committee had met for two hours each week during the last month. "I can't believe how much I have learned about what the goals for Christian schooling ought to be if they are in keeping with biblical guidelines," said Mark Wever, the father of a fourth grader. "I am truly grateful to the teachers on this committee for so carefully introducing the articles we were assigned. Having you people point out the central issues of each article before we read was helpful to those of us who generally read in areas other than education."

"I must admit that preparing for these discussions and listening to your points of view concerning what Christian parents expect of schools has helped renew my focus on the task at hand," answered Joan Fisher. "It would be great if every parent, teacher, and board member had the opportunity to participate in discussions like these."

Ken Heard nodded. "We will have to think of ways to make certain that happens. As we move forward in our discussion and writing we must involve the entire community, or at the very least we must make certain to keep everyone informed concerning each stage of our work."

"Perhaps we could try a strategy used in my company," board member Betsy Merrick proposed. "We presently have a committee of nine. Consider dividing into three groups for the purpose of involving the larger community in discussions. Each of our groups will consist of one parent, one board member, and one teacher. We have already decided on a series of tasks we must accomplish. Each small group might be assigned one or two tasks and it would be the goal of that group to think of a way of involving the larger community in completing that task."

"An interesting idea," said Ken. "But we will have to undertake each task with as efficient a use of time as is possible. Otherwise we run the risk of exhausting the community with meetings."

Nick Muffit looked up. "That's true. I also think it's important that, to as great an extent as possible, our group involvement always includes teachers, parents, and board members rather than separating them into categories. There is a natural overlap in the groups, anyway, because teachers and board members often either have been or will be parents. But our discussion plans must demonstrate that our entire community is working together on this project."

"Do you mean that for the teacher group, also?" asked Joan. "We were planning to ask them to work on goal statements."

"I still think they should be an important source for ideas for goal statements but when they work together I would like to have parents and board members participate. The school is the responsibility of all of us."

After the parents, working with the teachers and principal, have identified the biblical guidelines providing direction for the school, those involved in writing the mission statement will need to gather more specific information. Questions should be asked concerning the history of the school, such as: How did this school come to be? What motivated people to start this school? To what extent was this school started because of unhappiness with what was happening in the community schools? What was the original vision when this school was started? Do we believe that vision was appropriate?

The committee will want to gather information concerning its school community and the surrounding community: What kinds of people make up our school community? What are our students like? What kinds of interactions have our students had with the people of the community? What community resources are there that might be helpful in the education of our students? What services will be available for our students from the government-supported community schools?

The committee will seek information concerning the present conditions of the school: What do we consider to be the strengths of our school? What weaknesses are we able to identify? What attempts have been made in the past to capitalize on the strengths and to remedy the weaknesses?

While not all of this information will become part of the mission statement nor of the objectives, it is important to have a clear picture of the kind of school that already exists.

Involving the Teachers in Articulating the Mission Statement

After listening to a presentation by the teachers and Education Committee of Central Station concerning how they had developed a mission statement, the board members of Mountain City concluded that going through this process would be good for their own school. They appointed a committee of two board members, two teachers, and two parents to lead the community through the process. Next they divided into working teams with each team consisting of a board member, a teacher, and a parent. They then decided on the tasks each team would complete and agreed on a date for completion. They spent some time discussing how the teams would go about working at their tasks.

Joan Fisher's team had the task of involving the teachers in articulating the mission statement. She was to conduct the meeting with the teachers, and the other team members had promised to invite a few parents and board members and also to lend support in any way possible.

The day of the meeting arrived and Joan was well prepared. "I would like to begin by reminding you of why our committee was assigned this task. For a long time we have had a constitution that pretty much tells how the school will be organized. It describes the qualifications of the principal and the teachers, and tells who has what responsibilities. It tells what will be required of parents who send their children to this school.

"However, the board and some of the teachers felt that we needed a statement concerning our reason for being. The staff at Central Station School has worked hard at developing its own mission statement and the teachers there said that the process was very worthwhile. We need such a statement because there are parents who come to us and say they are looking for a school for their children and ask what we are about. We also need a statement that will provide direction for us so that we are not pulled around all the time by arguments concerning what our school ought to be doing." With that introduction, Joan began her report on the work of the committee.

"Because the committee recognizes that the articulation of a vision for a school is the work of representatives of all parts of the school community, they really would like to know what the teachers think the purpose of this school should be," Joan continued. "In preparation for our work today, you were asked to read the article sent to you. We are going to use that paper as a focal point in our discussion concerning the mission of this school and the result of our work today will be given to the committee."

"That sounds like a huge waste of time," said Glenn Prince, as he stood up and looked around the room. "I don't know about the rest of you but I've got too much on my plate as it is. I understand that Christian Schools International has just published a statement. I suggest that we adopt that one and get on with our work. Or otherwise, why not call around and try to get mission statements from other schools and use one of those?"

Ken Heard spoke from the back of the room. "At a later point in their work the committee will surely want to study that document and will also look at statements from other schools. However the committee members feel strongly that the process of reflecting on these matters will be beneficial to all of us, especially to those of us involved in the day-to-day activities of school life."

"To help us with our task we have asked Joe Morris to lead us through the activities of the day," Joan continued. "You all know Joe well. He is from the Education Department of Bethlehem College. Joe, we are in your hands."

Joe had been listening to the dialogue up to this point and, although he was aware that there was some tension in the group, he decided to ignore that fact and get to work. He began with a brief introduction concerning why a Christian school community should commit itself to creating a mission statement. When he had finished his introductory remarks he asked everyone to write three to five statements answering the question, "What are some of the issues facing your school?" For fifteen minutes the only sound in the room was the rustling of paper.

When most of the teachers had completed the task, Joe said, "At this point I would like you to form groups of three. It would be better if each group has one elementary school teacher and one from the high school, with the middle school teachers spread throughout the groups as much as possible. The task of each group will be to share the individual ideas. Don't discard any of them. If some of you have similar ideas you may combine them, if everyone agrees." The chairs scraped and creaked as the teachers redistributed themselves around the tables.

Joe watched the groups carefully and when he saw that most of them had completed their task he said, "Now I would like to have each group join with one other group so that we have groups of six. Again, your task is the same. Share your ideas but don't discard any. At this point, list the issues on a large sheet of chart paper. You may combine those that are similar."

The work continued and Joe was grateful that the tension of the earlier discussion seemed to have disappeared. He admired Ken Heard's ability to participate in the discussion of one group while keeping an eye on the way things were going in other parts of the room. Joe had led workshops such as this for schools in which principals either chose not to participate or else they did so while ignoring the working of the other groups. Ken had a wonderful way of showing that he thought the work they were doing was extremely important and Joe was grateful for this. He knew that the success of a day such as this depended greatly on the attitude and participation of the principal.

When the groups of six appeared to have completed their work, Joe had them form groups of twelve and repeat the process. After about ten minutes, he called everyone back together. He then presented to them a framework for articulating a vision for Christian schooling. He explained why it was important that they begin with trying to understand what they and others on their staff think are the issues facing Christian schooling today. He then invited the groups to explain the issues listed on their chart paper.

As they broke for lunch, Joe could hear the continuing discussion of the issues that had been listed. Kate Ladder, one of the secretaries, collected the chart papers; she had promised Joe that she would have typed copies of each group's list for use in the afternoon session.

Issues Facing Mountain City Christian School

Group one:
1. If we say that our students must learn to unwrap the gifts of responsive discipleship, what does that mean in very specific terms?
2. Should we be more interdenominational than we are? How do we need to change to make that possible? What could be the results?
3. What does it mean to say we are a *community* of learners?
4. What specific biblical interpretation do we as a school promote? Do we think of ourselves as creationists? Do we interpret Scripture in a literal way? in an allegorical way? Does that say anything about how we might think about the use of fantasy literature?
5. Are our daily tasks and activities really biblical? How can we strengthen our students' faith commitment?
6. Are there ways of assessing learning that are in keeping with our vision?
7. How do we promote fruit of the Spirit (compassion, forgiveness, self-sacrifice, etc.) in the midst of success and prosperity?

Group two:
1. Parents have so many different expectations of the school and not all agree with each other. How do we meet everyone's expectations when the expectations differ so much?
2. Does Scripture continue to be our first and primary source? What place does it have in our schools?

3. Do we place enough emphasis on our students' relationship to Jesus Christ? Do we care enough about spirituality?
4. What does it mean to "integrate faith and learning"? If it means that we teach with a "creation-fall-redemption motif," how can we do so effectively?
5. How do we equip our students to use the Bible to grapple with issues in the community and in the world?

Group three:

1. Are we providing quality education for all? At the advanced level, at the general level, and at the basic level?
2. What does it mean to design and model Christian curriculum? Is there a Christian way to think?
3. The rising cost of Christian schooling is encouraging two-income families. Is that eroding nurturing in the home?
4. What are specific ways we can help our students learn to share each other's joys and burdens? Do our current discipline policies help or hinder this?
5. Does the secularization of the community obscure the vision of the school?

Group four:

1. How do we prepare students for living in the world?
2. Shall we organize more student outreach as Christian teams to help in service projects both in our city and in the Third World?
3. What does it mean to seek God's shalom in a community of learners?
4. Our school follows a factory model of education. What effect does that have on the students?
5. Does decreased parental involvement in schooling mean less interest in the school?
6. The teaching staff does not have adequate time for reflection. How can we be reflective practitioners?

Joe began the afternoon session with a brief presentation on the importance of building a core of shared values in a school community. "Our basic question for this afternoon is, 'What guides our work here at Mountain City Christian?' In order to answer that I would like to have each of you begin by listing from three to five statements that complete the stems I will show you."

Joe turned on the overhead projector.

"Mountain City Christian School should be a place where . . ."

"The steps we should take to achieve that purpose are . . ."

After fifteen minutes Joe said, "Will you now again organize yourselves into groups of three making certain that your group contains one elementary teacher and one secondary teacher and also making certain that you are not working with anyone from your original morning group. Your discussions will be better that way. Your task is first of all to share and celebrate each other's ideas. After that, come to a consensus concerning five statements that present your group's vision for Mountain City Christian."

After some scuffling around and refilling of coffee cups the groups settled down to work. Joe knew that coming to a consensus was a difficult task for any group of teachers but he was delighted with the willing spirit that seemed to pervade the room. He was also pleased to see that Glenn Prince was taking a leadership role in his group.

The groups worked until it was time for a short break. They seemed eager to get on with things in spite of the fact that they had worked hard all day. After the break, Joe asked each group to present its goals.

Goals for Mountain City Christian School

Group one:
Mountain City Christian School should be a place where:

1. students can learn to live as Christians both in the Christian community and in the secular community;
2. students can understand the "whys" and "hows" that make the world what it is today and can learn to understand what their own place is in that dynamic world;
3. students are respected by their peers and by the entire staff;
4. students feel they belong, thus developing a sense of belonging to a larger Christian community;
5. students can explore creation and thus develop into mature adults.

Group two:
Mountain City Christian School should be a place where:

1. students learn a value system that will provide a framework for Christian living;
2. students learn life skills that will allow them to function in society in a meaningful way;
3. students come to know what it is to have a personal relationship with Christ and serve him joyfully;
4. students learn to unwrap the different gifts God has given them.

Group three:

Mountain City Christian School should be a place where:

1. students have experiences that allow them to make an active response to God;
2. academic excellence is promoted (What other kinds of excellence should be promoted in school?);
3. students and staff grow in their understanding of responsive discipleship;
4. students and staff experience Christian fellowship;
5. personal self-esteem is encouraged and promoted in obedience to God's calling;
6. students and teachers see God's shalom.

Group four:
Mountain City Christian School should be a place where:

1. students learn that Jesus is Lord of all of life;
2. students learn to be and become disciples of Jesus Christ inside and outside the school;
3. the Bible illuminates the stuff of life and where students learn to discern, evaluate, and learn from a Christian perspective in all subject areas;
4. students learn to share each other's joys and burdens.

Group five:
Mountain City Christian School should be a place where:

1. students come to recognize their personal talents, acknowledging them as gifts from God which they must develop, and including intellectual and aesthetic skills as well as other gifts;
2. students are encouraged to care for, serve, and respect others;
3. students learn what it means to make daily decisions in ways that reflect responsive discipleship.

Group six:
Mountain City Christian School should be a place where:

1. Christ is the center of education;
2. goals and values are clearly defined;
3. Christians of different persuasions feel welcome;
4. discipline guides students into the truth.

After the presentations, Joe gave them the task of combining similar statements. When the lists had been reordered as much as possible it was time to rank the goals in order of their importance. "When you move back into your groups," said Joe, "make a list of the sixteen goals that are left. Using a total of sixteen pennies, assign pennies to each goal in order of importance. You do not have to assign pennies to every goal but you may not assign the same number to any two goals." After the number of pennies assigned to each goal had been added together the group discussed the priorities that had been set. After they had made a few adjustments, the general feeling was that they had accomplished a great deal. Joe then led them through a discussion of the final goals they had set.

Joan brought the meeting to a close. "I know that some of you are wondering where all of this is leading," she said. "The mission statement committee will review the goals we present to them. The faculty members who are part of the committee will be there to answer any questions concerning our work. This information will become part of the puzzle that the committee is putting together in order to come up with a statement that will reflect the vision of Mountain City Christian School. Joe, we could have gone through these steps without you, but having someone from outside our group and particularly someone with your expertise helped us work our way through the task. Thank you for coming."

Describing the Dream of Your School

Next, each school community must answer the question, "What ought Christian schooling be?" This might be done by having a meeting of representatives from the teaching staff, parents, and board members. This committee could brainstorm answers to the question, "In light of what we know concerning how responsive disciples must live, what kind of school ought our Christian school be?" and "What are the truly important aspects of Christian schooling?"

Gathering the information and describing the dream will take time and energy and will be the work of a series of meetings. But once the discussion has taken place, the committee will have the background for stating the vision for its Christian school.

Writing the Statement

Articulating a statement that will work for the students, parents, staff, and community and for the glory of God can be accomplished in a single day if the background information has been gathered and if there have already been discussions of dreams and possibilities for a particular Christian school. At this point the committee might want to examine mission statements that other Christian school groups have written. Though schools differ, there are certain purposes and goals that all Christian schools share. These goals, along with the purposes that make each school distinctive, must appear with the mission statement.

The school's mission statement should be brief, with a tightly structured core of beliefs and values concerning students living and learning to live as responsive disciples of Jesus Christ. It should declare that the school will prepare students to understand the interrelatedness of the universe. It should state that students will be helped to understand God's will for all areas of the creation and for their lives and will learn to act in accordance with that understanding.

The mission statement has a symbolic value, providing a sense of significance and importance concerning the work of the school. It should capture the spirit of the community of believers setting forth on a journey together. It should include descriptive phrases that can be used frequently so that the vision will be woven into the fabric of the everyday operation of the school.

Stating the Objectives That Explain the Mission Statement

A carefully constructed mission statement does not provide details concerning how the purpose will be carried out. That is a matter for the *statement of objectives,* which will follow the mission statement. The objectives are a means of clarifying the mission statement. Each objective must be clearly defined in terms of what it means for specific areas of the school, such as school-as-community, pedagogy, curriculum, evaluation, student life, and administration. The Potter's House Christian Middle School again provides an example:

> In developing responsive disciples of Jesus Christ, in showing the interrelatedness of God's creation, and in encouraging a sense of community, each student will be helped to develop both personally and in relationship to God, others, and his creation.

Personal growth will be aided by

1. developing an understanding of self, a sense of self-worth in Christ, and the ability to accept talents and limitations gracefully;
2. developing an understanding of their emerging adolescence and an ability to make morally responsible choices, understanding that choices have long-term consequences;
3. developing intellectual discipline and persistence; learning to see error, as well as success, as a part of the learning process; valu-

ing the learning process by developing an intelligence that is active, inquiring, objective, open, flexible, critical, and decisive;
4. developing leadership potential through cooperative learning, student government, elementary tutoring, family worship, and a variety of community service projects;
5. developing creative capacity and the ability to enjoy a sense of freedom of expression through art, music, drama, and literature, thereby gaining aesthetic awareness through participation, appreciation, and evaluation.

Growth in relationship to God, others, and his creation will be aided by

1. developing the ability given by God to respond to him in reverence, wonder, joy, and affirmation with all of their being;
2. developing an understanding of and respect for others, and a sense of cooperation and tolerance; learning to accept and appreciate individual differences;
3. developing a social consciousness, a world view, and a sense of citizenship through various forms of community involvement;
4. developing an appreciation of God's awesome creation through responsive stewardship to the changing environment of our community and the world.

Comparing the Mission Statement and Objectives with What Is Presently Happening

After the mission statement has been written and the objectives have been listed and clarified, it is time to present them to the board as a whole. The committee representatives should be prepared to describe the procedure they used in coming to the final product.

When the board has discussed, modified, and approved the statement and objectives it is time for the committee to present them to the supporting community. Together, the members of the community will want to step back and compare the new plan for schooling with what is presently happening in the school. It is important that the parents, teachers, and board members work together in making this assessment. There are a number of ways in which this involvement can occur.

Memo from Ken Heard in the parents' newsletter:

Many of you know that we have been working hard at writing our mission statement. It has now been approved by the board for circulation to the society. We are eager to share it with you for your reactions so that we may know what changes should still be made. The board has decided that the best way to discuss the statement is to have small groups of parents meet with one board member and one teacher. The purpose of the meeting will be to review the mission statement and then to discuss the ways in which the school presently fulfills its mission and areas that need improvement.

All parents' names have been randomly selected and assigned to a particular meeting place and time. Your time and place appear on the flyer attached to this newsletter. If it is impossible for you to attend a meeting on the evening for which you have been scheduled, please call the school office and we will arrange for a time that fits your schedule. It is very important that all parents attend. This is the Lord's school but he has entrusted its oversight to you.

There may be a gap between many aspects of the existing situation in your school and your intentions for the future. Determine where these gaps are and list all the things that must be done in order to move from where you are now to where you will be when the vision has become a reality.

When the list has been made, determine your priorities. No school community can work at the same time on all of the changes that need to be made. Decide the order in which the changes must take place. Determine who has the responsibility for working on that particular piece of the whole. Spend some time in brainstorming ways each individual or committee might go about completing the assigned task. And, if possible, establish a time when you hope to have each change completed.

Groups or individuals who have been given an assignment could then create a plan for implementation and establish a time when they expect to have completed each aspect of the plan. The plan should be presented and approved by the committee that is overseeing the entire project.

Keeping the Mission Before the Staff, the Parents, and the Community

Unless the mission statement is woven into the fabric of the everyday happenings in the school, it will be little more than a worthless piece of paper. Every teacher and student must know the purpose of the school and it is the task of the principal to keep that purpose constantly before them. In the most effective schools, teachers speak clearly and easily concerning the mission of the school because they were involved in describing and shaping it. In the most effective schools, students are willing to discuss how everyday activities fit with the purpose of the school because their parents and teachers have involved them in discussions concerning it.

Interviewer: Is there ever a danger that the mission statement will become something of a slogan or cliché?

Principal: Of course that could happen. But it seems to me a far greater danger that the basic concepts of the mission statement will be forgotten or lost in the daily routine. Even if the kids make teasing comments about "servanthood" or "discipleship" or "building shalom," at least they will know that is what we are about and that we take our task seriously.

Interviewer: Now that you have your mission statement and objectives in place, will they be the guiding force for all time?

Principal: To the extent that a mission statement reflects biblical guidelines and the vision a community has for schooling, the mission statement will provide direction. However, while God's truths will be our guide for all time, what those truths mean for our lives must be a matter of ongoing discussion. Therefore, we have already planned that five years from now we will do this same kind of review of our purpose and goals.

Interviewer: Have you thought of changes you would like to make in the procedure you use when you are ready for your next study of the mission and objectives?

Principal: The process we have gone through has worked well for us. However, the next time we go through this procedure we plan to involve the students in our discussion. Exactly how we will work that out, I don't know. But we know it is important that students help us reflect on what our vision of a community for learning means for planning what happens in our school.

A school where teachers and students work together to learn what it is to be responsive disciples of Jesus Christ will be a school that is guided by a vision. The vision will be one of all the different parts of the school together creating an ethos of community in which students and teachers unfold the gifts God has given to them, share each other's joys and burdens, and seek God's shalom in order that they may live lives of worshipful kingdom service. Such a vision, clearly defined, will provide a mirror by which the school community may examine itself to see whether it is living and working according to its own stated purposes in keeping with God's plan.

Questions for Discussion

1. What is the vision that guides your school? Does your school have a mission statement? Are all teachers able to articulate that statement? Are they able to explain what each aspect of the mission statement means for curriculum and instruction in their classrooms?

2. Do you think children of parents who are not Christians should be allowed to attend your school? Why or why not? To what extent should the school emphasize the need for personal conversion? for reaching out to persons who are not Christians? for being involved in ministering to the poor or disadvantaged?

3. Using the steps that appear in table 2, plan a series of meetings by which your committee will develop a mission statement and a plan for implementation.

	Resources	Who	When
Table 2			
1. Identifying guidelines for Christian schooling			
2. Gathering the history			
3. Knowing the community			
4. Determining strengths			
5. Determining weaknesses			
6. Determining what a Christian school ought to be			
7. Describing the dream for your Christian school			
8. Writing the mission statement			
9. Writing the objectives			
10. Comparing the vision with the present			
11. Deciding what needs to be accomplished			
12. Determining priorities			
13. Developing a plan for implementation			

Recommended Reading

1. Hollaar, L. 1991. *Re-visioning and shared values.*
   Emphasizes the importance of the mission statement.
2. Van Dyk, J. 1985. *The beginning of wisdom: The nature and task of the Christian school.*
   Vryhof, S., et al. 1989. *Twelve affirmations: Reformed Christian schooling for the twenty-first century.*

Excellent starting points for articulating a vision for Christian schools.
3. West, S. 1993. *Educational values for school leadership*. Though the context is British, the argument and strategies for principals, boards, and parents together articulating a coherent value stance is directly applicable to Christian schools.

4

How Do We Set the Stage for the School Year?

Mountain City Orientation Session

"Just what we need," muttered Glenn Prince as he filled his cup with coffee. "An early morning meeting on a hot day in the middle of August. Well, what latest educational fad do you think we'll be talking about this year?"

"Joan Fisher said one of the things we'll be talking about is the new mentor program," said Cindy Schut.

"Joan told me you and she had already had some meetings." Jacqui joined the group. "How do you like the idea of having a mentor for your first year of teaching?"

"It's a great idea and I've enjoyed our meetings," said Cindy. "But I'm confused about her emphasis on teaching higher-level thinking skills across the curriculum. Of course we talked about that in my education classes but sometimes I think people are going overboard on that topic. Education, particularly Christian education, should be solid academic work. You can tell by all the national reports that schools just aren't as good as they ought to be. We can start worrying about some of the new fads after we've made sure that we really have our kids ready for high school."

"It surprises me to hear you say that," Jacqui said as she selected a pastry. "We've heard so much from the Central Station staff concerning the new middle school concept—I doubt that they would agree their first task is to get the kids ready for high school. I've always appreciated the direction they are taking with their curriculum. It shows a clear understanding of the vision for the school."

"There goes Jacqui again," said Glenn, "more talk about vision. Her next line will surely have something to do with either 'integration' or 'personalized learning.' Maybe that's all right for a first grade teacher. But the junior high kids that you and I teach, Cindy, need a firmer hand. Kids these days are spoiled and have no self-discipline."

Jacqui looked troubled. "I always worry when you talk like that, Glenn. I've really been looking forward to our week of in-service. While we are busy teaching we have so little time to reflect on how each piece of what we do relates to the whole school. It seems impossible during the year to find time to work hard at understanding how we can carry out the purpose of the school. At least this allows us time to talk about what it means to integrate faith and learning and how the mission statement of the school can be reflected in our design for curriculum and instruction."

Glenn rolled his eyes as they headed for the library where the meeting would be held. "You can tell Jacqui doesn't have children," said Pearl Stock as they walked along. "My teenagers at home give me enough trouble when I'm with them during vacation. Who knows what they'll get into with me away during this week before school starts for them. Ken should have thought of parents like me before he agreed to these in-service sessions." They found places to sit as Ken Heard began his opening devotions.

Getting Ready for the School Year

How can a school like Mountain City get ready for a new school year? Schools have often seen a few teachers drift in just ahead of the students. Teachers set up their own classrooms and prepared for the first few weeks of school. The principal allocated specific tasks during a staff meeting on the first day of school. But there was little interaction about the overall direction of the school or about the whole school as a learning community in which all members planned and took ownership of initiatives. Yet if we consider what the apostle Paul said about how the body of Christ should work together and also consider current educational research, we can only conclude that effective schools need to work at developing and articulating a common vision, using all members' unique gifts to contribute to the implementation of that vision.

Such working together takes time. It takes time that is not available while classes are being taught. This time must be found prior to the opening of school.

Some schools have a policy that the teachers will meet for a week at the beginning of the new school year. Other schools have a two-week planning period early in the month of August and then there is a break before school starts. Planning is essential for a cohesive program of learning and teaching. A unified community for teaching responsive discipleship cannot be created and sustained without adequate time together at the start of and throughout the school year.

Pre-planning for the August Meeting

If we use one or two weeks prior to the start of school for such planning, how can we use them effectively? First of all, the agenda for the week must not be imposed on the staff by the principal. Rather, it should result from discussions in meetings held at the close of the preceding school year, when learning needs are uppermost in the minds of the staff. As the teachers review the year, they should individually ask themselves questions that will provide direction during the coming year: To what extent does my teaching reflect the school's mission statement? Are students learning to unwrap their gifts in my classroom? Is my teaching helping my students deepen their faith? What changes do I want to make to encourage a spirit of responsive discipleship in my class? Which one or two areas of the curriculum will I focus on in order to make improvements? In what ways can I improve my teaching? Am I teaching in ways that truly help students learn to bear each other's burdens by helping each other learn? Are there new topics around which I will want to plan units? What new learning center will I develop during the summer? Where will I be able to find the resources? How can I plan for my own professional and personal growth in ways that enable me to unwrap my own gifts? What can I do during the coming year to encourage seeking and celebrating God's shalom in my school?

After each teacher has reviewed the year, team meetings or grade-level meetings should be held so that the teachers may share their personal responses and grow through conversations with colleagues. Often when teachers participate in such grade-level discussions they choose to revise their own personal goals and plans.

In addition to individual teacher review and team or grade-level meetings at the end of the academic year, it is important that the whole staff gathers to ask similar questions concerning learning and instruction during the coming year.

1. What do we as a staff want to accomplish next year?
2. What has the school climate been like?
3. Are there any ways in which the structure of the school (arrangement of schedule, calendar year, activities) prevents learning or contributes to a breakdown in community? What changes might be needed?
4. What one or two areas of the curriculum will we as a staff want to study and improve?
5. What study skills still need additional reinforcement?
6. Do we need a renewed focus on other skill areas such as critical thinking, problem solving, research, oral language, or written language?

In order that the most profitable discussion may occur concerning school-wide plans, the faculty might begin by answering the questions individually. The next step would be to have a meeting at which the faculty organizes into groups of four or five, each group consisting of teachers at the elementary, middle, and secondary levels. The groups will review the individual statements and record on a sheet of chart paper their consensus concerning three or four answers to each question. The sheets would then be reviewed by the full faculty, in order to come to consensus concerning goals, needed changes, and areas of study for the coming year, as well as to present different points of view where consensus cannot be reached.

When a faculty works toward consensus, there is always the danger of some people forcing their views on the others. Coming to consensus does not mean that those who are in the minority must give up their ideas to the group. Rather, it means arriving at an opinion shaped by all. Teachers who take seriously the concept of responsive discipleship in their own lives will work at actively listening to each other and asking questions until ideas are clearly understood.

One way to arrive at an opinion shaped by all has been described in chapter 3. Another way is by use of the nominal group technique, which begins with each person writing a list of statements on the issue at hand. Next, one statement from each member in turn is recorded on chart paper until all the statements have been presented. In that way every statement appears before the group without constant identification of source. The group then discusses all of the statements and assigns priorities to them.

An additional area that should be reviewed by the staff at the end of the school year is that of student life. Before initiating this discussion teachers may want to survey their students in order to learn their perceptions. If a survey is not conducted, other means must be found to involve students in the discussion, which might concern such matters as the following: Is the atmosphere of this school one that encourages students to grow in their faith? Do all students feel at home in this school or do some students seem to feel isolated and left out? Is the atmosphere of this school one in which students are encouraged to care for each other? What do you think about the way students act toward each other in school? Are all parts of the student handbook still appropriate? Should something be added or omitted? Do the teachers plan a variety of learning activities in each class so that students may respond to learning in different ways or are the assignments always the same? If more variety is needed, what suggestions can you make for improving instruction? Is instruction arranged in such a way that students will learn how to take responsibility for organizing their own learning?

Discussions such as these will allow the principal, committee leaders, and the rest of the staff to plan the agenda for the week in August. It will provide adequate time for ordering necessary materials. In addition, the teachers will have a direction for their own planning during the summer.

Cindy Schut's Journal Entry

My first day as a teacher is ended! It's hard to believe that it's all actually happening. When I first heard we were having a week of meetings I wondered how I would endure it. But I was surprised how interesting it really was. Some of the ideas we learned in our college classes are being studied here, as well. Only we are expected to make them happen. It's all so much more interesting when it's part of the real world.

For example, last year they studied "interactive instructional strategies" and had a series of workshops and readings throughout the year. This year different teachers have volunteered to report on how they are using these strategies in their classes.

The new topic for study this year is "using textbooks as supplements instead of as a basis for teaching and learning." They are basing this way of teaching on an inquiry model. The idea is that we will read a series of articles throughout the year and attend workshops on that topic. Then, next year some of us will be expected to show how we use the inquiry model to teach without textbooks in our classes. I never really thought of teachers teaching each other.

I really appreciate how, despite differences of views, our staff shows the bond of faith and love. They want to support each other because they know they are doing their work for the Lord.

The topic for tomorrow has to do with the mission of the school. It doesn't sound too thrilling but I hope it turns out to be as interesting as today.

Agenda for the August Meeting

An important part of the August meeting will be determining how the plans made in June will now be accomplished. During this week the staff should get a good start on working on the projects. Early in the meeting the teachers should address themselves to these questions:

1. When and in what order should we work on each project?
2. Who will serve on the team assigned to each project?
3. What are some ways each team might get started? How might that be followed up?
4. By what date must each team complete its work?
5. What kind of report or project do we expect will be the result of each team's efforts?
6. How will we use the end result?

This kind of discussion can provide direction for the teams to begin their work.

As the week progresses, opportunities should be made for each team to meet with the entire staff to inform them of their progress and to give an opportunity for questions concerning the work of the team. If all of the teachers are to use each project, it is important that they be informed and involved in the planning steps along the way.

In addition to these more formal discussions, the teaching staff must have opportunities for communal devotions and prayer, personal preparation, socializing, and team building. Some schools have found it profitable to use one-fourth of the time for meetings and projects involving the entire staff. Then they use another quarter for section meetings at the primary, intermediate, middle and high school levels or in grade-level and subject area meetings. They spend the remaining time in personal preparation for the coming year, meetings with parents, brainstorming units, and socializing.

Rebuilding the Team for the Coming Year

"Our staff is fairly large and we have a few new teachers," said Lynn Reese after the devotional time. She asked the teachers to each introduce one person to the new staff members and the resulting introductions soon had everyone laughing so hard she could hardly regain their attention. "I know that many of you have been engaged in worthwhile professional activities during the summer break. Some of you have taken graduate courses and workshops. Some of you have been involved in analyzing a survey of the parents in our supporting churches concerning why they chose a Christian high school for their children. Others have worked in groups planning curriculum for the coming year. And I've seen quite a number of you here during the summer working at your own preparations. An important part of responsive discipleship is recognizing and celebrating the gifts each of us has been unwrapping in our personal and professional lives.

"Let's take the next hour to tell each other what we have been doing. I have assigned you to groups of ten. Teachers from the different levels of the school have purposely been mixed together to help you come to understand the planning that goes on at each level. I've tried to arrange the groups so that there are four high school teachers, four elementary school teachers, and two from the middle school in each group.

"When you gather in your group make certain that everyone knows everyone else and what their teaching assignment is for this year. When you talk about your summer project be sure to explain it in enough detail so that everyone in the group will have a clear picture of the various strengths we are developing as a staff. If you have taken a course, talk about the high points of the course. If you have planned curriculum, describe the central focus, how it was worked out, and how it fits with the rest of the curriculum. I would appreciate it if you would include in your discussion suggestions of ways all of us might be able to hear about those projects that are particularly significant for our growth as a professional team. We will share experiences for the next hour and then we'll gather to hear suggestions from each group concerning future faculty or team workshops."

The groups gathered in their assigned areas of the library and settled down to conversation. Ken Heard moved from group to group listening and making certain that the groups were interacting productively. There were four strong people on staff who made sarcastic, negative comments about any kind of collaborative or community-building activity on the part of the staff. Lynn had carefully assigned no more than one of these people to each group, in order to weaken the influence they had. Ken was pleased to see that her plan was working. None of the four was interacting enthusiastically but neither were they hindering the participation of the rest of the group. At the end of the hour, they shared their ideas for future meetings and then it was time for a short break before beginning the next session.

"Our new teachers were introduced earlier and I think you should all know that this year we are using a mentoring program for the first time," said Ken after the break. "In the past we have usually assigned one experienced teacher to each new teacher to help with practical matters concerning how we do things at our school. But last spring a committee met several times to plan a more extensive program. I am very impressed with their work and we are already using their suggestions."

Though teachers' lives bring them into contact with a great many people, teaching can be a lonely profession. Most of the time teachers plan alone, close their classroom doors and teach their students alone, and when there is criticism often face it alone. When teachers keep their actions in teaching and feelings about teaching private they don't have to disclose their mistakes and insecurities but they also don't have the possibility of sharing real successes. This is not completely a matter of choice. It is simply a matter of the way schools often work and experienced teachers are concerned about this isolation.

Teacher: This is my third year of teaching and I know that I have a reputation for being a good teacher. But when I listen to talk about the need for building a spirit of community among the staff I feel uneasy. I am afraid to ask any other teacher for advice or help concerning ways to teach because I don't want to be perceived as someone who doesn't know how to teach. In the staff room everyone else talks with such confidence about their own teaching so I do the same thing. Also, I don't want the principal's evaluation of me nor my peer evaluation to say that I lack confidence or that I lean on others too much.

Interviewer: What about when you feel great about something that worked well?

Teacher: Well, I don't like to talk about that either for fear of sounding like I'm bragging. There are teachers who make everything they do sound perfect and that intimidates me. I always wonder if other teachers feel like I do about these things.

Beginning teachers in particular need support as they attempt to integrate ideas learned in their teacher education program into their first teaching situations. College teacher education faculty claim that novice teachers are often more strongly influenced by the practices and culture of the new school experience than by experiences that had been part of the teacher education program.

First teacher education student: My friends have told me that the first thing that happens when they go to student teach in a school, is that the teachers tell them to forget all that idealistic nonsense that they learned in college. "This is the real world. What would those professors know? Most of them haven't spent much time in a classroom anyway."

Second teacher education student: What can a first-year teacher do to change what happens in a school? It's just me against the system. I know from my own schooling, which is only a few years ago, how dull and deadening much of what happens in schools is. But what am I going to be able to do?

The way new teachers are initiated into the professional culture will in all probability determine the way they will go on, and how likely it is that they will grow in competence (McDonald and Elias 1980, vol. 1). The induction of teachers into a *collegial community* in which teachers stand in a defined relationship to one another is central to the growth of the new teacher. Without that induction beginning teachers often are unable to find avenues for demonstrating their vision and professionalism.

Teacher: What I see in the younger graduates is well-trained technicians. They know their strategies and technologies, but they are vision-less. I would expect and hope that they would come with dreams, hopes for educational reform. Instead, they come without questions, as if they were never taught to ask. They're sweet, compassionate, earnest, enthusiastic— humane. But there is no wrestling with the spirits of education.

The teacher who is speaking has had more than thirty years experience in Christian schools in a number of different states. But he is equally ready to admit that he does not see this type of questioning and probing among teachers of his own generation. We have met many dedicated teachers and administrators in Christian schools; not a few of these are also possessed of great vision. However, in too many cases school structures that keep teachers isolated from each other in their teaching have prevented them from demonstrating and pursuing their vision.

Teachers who are learners in a community for responsive discipleship will want to help each other explore new ways of teaching by sharing ideas, sharing the risk of attempting new ways of teaching, and providing support when teaching methods aren't as successful as hoped. If schools are to be *communities* for teaching and learning, teachers will need guidance in how to participate as colleagues. One way to provide such guidance and support is by having a carefully planned peer-associate program, in which each teacher is paired with another teacher.

Peer-Associate Programs for Teacher Induction

In a teacher induction program, each teacher new to the school (whether experienced or just out of a teacher education program) is paired with a teacher who has been with the system for at least three years. These peer-associates will help the new teacher to feel comfortable in the school and to understand the implications of the school's vision. Discussions concerning how the purpose of the school influences curriculum decisions as well as instructional methods are important aspects of the program. And, of course, information concerning the practical day-to-day matters is needed.

In working as peer-associates the new teacher comes to know the school and the long-term teacher becomes more reflective about the purpose of the school. Often the questions asked by the new teacher lead the associate to raise the same questions for discussion and reflection in a faculty meeting.

It is important that each staff develops a plan in keeping with the goals of the school. However, some general guidelines might be helpful. First, while every teacher will be involved in a peer-associate pair, the long-term partners who will work with new teachers will require certain qualifications. They should be teachers who not only understand the mission of the school but who are able to articulate that mission and relate it to daily activities.

The relationship between the long-term partner and the new teacher should not be one of "expert" and "novice." First, it is a relationship between two people who acknowledge the same Lord and who have been joined to one another by his Spirit: it is a relationship of equals in Christ. Second, it is a relationship in which two professionals work together in influencing each other by jointly reflecting on the task they share. The new teacher is becoming accustomed to the ways of thinking and acting in this community and the long-term teacher is becoming professionally rejuvenated through reflection and discussion.

The design for peer-associates should clearly specify the topics for discussion and the activities that will be undertaken prior to the school year. For example, in discussing how teachers must attempt to help students search out biblical guidelines for the areas of life being studied, the design might suggest that the long-term teacher provide three examples from his or her own instruction. Then that member might call in another colleague for additional examples. As the school year progresses, the peer-associates will have continued discussions concerning how this kind of teaching is being carried out and what joys and difficulties each of them is facing.

Among the important matters for discussion are these: helping students who have learning difficulties, providing for unwrapping of gifts unique to a few, helping students learn to help each other, planning meaningful classroom devotions, assessing students' learning and helping students evaluate their own learning, the teacher's self-evaluation, and conducting parent-student-teacher conferences. These topics and others should be part of an ongoing discussion at regular meetings throughout the year.

Peer-Associate Programs
for Experienced Teachers

Competent experienced teachers recognize that if the school is to be a *community* for learning, teachers must support each other as they learn. Healthy mid-career teachers shift from being concerned only with their own teaching to an increased fervor for the improvement of the school and an interest in guiding and supporting colleagues.

In addition to having teachers who willingly support each other, some schools are in the position of having one or two experienced teachers who appear to contribute little to the growth of the school and present obstacles that prevent change from happening. Neither the style nor the content of their teaching reflects professional growth. Their negative comments provide inappropriate models for younger colleagues. If such teachers are going to remain part of the teaching staff, it is the obligation of the rest of the staff to help them change.

Many mid-career teachers perceive fewer career opportunities and feel uncertain about the future. Mid- and late-career teachers often have an increased emphasis on material rewards and the quality of work life, feel less successful than they did earlier, and feel an increased sense of isolation. All teachers need a supportive, encouraging environment in which their personal contributions are valued. Teachers seeking to improve their teaching will be working in an environment of experimentation and risk-taking and will need to "find support in failure as well as in success . . . a trusting environment for learning" (Loucks-Horsley et al. 1987, 9).

Because all teachers need support and because some teachers have shown they are not likely to grow without support, we advocate that schools design a plan for every teacher to be involved in a peer-associate team. At the beginning participation should be on a voluntary basis. However, the goal is to involve every teacher.

How each partnership works will depend on the personalities of those who are on the team. Some of them will be very much like the teams involving the beginning teachers. They will provide support by encouraging each other and praying for and with each other. They will act as mirrors to each other's behavior, as observers and describers of student behavior, providing data for each other to employ in decision making. They may act in facilitative roles by active listening, paraphrasing, and asking questions that require the exercise of judgment and discernment. They will help each other learn to analyze their teaching.

Garmston and Eblen (1988, 24) suggest questions along the following lines:

What do you think the problem is?
How might you find out?
What do you need to do next?
When is another time you will need to do this activity?
Can you think of another way you could do this?
What do you think would happen if you changed the technique?

Whether the pairs involve beginning teachers or consist of mid-career teachers, participants will need leadership in learning to function as part of a pair. This is an area in which Christian school support organizations and Christian colleges can be of service. Adapting the suggestions of Odell (1989, 14), topics that might be part of a training program for teachers include:

rationale for teacher induction programs;
teachers as responsive disciples;
stages of teacher development;
fostering collegiality in teachers;
working with adult learners;
classroom observation skills;
career opportunities relating to teaching.

As he walked home at the end of the orientation week, Ken thought ahead to the rest of year. The agenda for staff development was full and he wasn't certain that there would be time to complete everything. Every item had been placed there and planned by committees of teachers, and he knew that most of the teachers agreed with him that the tasks they were working on together were important.

This was quite a different management style for him. Ken smiled to think that just before his fiftieth birthday he was willing to make such a major change in his approach to leadership. It was not that the old way hadn't "worked." Ken knew the school had a good reputation in the community, but he had begun to feel that the school community had a limited view of what was important. In the past year Ken had realized, in part because of the reading he had done concerning successful schools (Sergiovanni 1991), that teachers who find their work lives meaningful, who feel they are able to exert reasonable influence over work circumstances, who experience personal responsibility and are accountable for outcomes, are more committed to the school, harder workers, and more satisfied with their jobs.

More fundamentally, Karla Hubbard's work at Central Station had challenged him to think once again about the task of a leader in a Christian community. He knew that he had to focus on planning activities that would help his staff to experience God's shalom. Ken had promised himself to use this year as a major step toward that end.

Questions for Discussion

1. Think about your planning time at the opening of each new school year. Is it as helpful as you would like it to be? How could it be improved?

2. What educational topics have your staff studied recently? Which ones do you think merit discussion in the future? How can you gather the information necessary for an informed discussion?

3. Does your staff often have an in-service day in which an educational topic is studied but then it is left to individual teachers to work at applying the new information? Does the procedure of having one topic under study and another topic for demonstration, as described in Cindy's journal entry, seem workable for your staff?

4. Do the teachers in your school freely ask each other for advice and share ideas for teaching? Do they perceive requests for advice

as evidence of lack of confidence or offers of ideas as bragging? How can your staff work toward building a spirit of responsive discipleship?

Recommended Reading

Sergiovanni, T. J. 1991. *The principalship.*
Additional information concerning many aspects of school leadership.

5

How Do We Forge a Community for Learning?

Monday, 3:15

As Ken Heard made his way to the staff meeting, his eyes caught a glimpse of the picture of his first graduating class as principal. He could remember the first faculty meeting he had led . . . what a challenge that had been. Numerous interruptions over petty concerns. One teacher's suggestions had been met by soft but not inaudible comments by others. Even personal putdowns were frequent.

Now, almost ten years later, a different atmosphere pervaded most meetings. Teachers listened well; they were courteous and congenial in responding to each other's ideas. Nevertheless, Ken wondered whether the outward politeness hid some crucial differences of views about schooling, differences that hindered the staff from developing a better learning environment. One of today's agenda items, a request by the grade eleven students to be given a day off school to work at the City Foodbank, would certainly test the staff's willingness to work as a community. Ken set his sights on at least leading a well-focused and efficient meeting.

Friday, 3:15

At Central Station Christian School, Karla, Emmy, Ted, and Sam get together frequently to exchange ideas about their teaching, propose ways of extending or modifying units for particular classes, and consider the needs of particular students. Their meetings are held in a spirit of mutual trust and support as they encourage and challenge one another in their work. On Fridays they gather briefly to conclude their week of teaching. They share stories of the day's learning experiences. In communal prayer they bring praise to God for the gifts he has shown them in their students during that week and they present personal and student needs for his care. They also commit themselves to take some time away from school work.

Are schools collections of students who come together to be educated by teachers for individual self-fulfillment? Or do schools educate to submerge individual in societal needs? No one takes either extreme in this debate. Nevertheless, Mountain City and Central Station are at different points between these two poles. The way they structure learning, the way their teachers react to "outside" learning experiences, and even the design of their buildings indicate that a sense of community transcending North American individualism is more important for some Christians than for others.

Schools in our society feel the persuasive and pervasive effects of individualism. Students want to choose their own courses, decide their own amount of effort, and develop their own rules. Teachers want to decide their own methods and content, limit their own workloads, and control their own classrooms. Parents want schools to fit their personal purposes, to use their own reading preferences, and to allow them to decide their children's courses.

Although schools often lack an *official* common purpose, both the curriculum in use and the hidden curriculum show a great deal of commonality in North America. The implicit goals of schools are remarkably similar: to enable students to become productive members of an individualistic, consumeristic, and relativistic society. Frequently Christian schools promote "the Christian good life" more than they encourage the growth of discipleship. In these schools the frequent contradiction between our culture's goal of acquisition and a Christian life of service is not clearly explored.

Schools have developed well-organized ways to teach individual students. By grouping students according to age, ability, and class, and by dividing knowledge into separate subjects, schools process students systematically. To meet special interests and social needs, schools have established breaks from study to provide time for personal interaction, setting up a variety of extracurricular activities and sports programs.

Schools, however, foster isolation. Students most often study alone, even if learning the same subject at the same time in the same classroom. They hear one another asking the teacher questions. During class discussions they may address each other. But they typically work alone on assignments, especially when doing their "best" work (Goodlad 1984, 105–6). By making it a private quest, the curriculum camouflages the true nature of knowledge. Students experience learning in a distorted way when they are required to accumulate content just by themselves, with little discussion with classmates. Knowledge becomes something gained by individual effort and achievement and used for personal self-advancement (Bricker 1989, 49).

The present crisis in schools and in the lives of their participants is, among other things, a consequence of structuring learning primarily as a private, individual matter. Schools also require teachers to work alone. They must be effective individually in maintaining control of their classes. They are expected to come fully equipped with personal expertise in teaching subject matter and managing their classrooms. Such an individualistic conception of the roles of students and teachers frames most learning in our schools.

Christian schools need to examine how such a conception has affected us. We are called to a life of discipleship, personally and communally. Christian schools must become living examples of Christ-confessing communities. They must operate in ways that enable students and teachers to unfold the gifts that they have been given. They must develop ways of sharing each other's joys and burdens, looking out for the interests of others. They must give expression to seeking and celebrating shalom. They must be communities for learning rather than individual cells that happen to be together for the sake of efficiency, "a collection of classrooms surrounded by a common parking lot."

Varying Conceptions of Communities of Learning

Mountain City Christian School is proud of the way in which students and teachers can develop themselves in their own way. Yet in practice the school emphasizes its common rules, standard course requirements, and well-established patterns of knowledge transmission. Students and teachers clearly understand the shared expectations for individual success. On the other hand, Central Station Christian School emphasizes that each student and teacher is called to be part of a community for learning. Both teachers and students are engaged in learning together, often collaboratively. Knowledge and insight grows as they interact with one another and with the curriculum.

In the sense that in both schools groups of people learn, they can be said to be communities for learning, albeit very different ones. We can classify schools, including Christian ones, as contractual, hierarchical, or covenant communities (Kirkpatrick 1986).

In contractual schools, students and teachers are considered to be individuals who come together voluntarily to achieve their own ends. The community is seen as a social bond between independent individuals who subject themselves to each other while still primarily looking out for their own private interests. Students are viewed as rational, potentially autonomous individuals who can best develop their identity by building personal knowledge and values. These schools emphasize the self-actualization of students, constructing their own knowledge and determining their own values. The primary focus of classroom learning is on individual academic achievement. Even though constant negotiation has to occur to find a basis for consensus in classroom atmosphere, there is little sense of caring, compassion, or generosity. Rather, there is an acceptance that teachers and students are free to do what they want and to follow their own needs and interests.

In the hierarchical model of community, on the other hand, the social dimension takes precedence over the individual. Students are primarily social beings whose lives find their fulfillment in the community and therefore become subservient to it (Kirkpatrick 1986, 86). They are free when they adhere to the values and rules that the school maintains, giving up freedom for the good of the whole, for organic solidarity. There is a clear hierarchical delineation of function and role for administrators, teachers, and students. Teachers instruct; students obtain knowledge through taking courses and then meeting the requirements for graduation. Active student involvement centers on extracurricular activities and not on the nature and scope of classroom learning or the day-to-day functions of the school.

Neither of these models recognizes that community is at the heart of a person's relationship with God and with other people. A person is born to be cared for, born into a love relationship with other persons. With proper nurturing by parents, children will learn to form their own intentions and to acquire the skill to execute them and develop the knowledge and foresight to act responsibly as members of a community (Kirkpatrick 1986, 174). The basic unit of personal existence is not the individual but two persons in personal relation. We are not persons by individual right, but in virtue of our relation to one another. In this relationship, we image God. Only in community does the person appear in the first place, and only in community can the person continue to become (Palmer 1983, 57).

This type of community can be called a covenant community. Its members pledge to love and serve each other without conditions. They love others because Jesus first loved them. God affirms persons and thereby frees them to affirm the worth of others. Thus a covenant community is the work of both God and humans. United as one people in Christ, human beings covenant to support each other in loving interaction, functioning as unique but interdependent members of the body of Christ. Members exercise their gifts in humility, gentleness, and patience, striving for the unity that the Spirit provides.

Schools as Covenant Communities

August 29

Rob Boonstra glanced at his watch as he left the house. 7:15. Just enough time to walk to Central Station and be on time for the interview with a new family. Walking at a steady pace Rob recalled the first years of the new school. The frequent discussions and debates about developing the school as a community of learning had enabled parents, teachers, and students to re-examine their ideas about teaching and learning. Today's interview provided them with another opportunity to share and extend those ideas.

Rob reached the school after a brisk ten minute walk. What a welcoming feeling one experienced upon entering the bright, well-lit foyer! Green plants, student and staff art on the walls, several well-placed chairs, and the sculptured school logo all combined to make a person feel welcome.

"Hello, Rob," Karla said, "all set for a stimulating interview? The Manleys have some definite ideas about what a school should be like. Apparently in their previous Christian school they felt that they were never quite accepted."

When Sonya and Fred Manley arrived Karla greeted them at the door and introduced them to Rob Boonstra, the board representative, and Sam Freeland, the staff representative. Karla began the meeting with a brief overview of the school's goals, emphasizing that Central Station seeks to establish an atmosphere of trust through developing mutually supportive and caring relationships.

"Will our daughter and son be able to feel at home here?" Sonya asked. "In their last school they were given their desks and lockers and soon became just one of twenty-eight individuals in their classes. Little effort was made to help them get to know their classmates and they didn't meet the teacher until the first day of school. They are worried that it won't be any different here."

Sam Freeland welcomed the opportunity to describe the process the staff at Central Station used to build community among the students. "At the beginning of each school year each of us works with a group of students to establish an atmosphere of trust and respect for one another. We emphasize that all students share a common purpose, and they work together in their learning. By sharing their personal stories and encouraging each other individually and as a group, your children should develop a sense of security, a feeling of being 'at home.' In their respective groups, they will be paired with another student to assist them through the first weeks of feeling like a 'stranger.'"

"That sounds like a good process for them," Fred responded. "But how will we be able to become a part of the school community? Although we were in the previous school for four years, we always felt like outsiders. We weren't members of the same denomination and little was done to help us feel welcome; nor were we invited to make worthwhile contributions to the school other than assisting in fundraising activities. We feel that each of us has abilities and time to contribute to the school."

A parent himself, Rob sympathized. "We use a similar process for welcoming new parents and enabling them to feel at home. After this interview we will introduce you to the houseparents who lead a group of parents throughout the school year. They meet early in the year to share issues they feel are important to discuss during the year. As a group they affirm their acceptance of the goals of the school and establish their own common purpose by choosing the actions that they can take as they discuss each issue. Our house groups fill a dual purpose. They make it possible for parents in the school community to share in the school's responsibility for student learning and, secondly, through involving parents with one another in problem solving they enrich individual parents and decrease their feelings of isolation. We hope that you would soon feel at home among the parents that send their children to our school."

"What are some of the avenues that are open for direct involvement in the school?" Sonya asked.

"At Central Station, we are parents' partners in encouraging student learning. The roles of parents and teachers are complementary. Throughout the year there are many opportunities for parents to become involved. We have an outline of the themes and units that are addressed with each group of students. Some parents will be able to volunteer their assistance in the development and teaching of units. Students will choose some of the topics and issues they will study, both individually and in groups. They will work with their teachers and the parents who are resource persons for that unit. When students complete their work during the year we have several special occasions in the afternoons and evenings at which students present what they have learned. The adults that have been a part of that unit, as well as the students' parents, will be invited to share in the celebration."

The concept of the school as a community of learners, a place where all participants engage in learning and teaching, provides a way of thinking about schools that is different from the current framework (Barth 1990, 42). In a community of learners, adults and children learn simultaneously: posing and solving problems important to them, thinking analytically and critically, and so on. Students and teachers see each other learning; they see the principal learning. All members are visibly engaged with one another for the purpose of learning. They support and encourage each other in their tasks because all want to be responsive disciples of Jesus Christ. Their personal commitment to him enables them to develop a community for learning.

Schools that are covenant communities do not consist of individuals who work together because then they will each achieve more individual learning. Neither do they swallow up individuals into a corporate whole, losing all sense and experience of the riches of individuality. Instead, they foster an environment where students and teachers take delight in being with each other and build relationships based on a genuine desire to be with and for others. They cannot do so, of course, solely through their own efforts. Jean Vanier (1979, 73) points out that we must become conscious of "the limitations and weaknesses of human energy, and the forces of egoism, fear, aggression and self-assertion which govern human life and make up all the barriers which exist between people. We can only emerge from behind these barriers if the Spirit of God touches us, opens the barriers and heals and saves us."

Schools therefore should not seek to create independent learners but to increase the ways in which students develop their abilities and ways of interacting with and for one another. Schools should develop mutual interdependence among parents, teachers, and students. Each member should respond to others on the basis of common commitment, values, and purpose.

Leadership in a covenant community school is based on differentiation of tasks and responsibilities and not on hierarchical position. All members of the educational community have intrinsic worth as image bearers of God. Students, teachers, parents, principals, and board members are called to different meaningful offices. Each office calls for a particular kind of service, with authority and responsibility that is appropriate to it (Fowler 1990, 114). Parents are called to nurture their children so that they are able to live freely and responsibly in service to

God. Students are responsible for their learning and to discover the depth and the breadth of God's creation. Teachers provide opportunities for student learning in ways that empower students to exercise their tasks. Principals give direction and encouragement for teachers and students to fulfill their respective callings. Board members exercise communal oversight helping all members of the school community take on their responsibilities effectively (Fowler 1990, 118). All members of the school community are involved in building mutually helpful relationships as well as value orientations, perceptions, abilities, and knowledge that enable the members to function more fully in attaining both personal and communal goals (Benne 1990, 87).

Working in a covenant community is not without its tensions. Tensions arise from conflicts within each person and between different persons. Such tensions reveal flaws that require reevaluation, greater humility, and stronger support. As teachers and students work together to resolve the tensions that arise they need to develop a great deal of sensitivity, understanding, and patience. Growth begins when persons begin to accept their own weakness. Love makes us weak and vulnerable because it breaks down barriers that we have built up around ourselves. It lets others reach us and makes us sensitive enough to reach them (Vanier 1979, 18). A Christian school community will be one that accepts human weakness and honors the humility that Christ's life exemplifies.

Three Essential Ingredients of a Covenant Learning Community

Mountain City Christian School
Staff Meeting, January 15

The Staff Relations Committee was ready to present its report. At the end of June, Dennis, Linda, Greg, and Margie had volunteered to do some reading during the fall and to meet at the end of November and once more in December, in order to prepare a report that would initiate staff discussion in January. The committee's mandate had been developed during the staff's end-of-year reflections. Many staff members felt that personal relationships were fairly good, almost as good as could be expected. However, many also felt that professional relationships could be improved.

Ken Heard called the meeting to order, briefly reviewed the committee's task, and asked the committee to begin its report.

Linda made a few opening remarks. "We've had a number of meetings and discussions. We've talked with many of you individually, and read a number of articles and several books about staff relations. We placed a copy of our report in your mailbox last Friday. Today we want to highlight its major points and then begin a discussion about how we might improve our professional relationships with one another.

"Our report has four parts. Dennis will describe our current situation, Margie will comment on the hindrances to good staff relations, Greg will describe ways in which our staff could develop more collegial relationships, and I will conclude our report by introducing for discussion the actions we could take. Over to you, Dennis."

"Many of us have enjoyed numerous years together. We have shared moments of joy and celebration in graduations, school plays, and sport championships. We have shared moments of deep grief in the loss of loved ones among students and staff. Although we attend churches of different denominations we have been able to develop a unity of faith through prayer and common devotions in our staff room and in our classrooms.

"Yet when we talked as a committee and with you as colleagues, some problems came to the surface. It seems that there are disagreements on fundamental issues of schooling. As a further working out of our vision we need to come to grips with those disagreements, to own up to them, to find ways of talking about them, and to develop ways of accepting each other in a deeper sense than we do now."

Next it was Margie's turn. "We hinder the development of better relations with one another when we want our own ideas to be the one and only right way, the solution. We hinder the development of better relations because we operate on the basis of our established notions about fellow staff members. Unconsciously and consciously we relate with one another on the basis of opinions we formed the first day we came to this school. These preconceptions color the ways we perceive each other and block the development of better professional relationships.

"A crucial problem among us is our need to convert our colleagues to our own way of thinking. Many of us expressed feelings that suggested that if only so-and-so would be convinced that our idea or way of thinking was correct then everything would be all right. When we focus on converting others to our own view we block ourselves from seeing and understanding our colleagues as they really are.

"Finally, many of us reveal a tremendous need for control. We want someone to be in charge, to be responsible for what happens in our school and among the staff. In wanting someone else to be in control we hesitate to accept our own responsibility for the health of staff relationships."

Greg continued: "The committee wants to suggest that one way in which we avoid making staff relations stronger is when we flee from issues and problems when they appear. Remember last year when the issue of report card format arose? Many of us were quick to argue that we continue to use the present format because we were worried that discussing it would lead to a lengthy debate about evaluation.

"We know that differences exist among us but we pretend that they don't by continuing to use the present format. We hurt staff relations when we continue to battle over issues such as achievement tests, extracurricular duties, student attendance, and others. Instead of listening to each other and developing genuine understanding we press our views harder, hoping that we will convince others that we are right and they are wrong. At other times we develop alliances with colleagues who agree with us and form a subgroup that, sometimes quietly, sometimes overtly, hinders the development of community.

"In times of crisis, like the Smithson tragedy two years ago, we have experienced a rich sense of unity. However, that sense of community gradually disappeared as our lives returned to normal. Sometimes we experience moments of oneness as we work together on the school play, graduation ceremony, or school team.

"Our challenge is this: How can we expand those experiences of unity so that all of our teaching and learning is strengthened? Our committee would like to propose that we begin this process by developing a stronger sense of community among ourselves."

"Thank you, Greg," Linda said. "After this brief overview of our report, we want to pause before we begin our discussion so that each of us has a moment to reflect on our own experiences. . . ."

The issues facing the staff of Mountain City exist in many Christian schools today. Christian schools are called to be communities for learning, but frequently they are not the communities they could be. Some Christian schools have difficulties with personality differences among staff members. Some have problems with contrasting views of the relationship between Christianity and culture. Some have significant differences between older and younger teachers. Other schools may face a breakdown of communication between board and staff, or between the principal and the student body. In still others the structures discourage the meaningful participation of all members of the school community. When situations of brokenness exist, healing must occur by building trust so that mutually supportive and caring relationships can develop, and cooperative and creative action is fostered (Tucker 1987, 91).

Three essential ingredients for a school to be a covenant community are the need for a common vision, an atmosphere of love and trust, and an ethos of leadership for service.

First, a school covenant community needs to develop and experience its vision of shared values regarding teaching and learning. This covenant bond becomes the compass that charts the direction and inspires commitment and enthusiasm, with all participants being free to carry out responsively their aspect of the mission (Sergiovanni 1991, 179). The common vision is the catalyst that nurtures the quality of interpersonal relationships and the conditions that promote and sustain meaningful learning (Barth 1990, 45). School leaders should frequently and openly talk about the shared mission and commitment and encourage continued dialogue about what the school stands for and where it should be headed.

A Christian school community must regularly provide ways in which its members can reaffirm their shared commitments. Through story, ceremony, and celebrations of learning, its members can renew their commitments and strengthen their experience of working toward common goals. Each school has its own story of the people who launched it and their vision. The experiences of ex-students, teachers, and parents provide a rich source of memories. Accomplishments and failures alike stimulate thoughtful reflection about ongoing issues in schooling. The shared vision of today's school can be seen as part of the longer history of the Christians in a particular community. Indeed, the vision should be understood as part of the whole history of the people of God. Joyful celebrations such as graduations, assemblies, anniversaries, and reunions can all reinforce shared purpose, recognize diverse individual and group accomplishments and contributions as members have worked and learned together.

A second necessary component of a covenant community is mutual love and compassion. Members must accept each other as they are and encourage each other to fulfill their calling. In this way they are bound together in trust and service, using their gifts for the benefit of others. Such loving interaction also demands honest communication and conflict resolution. Members engage each other in dialogue in ways that express care and support and heartfelt respect for differences of views. Through careful listening, genuine consultation, and honest expression of views, members develop appreciation for each other's gifts and accept each other's limitations. Members offer support to one another through recognizing differences in ways that reconcile and strengthen common goals. The atmosphere of mutual concern and trust developed by communicating openly, sensitively, and with integrity is a necessary component in the continuous nourishment of the Christian identity of the school (Andersen 1989, 27).

Third, a covenant community is a community of servant leaders. Board and committee members, parents, principals, teachers, and students share opportunities and responsibilities for making decisions that affect learning. Decisions are made in a way that transcends individual differences and roles. Participants feel free to express themselves by offering their individual gifts at various moments in the decision-making process. All members of the body share opportunities and responsibilities for making decisions that affect the learning environment. Rather than a hierarchy of position there is differentiation of tasks. Whatever their capabilities or gifts or position, all members are respected as valued members of the community.

Persons in specific leadership positions lead in a spirit of love and nurture, enabling all members of the body to exercise their responsibilities. Leaders are spiritual models for other members, manifesting love, joy, peace, patience, kindness, goodness, faithfulness, gentleness, and self-control. A school community finds its unity in Jesus Christ through the Spirit. Its members recognize that the unity that they experience is a gift of the Holy Spirit. The Spirit enables each person to submit to the Lord and to each other. This unity does not mean uniformity. Each member has been given different gifts, each to be used in special, interdependent ways.

Love and respect undergirding the implementation of a common vision by persons who recognize that their special authority is given for serving the other members: here is the basis of the school as a covenant community. When the members of a community have established their common ground they can focus their attention on becoming that community, by caring, sharing, and working together. Through participation in setting group standards, discovering gifts and skills and clarifying roles, all members will feel that they have a voice and belong, and will experience the presence of other members. Members of the group are consulted and share in decisions that affect their work. Through shared leadership and participation members are involved in problem solving and in developing plans and activities for learning that are grounded in a common vision and yet allow the diversity of gifts to blossom.

Teacher-Teacher Relationships in the Christian School

The January 15 discussion about staff relations at Mountain City Christian School resulted in a proposal to hold a staff retreat. Margie had suggested that Pastor Mills of Hillside Community Church be invited to lead them in a community building workshop. Dennis contacted Stephanie Porter, the public school district's professional development consultant, to lead them in a workshop exploring ways of developing collegiality. The all-staff retreat was planned for February 21 and 22 at Elm Valley Retreat Center, a two-hour drive away. The retreat would provide time for personal and communal reflection, and build stronger community and closer collegiality.

At 6 A.M. on February 21, Pearl anxiously waited for a ride to the retreat. The staff had decided to car pool and she would be riding with Jim, Lynn, and Cal. Pearl wasn't so sure that this retreat was a good idea: what could be gained from sitting around talking for two days? She had lots of marking to complete, and a two-hour drive and sleeping in a strange bed could only mean trouble for her back. But, at least she was riding with people with whom she got along. As Jim's car pulled up she picked up her suitcase and headed out the door.

"Good morning, Pearl," Jim cheerfully said as he opened the trunk. "Good morning, Jim," Pearl replied, hesitantly. She had decided that her anxiety should not spoil the ride for the others, however, and as she entered the car she wished Lynn and Cal a more cheery "Good morning."

"So, what do you think, Pearl?" Cal said. "Will we be able to come to some agreement as we discuss community and collegiality?"

Pearl wished he hadn't jumped in with that question so soon. As she thought about how she should respond, Lynn joined in. "Well, I think we are in for two interesting days. Look at who's all going to be there. Can you imagine Greg, Willis, Glenn, Jacqui, and Valerie talking together about the same topic, let alone agreeing about something? At staff meetings they always argue vehemently about whatever comes up."

Pearl decided to be positive. "I believe it will be good to be away from school and home for two days. I can't remember when I last did that. February has always been a gloomy month for me. Just being away will make the whole retreat worthwhile. As for discussing community and collegiality, I hope that we can get beyond the griping about the administration and the school board or the endless talk about basketball or hockey games that so often dominate our staff room conversations. I hope each of us would think more carefully about our own students. What about you, Jim? What do you think this retreat will be like?"

"I'm really looking forward to listening to Pastor Mills. He's an inspirational pastor, very capable at leading group discussions. My neighbors really appreciate what he has done to enable their church to live as a community. And while Stephanie Porter is new in this area apparently she has led many successful professional development seminars on the East Coast."

"Hey," Cal interjected, "there's the Elm Valley turnoff! That seemed like a short trip."

Teachers in Christian schools have often been able to develop and maintain good working relationships. Their common commitments and respect for each other's abilities have enabled them to become a team whose focus is on providing a caring and warm learning environment. As a staff they meet regularly for devotions and prayer, encourage a cordial and friendly atmosphere in their interpersonal relations, and occasionally take time for mutual reflection and discussion of various teaching methods.

Yet Christian schools also face a number of problems in teacher-teacher relationships. In the present school structure, teachers are valued for being able to teach their own students in their own classroom. They are expected to know their subject areas well and, from their first day of teaching, to be competent in classroom instruction. They are expected to know what to do and to deny or hide failures since showing them would admit incompetence. Risking new approaches and failing is viewed more negatively than not trying at all.

If teachers do not provide each other with mutual support through pedagogical interaction, or if they do not have a safe place to air their uncertainties about particular teaching experiences, they will not receive the kind of feedback they need both to feel and to become good teachers (Lieberman and Miller 1984, 13–14). Yet in some schools teachers even agree to avoid sharing their experiences about teaching, classes, and students. By hiding their perceptions about teaching, teachers do not recognize their achievements, but neither do they lose face. Staff room discussions avoid pedagogical interaction and focus on news, sports, and personal concerns. In even more negative settings, staff rooms deteriorate into places where the dominant mode of staff conversation involves *griping* about the administration, particular students, or the school board (Lieberman and Miller 1984, 48). Observing each other's classes would be the equivalent of risky evaluation and is therefore not done. Teaching in such a school is a lonely experience. There is an urgent need for examination of present practices and for a process of renewal.

The experience of personal community that is God's gift to us in Christ needs to be expanded into an experience of professional community. Our spiritual unity is a solid foundation, but we need to build on it responsibly. Teachers need opportunities to interact with one another about teaching and learning. If the school is going to become a professional community the quality of interactions between teachers and between teachers and principals needs to be improved. This requires establishing a climate of *collegiality*, a high level of collaboration characterized by mutual respect, shared work values, cooperation, and specific conversation about teaching and learning (Barth 1990).

By breaking out of the isolation of the classroom, teachers find that working together on matters of curriculum and on learning activities makes them better prepared for leading students in learning. Through collegial work they find ways of recognizing their own strengths and the capabilities of others, as well as deepening their understanding of the school's mission. Through mutual effort teachers find support in their calling to be responsive disciples: unwrapping their different gifts, sharing each other's joys and burdens (including resolving conflicts), and fostering a shalom-filled atmosphere in their school.

The mutual respect and support that foster collegiality require that teachers engage in frequent conversation about learning and teaching. Teachers observe each other's classes and provide each other with specific, edifying critiques. They also regularly plan and design, reflect and evaluate, and prepare teaching materials together (Little 1982; 1990). In a helpful, trusting, and supportive atmosphere, teachers and principals in Christian schools can thus extend personal community into professional community, with collegiality breaking isolation and leading to teachers working together and becoming truly interdependent.

Developing such community takes time and effort, however. Holding a retreat provides a setting away from the day-to-day exigencies of home and school and enables the group to grow together in ways that often do not occur during the routines of school. Peer-associates, mentors, and coordinators can become catalysts in fostering a professional community. Schools can provide substitutes to give teachers some time to visit each other's classes, and professional days for joint planning.

Even then, as Scott Peck (1987) points out, the growth of community usually occurs in stages. At first, a group of teachers may be extremely pleasant with one another and avoid disagreement. Often unconsciously, teachers (especially Christian ones!) who want to care for each other do so by holding back some of the truth about themselves and their feelings in order to avoid conflict. The school is a "pretend community" that functions smoothly, but individuality, intimacy, and integrity suffer.

This is often followed by a stage where individual differences come into the open but the teaching staff tries to obliterate them. The dominant group of teachers works hard to convert other members to its view in well-intentioned but misguided ways, creating strife and bad feelings. The principal or another staff leader needs to point the way out when staff sense that they are going nowhere.

118

In the third stage teachers begin to see each other as unique and worthwhile, each with contributions to bring to the common mission. Up to this point people have not been communicating openly; instead, they have set up barriers. Therefore, teachers need to empty themselves, to give up things that stand in the way so that they can truly hear and experience each other. They must deny themselves and submit to the healing that Jesus provides. Becoming a community of teachers involves a recognition that together they have been called by God to teach together, to love each other, and to pray and work together in response to the needs of students.

Finally, the staff becomes a full *community* when members begin to talk about themselves, deeply and personally, with truthfulness and integrity becoming dominant. When members begin to express laughter and joy as well as sadness and grief about what is happening to them, then an extraordinary amount of healing begins to occur. Becoming a teaching community involves accepting being carried and loved by one another in a covenant relationship of interdependence (Vanier 1979, 27).

Christian schools reveal evidence of all four of these stages at different points and about different issues. A school may have developed a strong sense of spiritual community as staff devotions become a time of personal testimony of faith and sharing of burdens. Devotions may provide mutually edifying experiences and help develop a strong sense of unity centered around the gospel. Yet, simultaneously, the same staff may not have achieved the same sense of unity regarding their task for student learning. For example, discussions about the direction a school should take regarding student service projects or implementing learning activities that take students and teachers away from school property often reveal clear differences about the goals for learning. If a staff has not developed a shared vision and members have not made a commitment to work on that common vision, they will have a difficult time reaching agreement on issues that arise in day-to-day schooling.

Student-Teacher Relationships

The bell rang to indicate the end of English class and the start of the morning break. As the other students left, Janine lingered, hoping to talk with Mr. Holbrook about the journal assignment that would soon be due. Having completed back-to-back concluding lectures on Lord of the Flies, Cal Holbrook was anxious to get to the staff room for some coffee. Heading toward the door he saw that Janine was waiting for him.

"Mr. Holbrook, do you have a few minutes?" Janine had wanted to talk with him about the journal assignment for two weeks but hadn't been able to get up the nerve.

"Sure, Janine, what's on your mind?" he replied. "Are you having some trouble in one of your classes?" Students frequently confided in Cal about personal and school matters.

"Well, I'm not sure how to put this. But I'm having a lot of trouble completing the journal assignment. And now that it is due next week I don't know what to do."

"That really surprises me," Cal said. "You write so well. Your essays and reports are among the best in the class. Why would a response journal give you trouble?"

"I know that writing essays and reports are not a problem for me. But, journals are different. I am having trouble writing about myself, about my own thoughts. Each time I get about half-way down a page I rip it up and throw it away. What am I going to do? I'll never be able to complete this assignment."

What should Mr. Holbrook do? How should teachers and students relate with one another?

Teachers and students are called to work together for the purpose of learning. The relationship between student and teacher is a pedagogical relationship, not a parental or customer one. A pedagogical relationship involves teachers, students, and subject matter in an umbrella of learning experiences. The teacher intends students to learn and grow; and students must be willing to learn and must be able to do so in a particular way suited for them (Van Manen 1991, 76–77).

Pedagogical relationships between teachers and students thrive in a caring classroom structured as a Christian learning community. Such a classroom becomes a place where "children learn to accept and use their abilities in relation to themselves and others and to experience the joys and difficulties of working unitedly towards common goals" (Van Brummelen 1988, 65). Teachers help their classes to become communities of faith, hope, and love that encourage diverse gifts and abilities to be used interdependently. Working at being responsive disciples, students and teachers are involved in developing group unity, learning collaboratively, sharing joys and burdens, appreciating diversity of gifts, and celebrating shalom.

In a community of learning each member has special tasks. Each contributes to the learning success of other members. Expressions of individuality are encouraged in ways that affirm gifts and stimulate the learning of other members in the class. All activities, classroom devotions, communal prayer, sharing time, working together on learning tasks, and interacting about discoveries and products are developed in ways that contribute to building the classroom into a community of learning.

Many elementary and some middle schools have successfully developed such communities. However, studies of high schools paint a bleak picture. One reason may be that adult/youth relationships in school often involve serious misperception: "Whenever [students] consulted any of the adults that were supposed to help them the adult's assumption was that something must be *very* wrong. All they wanted was to talk to a caring adult, but the price of a conversation was that they would be considered a problem case" (Powell, Farrar, and Cohen 1985, 47). It is not easy to build community on the basis of differences rather than similarities. Schools too often settle for the absence of conflict as the definition of community. Frequently, this means "to live and let live." A community of shalom, however, is one in which the members actively work together and support one another in dynamic interaction.

Powell, Farrar, and Cohen (1985, 67) go on to argue that in many high school classrooms teachers and students have subtle ways of accommodating either differences or similarities: they arrange deals or treaties that promote mutual goals or that keep the peace. The focus for teachers and students then becomes the avoidance of learning. In its most negative sense teaching becomes limited to covering the content and maintaining control for the duration of the class. For students, learning becomes reduced to meeting the minimum requirements of a course and putting in the appropriate amount of time. Teachers and students, caught in their own webs, develop treaties by which students regard subjects as materials to be endured and teachers fail to require students to engage seriously with the subject material (Powell, Farrar, and Cohen 1985, 105–6).

Research and student experiences clearly reveal the brokenness that pervades learning at the high school level. Yet renewal is possible if teachers and students take time to develop classroom communities of learning. Classrooms should be places where teachers and students are present for each other, hearing and responding to one another, establishing an atmosphere of trust, support, cooperation, and mutual concern about learning.

As presently organized, many teachers continue to have a domineering role in classrooms in Christian schools. Many teachers maintain complete power over the entire learning process of students. Teachers make so many of the decisions about learning activities, assignments, and evaluation that there is little room for students to make decisions in matters that directly affect their learning. Students' learning, in fact, is reduced to following instructions and completing assignments as designed, leaving little room for them to be involved in creating and directing their own learning. Such teaching takes away from students the authority they should have over their own learning.

Students must be able to make decisions and judgments that rightfully belong to their office and calling as students. Fowler (1990, 116) argues that teachers must empower students to be able to experience for themselves the ordering authority of God's rule in creation. In order to be able to do this, students must be free to explore the boundaries that God has set in the creation by investigation and experiment. Teachers empower students by providing them with the means for a responsible exercise of the authority of their calling as students. Courses and units should provide opportunities for students to explore topics and problems that arise in day-to-day teaching and learning. Opening up the typically closed content requirements will enable students to deepen personal insights and challenge them to develop their own learning beyond completing minimal requirements.

Noddings (1984, 179) states that teachers must establish a caring relationship with students through modeling, dialogue, practice, and confirmation. In modelling teachers must show themselves as caring, not by "talking" caring but by living it, being there personally for the student. This does not require a deep and lasting personal relationship with each student. Rather, it means that a teacher must be totally and nonselectively present in each interaction with a student.

Teachers establish a caring relationship through dialogue. In order to engage in true dialogue with our students, we will also have to engage in true dialogue with their parents. Noddings (1984, 184) argues that teachers need to take up their common humanity and give up a narrow professionalism that establishes distance between teacher and parent. Through talking, listening, and sharing we are able to establish caring relationships that enhance understanding and build common goals. Parent-teacher-student interviews, for example, need to be set up in ways that encourage people to share their ideas and feelings about learning; this will require teachers especially to be vulnerable, refusing to hide behind their professional roles. In open dialogue, each person should gain a deeper understanding of each other and work toward the common goal of learning.

A third way to establish a caring relationship is through practice, providing opportunities for students and teachers to care for each other.

Students might be expected to participate in regular service activities with an emphasis on developing skills that contribute to competence in caring. Such opportunities would involve adults in all kinds of occupations with students, with each adult functioning as teacher in his or her own area, taking special responsibility for nurturing a sense of caring (Noddings 1984, 188).

In classrooms, students will be encouraged to learn from each other as well as from teachers and books. Teachers will provide multiple opportunities for students to demonstrate that they have learned the material. Class presentations, group research and discussion, individual writing, designing and completing projects, and demonstrations are rich alternatives to the standard textbook and worksheet practices that prevail in many classrooms. If students have difficulty the first time around, we need to try again with renewed support, perhaps in more imaginative ways. If learning really is our goal, there has to be a mutual effort by teacher and student.

Finally, a caring relationship needs to include affirmation. Teachers have to reveal to students that they can become more than they are. As they evaluate student progress in learning, teachers can encourage and show students how they have grown. To achieve this, teachers will need to reexamine many traditional grading practices. To affirm students, teachers must see and receive them: they must see clearly what they have actually done and receive the feelings with which it was done.

A teacher should lead in establishing a caring environment in which each student feels invited personally, is encouraged to be actively involved, is recognized for making valuable contributions, and experiences the benefits of learning individually and collaboratively.

Principal-Teacher Relationships

The Christian school must be a community of learning where students, teachers, and principals have different and complementary responsibilities for making decisions regarding learning. Leadership by the principal is crucial for developing such a community. Principals in Christian schools are called to lead in ways that empower teachers and students to fulfill their respective offices. The primary task of the principal is to keep the vision of the school at the forefront of the daily work of all members of the school community. The vision helps members in the school community "to regularly define and clarify what they are seeking to accomplish; it helps them envision how each can contribute to the purpose of the whole school; it is a vision which encourages and assists in personal and communal growth and renewal" (Mulder 1990, 99–100).

The principal should encourage teachers to discover, develop, and use their gifts in teaching and learning. As head learner a principal is engaged in "experiencing, displaying, modelling, and celebrating what it is hoped and expected that teachers and students will do" (Barth 1990, 46). Principals carry out specific practices if the school is to become a community of leaders. They articulate the school's goals in staff meetings, conversations, newsletters, and community meetings. They involve teachers in making decisions and entrust them with authority according to their responsibilities. Principals also set in place a way of sharing the responsibility for failure. The important issue is not who should be blamed for failure but to consider how we can learn from it. By being willing to say "I don't know," a principal makes a powerful invitation to teachers to participate in leading and at the same time gives them room to risk saying "I don't know" themselves. Finally, principals provide teachers with opportunities to share responsibility for success and enjoy recognition from the school community. Sharing school-wide success replenishes teachers personally and professionally as they experience being members of a community of leaders (Barth 1988).

A principal who lives out the vision of a Christian community for learning evokes authentic community that makes space for other people to act: "[W]hen a leader is willing to trust the abundance that people have and can generate together, willing to take the risk of inviting people to share from that abundance, then and only then may true community emerge" (Palmer 1990, 138).

School-Parent Relationships

Lynn Reese is having coffee with board member Barbara Travers after a Mountain City board meeting. "Barbara," she asks, "what do you think we could do to make parents feel more welcome at school?"

Barbara thought back to the first year she had sent her children to Mountain City after teaching them at home through third grade. She had hoped to maintain her interest in their learning as they progressed, but somehow she had not felt free enough to tell her children's teachers that she wanted to be involved.

"Well, Lynn, we do need to break down some of the barriers that presently exist. As parents many of us feel that relations between parents and teachers are set up too formally. Our teachers adopt too professional a manner in conversations about our children's learning. We each seem to say what we are supposed to say as parents and teachers but I don't feel we communicate as well as we should. I believe we should take a careful look at what we could do to improve parent-teacher relationships at school. How do the teachers feel about parents?"

"To be honest, Barbara, many teachers really appreciate the support they receive from parents. They are obviously thankful that most children have stable homes. But teachers are sometimes frustrated by lack of parent response to the papers and newsletters that children take home. They wish that once in a while parents would phone with a comment or question about what their child is learning. Maybe it's time for a parent-teacher evening that focuses on how we could improve communication between home and school. Let's see, as a parent, what do you need to know?"

"First of all, for me it's important to know what's happening in school and how my son and daughter are doing. When I taught our children at home I knew what they were learning. I know that now I won't be able to stay as involved in their learning. However, I believe that as a school community we need to build stronger connections between home and school as far as learning is concerned. Also, parents want and need to know how the school 'works' and how they can be involved, directly and indirectly, in their children's learning. Parents want to know what they can do at home to help their children with their learning. I feel that this becomes more important in the higher grades. Sometimes it seems that teachers hide behind their specialized knowledge in order to avoid addressing what could be done at home."

"It's interesting to hear you express parent interest in that manner. It would be good for teachers to hear parents talk about that. Teachers often argue that parents would rather not hear from school because it might lead to one more difficult issue to talk about with their teenage children. Let's keep in touch, we need to pursue this further."

Christian schools have a well-established record of parent involvement in school. Annual membership meetings for budget approval and election of board members provide an avenue for parents to participate in decision making and governance. Regular parent-teacher meetings offer parents opportunities for direct interaction with teachers about student achievement. School newsletters provide regular communication to parents regarding school events and noteworthy activities. Many Christian schools invite parents to volunteer for a variety of needs in libraries, for playground supervision, and for numerous fundraising activities.

Although these avenues of involvement are often available, many Christian schools increasingly suffer from the same serious problem faced by public education: there is often a strong separation between the professional world of principals and teachers and the personal world of parents.

In such a situation, principals and teachers see themselves as offering a service to the parent customers who pay for it. Parents see themselves as buying a service for a fee and hold the school responsible for their children's education. Sometimes they want to avoid the problems of teaching their children, especially as they become teenagers.

This separation between the professional world of the school and the familial world of the home results in discontinuities in children's learning. School learning becomes disengaged from the life experiences that for most children are centered in the home. Teachers grumble about apathetic parents and are relieved in part by the presence of the committed ones who faithfully attend school meetings. Parents complain about principals and teachers who appear distant and seem to do little to help their children's personal problems.

The separation between school and home is exacerbated by the increasing costs of Christian education. As tuition increases parents ask more questions about the "services" that are being provided. If a Christian school has not developed a strong sense of community and has little basis or motivation for building community, parents begin to look elsewhere. They look for schools that appear to have more caring principals and teachers and provide better facilities.

As costs increase, pressure builds for maintaining or sometimes reducing teacher salaries. Teachers begin to ask questions about the value of their work and their dedication to student learning. They wonder whether it continues to be worth their effort to teach in Christian schools for salaries that are lower than those in public schools.

Christian schools need to reexamine the relationships between parents and teachers. Family-school relationships are a dominant influence in the lives of parents and teachers and a major factor affecting learning (Lightfoot 1978). Christian schools, therefore, need to be designed and developed as Christian communities of learning. Teachers and parents are called to be joint members in a community that has a common mission and responsibility for children's learning, a community that builds meaningful relationships between teachers and parents for the purpose of fostering learning.

What can Christian schools do to improve parent-teacher relationships? Berger (1991) lists a number of aspects that have to be addressed. Parents must be seen as partners and supporters of the educational goals of the school. They need to be involved in making decisions about the direction and purpose of the school and in maintaining a liaison between home and school to support their children's learning. Parents should be encouraged to participate as volunteers or paid employees at school. Finally, they must be involved as active partners in promoting children's learning at home and at school.

With such involvement, schools can help parents more effectively in nurturing their children. Schools can host orientation meetings in the spring at key points in a student's learning, before kindergarten, before middle school, before high school. These meetings should provide an opportunity for parents to visit the school and meet the staff, and a way for teachers and parents to share their vision for the school.

Throughout the year Christian schools must have avenues for parents and teachers to communicate with each other regarding student learning. Regular newsletters, timely parent-teacher interviews, meaningful report cards, and student-parent-teacher conferences must be used to reinforce the common vision that has been established and is constantly being renewed. Not all teachers must be involved with parents to the same degree, nor should all parents be expected to be involved in schools to the same degree. But each school community should see to it that feelings of trust continue to grow between teachers and parents and that there are ways for parents and teachers to work together in enhancing children's learning. There must be avenues for working out problems and difficulties as they occur and processes for confirming and renewing mutual goals.

Forging a covenant community for learning requires that teachers, principal, students, and parents continually renew their common vision for Christian schooling. They must maintain an atmosphere of mutual love and compassion. They must share opportunities and responsibilities for making decisions about learning.

Questions for Discussion

1. Examine your own school in terms of the three essential ingredients of a covenant community: a common vision, an atmosphere of love and trust, and leadership for service. Are the conversations in halls and classrooms evidence that your school is a community for learning that lives and works toward responsive discipleship?

2. Initiate a discussion and develop guidelines that enable all of the relationships in your school to be grounded in the princi-

ples and practices of a community of learning. Address each of the following:

a. teacher-teacher
b. student-teacher
c. teacher-principal
d. parent-teacher

3. As a teacher, do you feel isolated in your classroom? Do you experience the support of colleagues? As a staff, become involved in discussions that work toward strengthening community among teachers. You may find it helpful to engage an outside resource person to lead a number of workshops that help to build a collegial community in your school.

4. Set up a forum for examining the role parents presently have in your school. Gather resource articles, phone other schools, involve parents and teachers in a review of what those roles might be in a community for learning.

Recommended Reading

1. Berger, E. 1991. *Parents as partners in education.*
Contains valuable ideas and practices about parent involvement in school.
2. Peck, M. S. 1987. *The different drum.*
Includes sections describing the meaning of community, the stages of community building, as well as the dynamics of community.
3. Vanier, J. 1989. *Community and growth.*
A personal account of experiences in building and maintaining community.
4. Barth, R. 1990. *Improving schools from within.*
Particularly helpful for looking at schools in terms of adults as learners.
5. Sergiovanni, T. J. 1991. *The principalship.*
A valuable resource for school leaders involved in examining the mission of schooling, teaching and supervision, and school leadership.

6

How Do We Learn?

"Is anybody else as bewildered as I am?" asked Greg Fouts as the staff gathered for coffee during the break. "Here we are having another seminar on how our students learn. This time we are hearing that Gardner says they have different intelligences and we must keep that in mind as we teach. Last year we had someone come and tell us about cooperative learning. The year before we talked about their different learning styles."

"Don't forget the session we had about five years ago concerning right-brained and left-brained students," Margie Phipps joined in. "I was quite excited about that for a while because it fit so well with what I saw happening to students. But I haven't heard much about it lately. Some of these new ideas seem nothing more than passing fads. Others are important insights and should remain with us. But I, for one, have no way of knowing which is which. And what is equally frustrating is that I just can't get a handle on which ones match our Christian school philosophy."

"I don't know about all these new ideas about learning," Pearl Stock said. "We never talked about things like this twenty-five years ago when I began teaching and we did just fine. The kids learned what we told them to learn and it wasn't all such a hassle. Back then we knew exactly what to do when we taught."

The older faculty smiled and nodded. Geoff Schmidt said, "I'm a little embarrassed by how much I want to agree with you, Pearl. It certainly used to be easier but I'm not at all sure it was better. I know they say that ignorance is bliss but I don't know how blissful it was for the students who needed help and understanding that simply wasn't provided for them."

"But you can't do everything, can you?" asked Greg. "I spend a great deal of time talking with kids, but I really don't know how to teach in ways that take into account their individual learning styles and individual intelligences. Most of the people who come here to lead our in-service sessions tell us that we must teach in those ways and tell us that we must use interactive learning strategies so that the students will be involved in learning. But rarely do they show us how to do it. And when they do lead us through a workshop in how to teach that way, it is only a one-time session. Teaching is such a daily task. You always have to be ready with interesting material and with exciting ways of teaching that material. If teaching and learning are ever going to change and reflect the new research concerning how students learn, we teachers will need much more intensive and extensive training."

Learning Is Active Responding

Many parents and teachers think that students learn best by acquiring factual knowledge, bit by bit. Paulo Freire (1972) refers to this as the "banking model of education" in which teachers "deposit" information in the heads of passive students. The thesis of this book, that Christian schooling should be for responsive discipleship, demands far more than such banking of information. Students as image-bearing subjects are called to respond actively to God's will for their lives. They actively unwrap their gifts, share their joys and their burdens, and nurture shalom wherever they are able to do so. A biblical view of knowing implies a many-sided engagement with creation. God taught his people in a variety of ways and Scripture emphasizes active response to these teachings. Jesus also called his hearers to act on what he taught. All this implies that learning is always dynamic rather than passive in character.

We teach so that our students will be able to live as responsive disciples with wisdom and insight. To have wisdom means much more than simply knowing things in the abstract. To be wise means to know how to *act* rightly in specific situations. To act *rightly* means to respond obediently, to act in conformity with God's will.

To be wise also means knowing why we believe some things are important and how this understanding can help us live (Nozick 1989). Wisdom finds its meaning and coherence in Christ, in whom are hid all its treasures. If we are truly wise, we have the insight to see all things in terms of their relation to Christ and his service. Then we are able to place things in their proper perspective, to understand what is of lesser and greater importance. Setting our minds on things that are above transforms how we view all things. Wisdom is thus rooted in faith and leads to a walk of faithfulness. With wisdom comes a passion to know more, to understand more, and to be able to do more, in a world we recognize as an abundantly rich home for God's people.

Wisdom brings insight, the ability to see into the real meaning of things. While facts and skills are facets of learning, with insight comes a sense of joyful discovery, of challenge for future learning and willingness to be absorbed in activities that promote learning. Memorization does not ensure insight. Rather, it ordinarily carries with it only relief that the task has been completed. Learning a new skill does not in itself ensure insight. It is possible to learn to read without appreciating the riches of reading, to learn to sing in key without experiencing the joys of music.

Teacher: The thing that bothers me so much about schools these days is that there is far too much emphasis on "meaning" and on "critical thinking." I have always believed that if students have enough facts at their fingertips then meaning and understanding will follow.

Interviewer: On what do you base that belief?

Teacher: It seems to have worked that way in my own life. My own schooling included a great deal of memorizing of facts. This idea that facts aren't important is the downfall of our education system.

Facts, of course, are important—but only because of their place in a larger framework of understanding. During the last twenty years research conclusions about how students learn, while sometimes tentative, indicate that narrow "banking" education is generally unproductive. Rather, effective learning requires the active and dynamic involvement of the learner. Middle schools and, even more so, high schools have lagged behind elementary ones in improving teaching in light of this understanding of how students learn.

God has created us so that we long to find meaning in the experiences of life, to see how things relate to each other and how things hang together. This is because the meaning-full creation speaks of him and is designed to bring us into and deepen our personal relationship with him. God invites us through creation to respond. Learning therefore always involves relating things to God—or if not to him, then to an idol. Today, we have supporting research conclusions about this need to see things in relation to one another. This research concerns how students

131

think about what they have read or heard, the process they go through when they relate new experience to prior knowledge, how students break down new information into its constituent parts and then put it back together again into a new pattern, and how they use abstractions and ideas in particular situations.

Brain research confirms this need to search for how things make sense. For the individual, the recognition of relationships is experienced as an act of invention. It is indeed a creative response to the structure of creation, a personal response that however always occurs within a communal context, as when a child learns to speak a word within an English-speaking culture. But the validity of our "inventions" depends on their faithfulness to the order of God's world.

Learning that has long-term benefit can be thought of as a three-fold rhythm of immersion, withdrawal, and return (explored in greater depth in chapter 7). We immerse ourselves in experiencing an aspect of God's world, then withdraw by standing back to focus on a problem and draw connections, and return by encountering creation with deepened insight. Each phase helps to enrich and extend the connections that students gradually make as one phase builds on the previous.

For example, children build a rich experience of shapes and figures through their daily interaction with the world. Much of this knowledge is implicit or tacit. At some point they meet the notion of "triangle," a figure with three sides. This relatively simple concept poses a problem for them. They now face the world with a new challenge, that of deciding what is a triangle and what is not. Very often, when children learn new words, they enthusiastically seek to label everything in sight that appears to fit their understanding of the term. They test the concept, using it to guide their exploration of the world. Having learned that all triangles are alike with respect to their number of sides, they see triangles on a sheet of paper or on the side of a huge building or as a piece of metal that makes an interesting sound. Adults may tell children all kinds of information about the characteristics of triangles but it is not until children effectively reintegrate this information with their everyday experience, so that it is informed and deepened by the concept, that meaningful learning will have taken place. This may come as a flash of insight or as a gradual process of recognition: what is significant is that it is *what the child does* that counts for learning. It is the moments of "Aha! I understand that triangles are alike in this way, even though they differ in other ways!"

This is true of learning at any level. All learners try to make sense by looking for patterns and relationships. Helping students respond to the relationships that God has created and that humans have creatively shaped is an important goal of effective schooling. A teacher may insist that students memorize the causes of different wars and the students may do so but this does not mean that learning (properly defined) has taken place. Even if it is a common strategy, memorizing lists or definitions without reflection on the connections between the items and without connection to the students' own experience will not only impede understanding but may well lead to rejection of the information that has been delivered and then stored only for its utility in passing a test (McNeil 1986).

Teaching that leads to understanding enables students to make appropriate connections and recognize patterns. Students often find it difficult to take new information and then see how it fits with the relationships that have already been established, or to rethink old ways of knowing to accommodate new experience. Scientific explanations, for instance, may conflict with the intuitive way students feel that things happen or work. Students need to predict, to test, to witness the evidence before they will resolve their misconceptions. Similarly, teachers need to help young and poor readers make connections between new and prior knowledge and to provide the opportunity for lively discussion and interactive processing (Bennett 1986, 22–23).

Only when students have had significant experiences allowing them to make connections between various situations—say, between the causes of World War II and the probability of military conflict ensuing from the collapse of the U.S.S.R.—does real learning occur. At that point the student has "experienced" the causes in several contexts, analyzed them and focused on their consequences, and projected and tested a pattern for relationships in human behavior. Note that in this way theoretical or abstract concepts are rooted in concrete experience and, after more distanced focusing, once again lead to concrete understanding. Such particular understanding is not restricted to the senses but will also include social, ethical, aesthetic, and spiritual insights.

Active processing and integration of old and new understanding is enriched through "metacognition," the process of thinking about thinking. Students with strong metacognitive abilities can explain not only what they have learned but how they have come to learn it. They are conscious of what they are doing while they are learning. They are able to describe the assumptions they once made and how they differ from the assumptions they make now, as well as explain the steps they went through in changing their assumptions. Students develop this ability to reflect on their thinking by speaking, listening, reading, writing, viewing, and acting under the direction of teachers who know how to help them to ask reflective questions and who will also model this process for them. Through such activities and by such questioning, students rethink and rearrange old categories in ways that allow the learner to make new meanings.

Some of the information we need for our daily lives, once acquired, needs to be consolidated through practice and rehearsal. The more seemingly random and patternless this knowledge is, the more this repetition is required. We need to memorize telephone numbers if we wish to remember them, although even here the continual use of them in actually making phone calls will be more efficient: either way, we establish a pattern of behavior. And if we can invent some meaningful relationships between the numbers, our task is all the easier. All knowledge is stored with less effort if it is perceived as meaningful, if there is a context for learning or if the person understands the need for it.

Unfortunately, far too often teachers act as though most learning in school is disconnected from personal meaning, context, or intrinsic motivation. They promote the idea that learning itself is not inherently meaningful, and that it takes practice, drill, threats, and rewards to get students to memorize information. The student's need for information is then satisfied by performance on tests, at which point the information is released from memory. Such teaching tends to burden students' memories with unorganized facts that are rather easily forgotten. Facts and skills are important, but mainly if they are available in a meaningful context to deepen insight or enable more informed thinking and acting.

Parent: We really don't seem to benefit very much from simply memorizing information, do we? It's all connected, but when we are kids we can't see the connection. For example, I remember being held on my German grandmother's lap while she sang songs of her country. And standing on a chair in the kitchen watching while she made wonderful desserts, both of us singing, "Gott ist der liebe." I remember fearing for the life of my uncle who had been sent overseas to fight the Germans. And watching the children of German parents being excluded from games on my school playground during World War II. Some very conflicting emotions resulted from all of that. Yet, when it came time for me to study German history in high school, I thought of it as facts that must be memorized. I was much older before I made the connection between the happenings in my childhood and the happenings in modern German history.

Most teachers recognize that relationships in experience cut across the knowledge from several disciplines. The disciplines focus on particular kinds of relationships abstracted from everyday experience. When we teach primarily within subject boundaries students have difficulty recognizing the relationships that cut across the disciplines and internalizing them in a personally meaningful way. Using integral units to organize a large proportion of school learning is necessary to help students grasp the interconnected patterns that help us understand and respond to life's complex situations. This, of course, will require rethinking many aspects of the structures of schools.

Providing for Diversity: Unwrapping Different Ways of Knowing

Treating students as if they are identical promotes conformity and flies in the face of the richness of individuality that they are called to contribute to the body of Christ. Students differ from one another, for instance, in personality traits and learning styles as well as in the degree to which they possess certain gifts. If we are to help students to develop their various talents and abilities, we must be alert to these differences. At the same time, to assume that all differences are relevant to learning promotes discriminatory practices, which once again will stifle individuality and the unwrapping of gifts. In the next sections we deal with the implications of current research for these concerns.

For a long time teachers have known a great deal about the physical development of children and young people. They know that students go through the stages of physical development at differing rates. They are aware that certain types of behavior such as restlessness and inattentiveness occur more often in some stages than in others. Elementary-level teachers who spend the whole day with a group of children tend to teach in ways that are in keeping with these physical characteristics, allowing more movement for restless children and providing concrete learning experiences for inattentive ones. Sensitive teachers cannot help but be aware of physical differences among their children and teach accordingly.

Teachers, however, find it more difficult to observe intellectual characteristics. Even defining what we mean by "intelligence" is difficult. Is it an ability to understand things, to solve problems, and to figure things out cognitively? Or is this too limiting since it focuses only on logical-mathematical and verbal intelligence? Does intelligence also include the ability to withstand distraction, to be socially competent, to have

an interest in learning, and to be motivated toward academic performance (Snyderman and Rothman 1987)?

These definitions, however, are narrow in that they reflect only the
types of learning generally emphasized in schools. We use tests to measure such learnings, and assume that the resulting test scores indicate
some inborn characteristics. That assumption is not warranted. We
harm students by equating scores on "intelligence" tests with a student's innate ability. An "I.Q." score depends significantly on the learning experiences a student has had at home and at school. Thus, an intelligence test is in part an achievement test, one that is limited in scope.
Its score has some meaning but not necessarily the meaning the teacher
or parent assumes.

Another problem with this view of intelligence is that the different
ways in which people know are far more delightfully complicated than
these general descriptions and measurements would lead us to believe.
Howard Gardner (1983) has given us a more helpful description of the
wonderful array of ways of knowing or intelligences. Gardner suggests
that we can identify at least seven different ways of knowing that we all
possess to some degree, and that these are only slightly interdependent.
The linguistic way of knowing involves, for instance, using vocabulary,
playing with words, and applying metaphors. The logico-mathematical
way of knowing allows people to manipulate numbers and symbols.
The musical makes it possible to enjoy and make music, while the spatial enables persons to perceive and reproduce the visual world. The
bodily-kinesthetic way of knowing leads to an awareness and control
of one's body. Finally, the intrapersonal and interpersonal ways of knowing involve, respectively, self-knowledge allowing access to one's own
feeling life, and "people skills" such as the ability to make accurate
assessments of other people based on subtle clues.

It is likely that more ways of knowing exist than those Gardner
describes. We should probably recognize aesthetic and spiritual modes,
for example (Eisner 1985), as well as ethical, technical, and economic
insight (Blomberg 1980a). However many there are, each person
uniquely combines varying degrees of each. In order for their multi-
faceted abilities to develop as richly as possible, students need mentors, including teachers, who value their particular constellation of
intelligence gifts—and an environment that encourages such development. If a particular way of knowing is considered important in the
culture of the child, if considerable resources (time, thoughtfulness,
and money) are devoted to it, if the child is willing to develop in that

area, and if proper means for learning are available, nearly all normal individuals can attain impressive competence in that area.

At present, most schools encourage especially linguistic and logical-mathematical ways of knowing. We do not do a very good job with musical, aesthetic, spatial, or intrapersonal ways. The value of Gardner's work is that it encourages us to recognize that students have a variety of gifts and must be helped to capitalize on their particular strengths in the ways of knowing and learning. But teachers and parents who fail to understand the complexity of the combinations of intelligences may well thwart students in their unwrapping of the gifts of responsive discipleship. Christian schools do not need to ascertain that each student reaches some particular level or standard in any particular intelligence. Rather, our task is to provide an environment in which every way of knowing is valued, and to help students nurture and unfold the potential in themselves, in others, and in God's creation.

Providing for Diversity: Affirming Learning Styles

Ever since 1968, when Sperry and his colleagues studied the perceptions of patients who had had the connections between the two hemispheres of their brains severed, a flurry of articles and workshops has advised teachers how to teach for both sides of the brain. Persons with left-hemisphere dominance were verbal, rational, and sequential learners; those with right-hemisphere dominance, intuitive, holistic, and sensory ones (Caine and Caine 1991, 33–34). Today, many educational psychologists agree that while there is something to these distinctions, both hemispheres are involved in all activities to such an extent that simplistic explanations of the activity of each has not been helpful (Levy 1985). We are marvelously complicated beings.

What is important for teachers to know is that students are capable of thinking intuitively, synthesizing, and learning through guided imagery. Teachers also need to recognize that those same students are capable of logical and critical thinking, verbal articulation, and written expression. In order to teach well, teachers do not need to understand how or where these functions occur in the brain. The classroom must be a place where instruction is arranged so that opportunity and guidance is provided to develop all abilities and where the development of each ability is recognized and appreciated as a valuable part of learning.

Perhaps the most important implication of split-brain research has been the interest educators finally began to take in the relationship between the brain and ways of classroom instruction. For a long time sensitive teachers have recognized that students respond to instructional environments and activities in unique ways that have little to do with their intelligence. Research concerning learning and perceptual styles (McCarthy 1981) as well as reading styles (Carbo, Dunn, and Dunn 1986) has done a great deal to show that students respond differently to dissimilar kinds of instruction. Learning style preferences have been described as principally visual (reading), aural (listening), or physical (activity). Rosenberg (1968) labeled learning patterns as rigid-inhibited, undisciplined, acceptance-anxious, and creative. Other researchers presented alternate categorizations. Van Brummelen (1988, 46–60) provides a helpful description of how information concerning learning styles and phases can help Christian teachers develop a model for meaningful learning.

People come to know in diverse ways. For example, many people are unable to arrive at carefully thought-out conclusions about issues until they have developed an argument in writing. They outline the issue at hand, present the arguments concerning different aspects of the issue, gather new information and evidence to help them with the arguments, present their reasons for valuing the evidence which they do, and finally state the position they have decided upon. In the writing, discarding, and rewriting they arrive at what it is that they know. Others find it more profitable to read, reflect, discard some of their earlier ideas, and discuss their way toward the resolution. The discussion in turn leads them into further reading and reflection. Still others learn better by observing, interacting with many different concrete examples, reflecting on that interaction, and going back to observing.

Teacher: My eleventh-grade class was studying U.S. history and for one of their assignments I asked them to make twenty-five sketches of buildings or bridges in our city. There was a great deal of moaning, of course, particularly from the students who are the best at writing and discussion.

Interviewer: What exactly did you want them to learn from that assignment?

Teacher: Our city is quite old and the construction is from different periods. In the sketching, I expected students to notice details that appear in construction of the same period. In the discussion that followed the completion of the assignment they became aware that the way people think and the values they have influence many areas of their lives.

Interviewer: Would you consider allowing students to choose whether they will sketch, or write, or produce some other evidence of learning?

Teacher: No. I do encourage that in some other assignments, of course. But I also want students to be forced to struggle with the unwrapping of gifts that aren't their strongest. In doing so they gain appreciation for gifts that others have, compassion for those who struggle with tasks that are traditionally part of school learning, and an understanding of new ways of learning. I continue to think this is a worthwhile activity.

Caine and Caine (1991) warn that no teacher can adequately deal with all the variations in learning style and that we shouldn't attempt to customize our teaching methods for the needs of each child. Instead, they affirm that teachers must have a thorough knowledge of content, a variety of ways of teaching, and a strong spark of creativity in order to provide a school environment that is supportive of meaningful, challenging, relevant, and, above all, different types of learning. Once again, purposely providing a rhythm of immersion, withdrawal, and return will animate a variety of learning activities so that each learner has opportunities to feel comfortable and shine.

Imaging God as Males and Females

Schools must respect the similarities and the differences between female and male students in ways that affirm that together they are made in the image of God. What has become glaringly clear during the last two decades, however, is that our stereotypical image of how boys and girls differ in the way they learn has little support in our knowledge of innate ability. Differences in the ways males and females learn as groups are slight compared with individual differences within each group. Furthermore, in interpreting any differences we find between the learning of males and females, we rarely can separate genetic influences from environmental ones on the behavior of each group. We simply do not know what each gender would be like if there were no cultural conditioning.

Where gender differences in learning occur they are slight. For example, in mathematical, science, and verbal abilities, only 1 percent of the variation that exists in students can be attributed to gender—a slight difference, indeed (Hyde 1981). An inappropriate and unwarranted emphasis on the differences between males and females in verbal and mathematical skills is likely to lead teachers to lowered expectations of one group or the other, expectations that may strongly influence student performance (Rosenthal 1974).

While the gender differences in cognitive abilities are slight, if they exist at all, there are differences in personality variables that we must take into consideration. Males tend to be more aggressive than females in all ages and in most cultures; females and males react differently when it comes to conditions concerning conformity, achievement, and how emotional problems are manifested. We cannot examine all of these variables here but for a biblically based approach Mary Stewart Van Leeuwen's *Gender and Grace* (1990) is a helpful starting point for faculty discussion.

What does this mean for classroom teachers? The current debate about schools in North America would lead one to believe that the experience girls and boys have in school is virtually the same. However, a recent report commissioned by the American Association of University Women Educational Foundation (1991) challenges that assumption. This report, which synthesizes the research on the subject of girls in school, presents compelling evidence that girls are not receiving the same quality or quantity of education as boys.

According to the research, teachers give more classroom attention and more esteem-building encouragement to boys than to girls. Often, when boys call out answers to questions, teachers listen and encourage. When girls call out they are told to "raise your hand if you want to speak." Teachers tend to choose classroom activities that appeal to boys' interests and present material in ways that appeal to boys. Teaching methods that foster competition continue to be used, although research indicates that girls learn much better when cooperative activities are used.

In many schools the curriculum and textbooks often ignore females or reinforce stereotypes. Differences between the achievement of girls and boys in mathematics and science are small and declining. Yet in high school, girls are less likely than boys to take advanced courses in those areas. Even girls who are highly competent in math and science are much less likely than boys to pursue careers in those areas. In part this is because of lack of encouragement to make decisions that are not in keeping with the stereotypes and in part it is because the manner of instruction in math and science courses is often oriented more to boys than girls (Stronks 1984).

Are Christian schools different? Do teachers in Christian schools encourage boys and girls equally in the unwrapping of gifts in every area? There is no evidence to reassure us that they do. Inappropriate interpretations of biblical norms for family living as well as cultural traditions have regrettably restricted the unwrapping and employment of women's gifts. In fact, a recent survey of male seminarians has shown a high correlation between sexist attitudes toward women and strength of theological convictions about male headship (Dorner 1990). Schools may not use differences between boys and girls as a basis for discriminatory behavior. In terms of the school's task to promote learning systematically, the differences are so slight as to be insignificant. Thus, rather than emphasizing presumed differences, schools and teachers must take steps to overcome the effects of discriminatory practices and structures as these have affected the children we now teach in their earlier experiences and as these continue to be reflected in our current procedures.

Grouping for a Responsive Discipleship Community

"Ability grouping" is the practice of placing students in low, middle, or high groups for specific subjects such as math or reading, and then instructing in ways presumed to be more in keeping with their ability. It is planned by a school and therefore differs from either the self-selected tracking that occurs when students choose specialized studies such as advanced business or calculus, or from flexible groups that are formed temporarily for instruction in a specific skill.

One of the problems with ability grouping is that teachers tend to have inappropriately low expectations of students in the low ability groups (Good 1982). Students in the lower groups fall increasingly behind students of equal ability who were placed in higher groups.

A related problem is that plans for instruction are more often based on the presumed instructional needs of children at that level rather than on actual needs. As a result, lower-level reading groups receive much more instruction in decoding and comprehension skills whether or not a careful diagnosis has determined they need such instruction, and they are instructed in less stimulating ways than children in other groups (Shavelson and Stern 1981). A much less adequate literacy results, one that stresses narrow skills but not meaningful engagement with and response to content and ideas.

Students' perceptions of themselves and the perception that others have of them are affected by such practices. Teachers and students view students in higher ability groups more positively than students in lower groups, regardless of academic achievement. Students in low groups as a result of the teachers' judgment of their current ability as well as their self-perception, usually begin to behave according to those expectations (Oakes 1991).

In spite of the disadvantages, ability grouping might still be defended if it resulted in increased academic achievement by most students. However, research does not support such a defense. When achievement is compared, students of high ability benefit but students of lower ability suffer; furthermore, the gain by students in the high ability groups is much less than the loss experienced by students in the low groups (Kulik and Kulik 1984).

Christian schools should give special honor to the weak and the needy and should organize instruction to their advantage. Furthermore, students who are living and learning to live as responsive disciples need opportunities for helping each other with difficulties and for celebrating each other's gifts. Ability grouping neither allows such opportunities nor enhances the learning environment of those of "lower ability." As Paul put it, we have been given different gifts, according to the grace given us, but we must give greater honor to those parts of the body that lack it, so that all may contribute according to their particular talents (Rom. 12; 1 Cor. 12).

At the same time, our discussion of different ways of knowing should remind us that "ability" is a function of the kinds of ability we choose to acknowledge. Our schools should be organized in such ways that excellence in many different kinds of intelligences and ways of knowing are encouraged. Above all, this implies the recognition that the "excellence" that ought to pervade all that happens in the school, and without which even being able to fathom all mysteries and all knowledge is nothing, is the excellence of love.

School board member: I visited the high school recently and saw that the social studies teacher had his class working in groups. I know group work is more the thing to do these days but how can you tell whether the kids are really learning? Is group work always productive?

Rather than grouping students according to their ability, many teachers have discovered that teaching students of different abilities to work in collaboration can create a productive learning climate. Collaborative learning is known by many names: cooperative learning, peer tutoring, group learning, or mentoring. Research has shown that students' work tends to improve when they get help from peers. Not only that, but the peers offering the help learn from the students they are helping and from the activity of helping itself. The reason this is true is that the act of telling information to another, or explaining a concept, or describing the steps of a procedure to another reinforces and extends the learning of the one who is speaking. Teachers know that the best way to learn something is to try to teach it!

Collaborative learning is an important element in a classroom where students are expected to learn responsive discipleship. Its importance lies not only in the fact that learning is strongly reinforced through collaboration but also because through working together students learn to take responsibility for each other's learning and understanding, rather than simply being concerned with their own.

Some collaborative or group activities are designed to provide appropriate interactions that will lead to metacognitive and reflective abilities. These are the activities that *must* be part of teaching and learning in a classroom. Other group activities are designed simply to encourage social interaction. These activities are at times appropriate for a classroom but may also be a waste of time. A teacher needs to know which kind of group activity is appropriate for a specific purpose. For a teacher, principal, or workshop leader to talk about "cooperative" or "collaborative" learning activities is not helpful unless the purpose of each activity is clearly kept in mind. Both the teacher and the students must understand at all times why they are using particular teaching and learning strategies.

Growing in Faith

Saving faith is a gift of the Holy Spirit. The gift of faith is a mystery that we receive in gratitude and work out with fear and trembling. In school, faith is at work in all areas of the curriculum just as it is in all areas of life. In Christian school circles, it has become common for teachers to participate in meetings and convention sessions on the topic of "integrating faith and learning." But such deliberations are often restricted to integrating God's revelation once delivered in Christ and Scripture with various facets of curriculum perspective and content.

Several questions arise at this point. Isn't the phrase "integrating faith and learning" misleading in that, rather than bringing together two distinct things, everything we do in life and in school is based on our ultimate faith commitment? Further, in all the attention we give to such integration in the curriculum, do we pay enough attention to what faith itself involves, and to how faith grows and develops? To what extent and in what ways can the mystery of faith and faith development be analyzed to help us in the classroom?

Growth in faith is difficult to explain. Understanding certain patterns of a life of faith to the extent that that is possible, however, will enhance the possibility of teaching in ways that broaden and deepen students' response of faith. Students have different kinds of questions and concerns about their beliefs at different ages. Knowing the typical characteristics of students' journeys of faith will help to inform our curriculum planning. We cannot describe in any depth the journey people make in coming to a mature faith. Rather, our intention here is to explain some of the kinds of questions and concerns students have about their beliefs at different ages that should inform curriculum planning.

Preschool

Beth: If God made everything, did God make the wheels on our car?

Elise: When I pray I always think that God wears a white shirt and grey pants. But why does Jesus always wear a dress?

Todd: If God is really good why did he let my pet rabbit die?

Monique: Well, where is God now?
Mother: God is in your heart, darling.
Monique: Oh, then is God in your tummy with the new baby?

During the preschool and kindergarten years, children tend to think of God in literal terms. They will look for pictures of dignified or awe-inspiring people and ask, "Is this God?" or draw God with a white robe and a long beard. We should not be disturbed by this very literal level of understanding nor by the matter-of-fact questions children ask and the categorical statements they make. Rather, we need to keep in mind that these children grow spiritually when they have affirmative experiences that help them form positive attitudes about God, the Bible, and worship.

In school, teachers need to remember that children at this age can learn to love Jesus, but not as much through words they hear spoken as through the experiences they have (Westerhoff 1976). They can easily learn to pray and sing songs of faith, and enjoy participating. The physical ritual elements such as folding hands and bowing heads and holding hands with each other in prayer and action involvement while singing are important for them. Similarly, sitting in a close circle while listening to a Bible story or praying or singing is significant for them. Children at this age grow in faith and the understanding of its implications as they hear concrete stories, particularly Bible stories with a clear theme. Visual aids that can be touched and manipulated will also reinforce words and ideas about faith.

144

Elementary Level

Michael: Did Aunt Mary go to see Jesus right the very second she died or did she have to wait a while?

Patty: I am so worried about Suzy's family. I'm pretty sure they aren't Christians because they don't go to church. But I saw angels on their Christmas tree so maybe they are, after all. It's so hard to know.

Billy: That man is painting his house on Sunday. Is he going to go to hell?

Valerie: If you don't close your eyes when you pray will God still listen?

Jim: Do dogs go to heaven when they die? Will there be any animals in heaven?

Michael: I don't understand about this thing they call the Trinity. How can something be three things and one thing at the same time? It isn't possible.

As children enter the early years of elementary school, they have a great desire to learn about God and heaven, and their questions and comments reflect their interest in thinking about a power that is greater than themselves or their parents and teachers. Rules become important in their faith life, just as they do in games (Shelly 1982). With this early understanding of rules, conscience begins to mature. Children compare the actions of their friends and family with some standard they have learned. While children often sound disturbingly rigid and judgmental, in reality they may be worrying and trying to sort things out for themselves. They no longer take for granted that everyone is a believer and they want to know what people believe if they don't confess that Jesus is Lord. What is particularly important at this age is that teachers answer their questions and concerns as seriously and as straightforwardly as possible.

Younger elementary school children also continue to appreciate recurring rituals like standard prayers at standard times and may feel uncomfortable if they are omitted. Teachers should encourage the willingness of children during these years to speak openly and freely about God and their faith, and support their desire to approach God with more personal prayers that will often contain requests for specific things and thanks for specific people and things they like very much.

Middle School

Joe: Well, I worry that Jesus isn't real and that some weirdo wrote the Bible. He just made it up or something. I have so many doubts and it worries me that I won't go to heaven or something.

Mark: One thing I wonder is this. If others believe so strongly in things like Buddhism and they believe as strongly as we do then can't we be just another group of believers with a God that really doesn't exist, like Buddhists?

Nathan: I worry if my faith is strong enough. How strong is the faith of all those who went to heaven and how weak was the faith of those who went to hell? And where do I fit in?

Bill: I am worried that my faith should be better. Since I believe in God I shouldn't do bad things. But I might sin over the limit and won't be forgiven any more. Is there a limit?

Students in middle school remember that when they were younger their faith was simple. Their faith was the faith of the family and church and it provided clear-cut answers to life's questions. But now they are beginning to think in more complex ways. If they don't come to see how their faith in Jesus Christ relates to the problems of the world around then they are in danger of discarding the simple faith of their early childhood years. Their new ways of thinking and questioning tend to encourage them to discredit anything that doesn't make sense to them (Stronks 1991).

Students at this age are very idealistic and are to some extent willing to talk about what they believe but they are not very good at connecting what they believe with what they do. David Elkind (1983) calls this inability to carry out actions that follow from professed goals an "apparent hypocrisy." It is not a real hypocrisy because young adolescents have not yet completely developed the ability to relate their walk with their talk. They will express extremely strong views about injustice and unfairness on the part of teachers or politicians but have a very low standard for just and fair behavior for themselves. Many of them recognize this lack of consistency in their thinking.

It is part of the paradox of these years that students know what to do but have great difficulty doing it. They still believe that good Christians do not sin much but they are mature enough to know that their own lives now are filled with sin. They want to change that and don't know how. They want their lives to count and have a strong desire to be committed to their beliefs. That is why it is so important that schools plan and give them many opportunities to serve others. If their idealism and eagerness to commit to a worthwhile cause do not find expression during these years it is likely to diminish as they get older. They need to know that they have a task in God's kingdom right now.

During the middle school years teachers need to recognize that students may experience some skepticism. That doesn't mean that they must work toward answering every question they have or eliminating all doubt. Teachers can help by showing them that their doubts and questions are normal and that God is leading them through new ways of thinking and wondering. Because of students' concern that their family's beliefs may reflect no more truth than any other belief system, it is appropriate for them to learn about the beliefs of other Christians and other groups of people. They can begin to understand different world views and the implications they have for the way people live and make decisions.

Emotions during this period fluctuate and students are able to recognize that while faith can make one feel confident or euphoric, it is not dependent on feelings. However, it helps if teachers discuss those emotions with them in class in an environment of trust so that they will learn that others have the same kinds of thoughts and feelings about faith.

In their search for living according to their ideals, students need to have models of the Christian faith to help them see ways they can live their own lives. That is why they seem to be hero-worshipers, giving their allegiance to singers and actors, who are of course marketed for this very purpose. Because of their need for models, it is extremely important for them to have teachers who live exemplary, healthy Christian lives and who are willing to share their lives with their students. These teachers will not be perfect but they will be watched by students who are quick to see contradictions between what they profess and the way they live. Most importantly, teachers can model a willingness to ask for forgiveness and to forgive, an attitude that authority is to be used in humble service, and a respect for all individuals, and adolescents especially, as persons made in the image of God.

High School

(college students reflecting on their high-school experiences)

Sarah: What bothered me so much during my high school years was all the bickering and infighting there seemed to be in my church community. It

was as though each group was trying to prove it was just a little more correct and a little more Christian than the other group. With all the problems
in the world, you'd think they could have concentrated on solving some of
them. It all seemed so petty and my faith was really shaken.

Mark: I know what you mean. That happened in my community, too. And
what really got to me was there were complaints that our high school youth
group was too emotional in the songs we liked to sing and the things we
liked to do. Talk about emotion! The church people were terribly emotional
in the way they dealt with their conflict. It was the high school group that
really carried me through.

John: There was this one teacher who talked so openly about his own struggles with faith. The way he described them helped me see that other people
had gone through what I was going through. You know, recognizing that
my parents and the other church people were wrong about a lot of things
but they were right about some other things, too. It made me see that
probably our children will think the same things about us when their time
comes.

Sarah: I had a teacher like that, too, who really tried to be honest. But she
scared me a little because it was clear that she was still in pretty much of
a struggle. And I wondered whether my own struggle would ever end.
Maybe on this earth it won't and shouldn't completely end but we will want
to be sure to provide some comfort for our own students that the struggle between one's walk and one's talk doesn't always hurt so much and
that there is help from other Christians.

The faith of the older high school student may include aspects of
what has been called "searching faith" (Westerhoff 1976). For many students this is the beginning of a time of doubt and critical judgment. The
faith they acquired earlier as part of the family and the community of
believers is examined in terms of its personal meaning. They critically
examine the beliefs and actions of their families and communities. If
they discover that persons around them lead lives consistent with their
faith, then they will develop a deeper, more mature personal faith. Sometimes, however, students discover an enormous gap between their own
professed views and everyday actions. If they perceive a similar clash
between the views and actions of the surrounding community of believers, their faith may be shaken and perhaps discarded.

Young people at this age have an ever-growing realization that in one sense they stand alone before God, no longer buffered by family and community. They feel strongly about many things, including major life decisions such as how they will find intimacy, how they will take responsibility for their own lives, what kind of work they will do, what kind of social interactions they will have as school friends separate. In high school, students need help recognizing and answering these questions.

High school students often do not even verbalize their deep questions about faith: What is truth? How can God be loving and yet allow so much evil and sadness on earth? Who am I and what is my place in the total scheme of things? What causes are important enough to fight or die for and what should that fight be like? How does a Christian know what needs to be changed if we are to live as the salt of the earth? How does a Christian confront what needs to be changed and still remain a loving person? Even when they do not doubt the basic tenets of the Christian faith, students do question the meaning of that faith for life.

The school should be a supportive environment that encourages students to express their questions and search for answers to them as they struggle to find personal meaning and direction for life. The curriculum at this level of schooling should provide a context in which students may explore these questions, not as issues separate from the main curriculum, but as central to it. The Christian school curriculum and ethos will present a continuing challenge to acknowledge the lordship of Christ over the whole of life.

A sensitive teacher can become one of the most important supports for helping the young person come through this period of questioning with a strong, mature faith. Especially those students who struggle with school need to feel free to talk with a teacher about their boredom and loneliness in the school and church communities. Students who feel "unspecial" in school and church may come to recognize their importance and individuality before God by experiencing what it is to share the burdens of someone else. Students who do not take academic work seriously nevertheless may think seriously about other important issues of life! The assumption that they do not ignores the need for direction on the part of these students.

Christian schools must take with utmost seriousness their students' search for what it means to walk in whole-hearted commitment to Jesus, for it is this that gives life to all else that a school attempts. Faith leads and motivates human life, providing its direction and its coherence. We were made to be in relationship with God but if we are not, we will place our faith in a substitute. Trust in a source of order and meaning

149

is the dynamic that drives us, whether we are young or we are old. A school that ignores this dynamic, this active responding of students to the world, will be a poor place indeed.

Growing as Responsive Disciples of Christ

What we have learned about learning during the last two decades underscores that how people learn is a far more complex and wondrous phenomenon than we once realized. It was not surprising that, in the vignette that introduced this chapter, Greg Fouts expresses some frustration about implementing all the strategies that he has heard about during the past five years.

Greg and his colleagues, nevertheless, will improve their students' learning when they take into account, for instance, the various considerations we have discussed thus far in this chapter. We suggested that teachers help students relate concepts and ideas to each other so that the learners form patterns of meaning. Teachers should encourage the development of different ways of knowing and provide learning experiences that reflect a spectrum of learning styles. Moreover, they enhance learning when they avoid gender stereotyping or labeling students through forced ability grouping. Finally, they support students on their journey of faith when the pertinent learning experiences take into account levels of faith development.

In this concluding section, we will elaborate on how students learn differently as they mature. As we have already indicated, the reaction of students to issues involving faith is distinct for learners of different ages. But such reactions—and therefore the types of learning experiences that are suitable—vary not only for faith as it unfolds, but for all matters that students explore in their learning. Piaget and his followers have made it abundantly clear that we cannot afford to neglect developmental levels in our teaching. They have been less helpful, however, in providing guidelines for planning teaching and learning. For one, it is unlikely that students pass through Piaget's stages as neatly and sequentially as his followers claim (as is the case for Kohlberg's stages of moral reasoning and Fowler's stages of faith development). More seriously, Piaget's focus is narrowly rational/cognitive, neglecting most of the ways of knowing that Gardner and Eisner, for instance, have shown to be important in school learning.

The work of Kieran Egan (1986; 1988; 1990; 1992) is more helpful for classroom teachers. Egan defines three broad "layers" of understanding in school-age students. Unlike Piaget, he does not claim that these are clearly distinct, but believes that students move from one to the next gradually, with the next level incorporating the former in a richer, more complex way. We will briefly consider each of these layers with some implications for the classroom.

Sarah (age 6): I liked the story about Robin Hood. The sheriff was so mean and I'm glad that Robin Hood helped the poor.

In the primary layer of understanding (ages five to nine), children discover themselves, Egan believes, by focusing outward on the world and on others. They can confront the mysteries of life and learn a great deal about abstract "binary opposites" such as good and evil or courage and fear as long as these are embedded in concrete story settings that provide a sense of adventure and wonder. For children, the story form is fundamental to their understanding, and imagination supports their rational development. The curriculum, therefore, should consist of a set of great stories to be told, fictional ones as well as the great true stories of the Bible, history, science, and mathematics.

That does not mean that teachers just tell a large number of stories in class. Rather, Egan continues, it means that teachers plan their units in story form. They identify the importance of a topic; they find binary opposites that express the importance of the topic in a way that is accessible to children; they articulate the topic into a developing story form; and they structure the unit so that it leads towards resolving the dramatic conflict inherent in the binary opposites. In this way topics of keen interest may be explored in meaningful ways by children. In grade one, Egan points out, children are far more interested in themes with clear conflicts, even when foreign to their experience, than they are in "helpers" in their local community (e.g., survival/destruction of North American native peoples).

Jonathan (age 11): I read about how they built medieval cathedrals. Were they ever huge! My church would fit into some of them about twenty times! Some took more than one hundred years to build. And then one of them wasn't built properly. When there was a big storm the part between the church and the tower collapsed. They never built it again, and today you can still climb the tower—it's the tallest tower in Holland.

The next layer, which Egan calls the romantic one (ages eight to fifteen), does not leave the previous one behind but adds a new level of understanding while incorporating the primary one in a re-formed way.

Students are still interested in stories, but now units in story form can involve more theory. At the same time, nonnarrative sense-making techniques that deal with reality become increasingly important for students. They often have an intense drive to understand something in detail, and want to explore the limits of reality—the exotic, strange, and mysterious. Egan chooses the term *romantic* because learning at this age has powerful emotional components even as the rational grasp of particulars and the growth of self-consciousness continues. Students often display a flexible, vivid, and energetic capacity in the various ways of knowing; that is, they want to use their imagination to the fullest (Egan 1992, 65). For effective learning during this broad age group, Egan therefore continues, learning must provide opportunities for detailed study, focusing on the extremes of the real world and the limits of human experience. This should be done in a context where students consider human motives and transcendent qualities such as faith, hope, compassion, justice, courage, beauty, and self-sacrifice. Such content must also affect the emotional, intrapersonal life of students, and stimulate awe and wonder. Thus the science curriculum, for instance, should emphasize making the familiar strange and wonderful, with theories and experiments being introduced "through the lives, hopes, and intentions of those who first designed and constructed them" (Egan 1990, 233). A key point that Egan makes is that while education is crucially tied up with knowledge, we focus too much on knowledge content itself. Especially for this layer our emphasis should be imaginative learning that affectively engages the learner (Egan 1992, 53).

Donna (age 16): I wonder about the way the church and the nobility in the feudal age built themselves cathedrals and castles. I suspect it was done at the expense of the common people. They probably became even poorer because of the grand dreams of the elite. Why is it that the rich and powerful seem to have so little regard for the struggles of the poor?

In Egan's third layer of understanding, the philosophic one (approximately from ages fifteen to nineteen), students use the patterns and associations they have formed in the romantic layer to develop causal chains and networks. They begin to redirect their intellectual attention from romantic fascinations and associations to the laws and general patterns whereby the world works, whether that be for history, human behavior, or the natural world (Egan 1990, 177). Students now turn to surveying and analyzing what their romantic patterns of meaning were all about. They do not discard the understandings of particulars of the romantic layer, for example, but use them to provide a basis for a much more general, philosophic understanding of life. In this layer, the meaning of specific concepts is "most commonly derived primarily from its place within some general scheme" (Egan 1990, 179). The curriculum now puts much more emphasis on general principles that guide and direct our lives.

Egan's scheme is not the only valid way of categorizing developmental layers. The point of considering it as we plan learning, however, is that it helps us enable students to be responsive learners at their own level of development. Therefore we capitalize on the particular types of learning that stimulate them at certain ages. We cannot expect six-year-olds to discuss the principles of justice that should be embedded in a constitution, but we can have them respond to what is just or unjust in fictional and real-life stories. We cannot expect eleven-year-olds to be interested in a detached, abstract study of European geography, but we can expect them to respond enthusiastically and imaginatively to investigating the geographical challenges that David faced as he travelled from southern Yugoslavia to Denmark in Anne Holm's book, *I Am David*. And for sixteen-year-olds the study of a particular technological development related solely to human motives and ingenuity will often be insufficient; they will also want to consider how this relates to more general scientific principles as well as to the general impact of the innovation on human life.

In short, learning needs to be planned so that students can respond meaningfully. To do so, we have to take into account factors such as the diverse ways of knowing, learning styles, layers of understanding, and how we group students. If we fail to do so, then the learning in our classroom will unwrap our students' gifts inadequately: learning, for many of them, will become a burden rather than a joy. And that would undermine the habitat of shalom that God intended students and teachers to experience as they learn about him and his world.

Questions for Discussion

1. Do you think Christian education ought to be about nurturing or ought it to be about letting go of old attitudes? Do these two purposes work against each other?

2. To what extent should students learn in our schools that to be a Christian is to be countercultural? Is there a danger in teaching for that kind of understanding?

3. What patterns and relationships shared by different disciplines have you recognized in your curriculum? How can you as a staff discover where others occur?

4. What examples can you give to show evidence that you as a staff recognize and celebrate different ways of knowing? Which of the ways of knowing need more attention in your school?

5. The home, church, and school all have a role to play in the faith development of students. What should be the focus of each agency? To what extent should the school deal openly and explicitly with the growth of faith in students? Which activities in the school can and should foster such growth?

6. Consider a topic that could be taught to students at different age levels. In terms of Egan's view of layers of development, how would you design the unit to suit learners in each of the three layers of development?

Recommended Reading

1. Dillon, R. F., and Sternberg, R. F., eds. 1987. *Cognition and instruction.*
   The implications of information processing research for instruction in reading, mathematics, second language learning, social studies, art, and music.
2. Elkind, D. 1983. "Teenage thinking and the curriculum."
   Describes the instructional need for a better match between the learner's cognitive level and the material to be learned.
3. Van Leeuwen, M. S. 1990. *Gender and grace.*
   An excellent analysis of gender differences from a Christian, psychological perspective.
4. *The AAUW report: How schools shortchange girls.* 1991.
   Provides information from research on girls' experiences in schools.
5. Shelley, J. A. 1982. *The spiritual needs of children.*
   Discusses faith development in children.
6. Stronks, G. G. 1991. "To see the church through their eyes."
   Describes the way middle school students think about their faith and their relationships with the church and school.
7. Good, R., and Smith, M. 1987. "How do we make students better problem solvers?"

Whitney, D. R. 1987. "On practice and research: Confessions of an educational researcher."
Suggests ways in which teachers can be involved in classroom research.

8. Egan, K. 1986. *Teaching as storytelling.*
———. 1992. *Imagination in teaching and learning.*
These two books give Egan's most practical advice for teachers.

7

How Do We Know?

The Science Curriculum Committee met on six or seven occasions last year. Over the summer, Joan Fisher has drafted a report for the group to consider. The reaction to it has not been promising, seeming only to crystallize the differences between the committee members on some fundamental issues.

On this occasion, Ted Pakula (Central Station's representative) is the first to weigh in. He is appreciative of the work that Joan has done "on her own time." "But, Joan," he said, "if we adopt an approach like you've suggested, all the kids are going to end up with is the ability to play with ideas, but no sense of what the ideas are for. It's all very well to opt for virtuoso intellectual performances, but how do we know the kids are not just going to use their skills for pagan ends? How are they going to learn to use their scientific abilities in service of their neighbor and to the glory of God?"

"I want to back Ted up on this one," Jim Deboer chimed in. "You may think I'm thinking too much of elementary kids, but what is really important is not that they master certain skills but that they get turned on to the wonder and beauty of God's creation. We have to emphasize more the excitement that can be found in exploring God's world. I want kids to feel as though they're a part of the world and that the world is part of them. After all, most of them are not going to be scientists or even use science in their jobs and everyday lives. What they need is a sense of what the world can give them, the fulfillment that can come from staring at a stormy sky and knowing all the forces that are at work there, or wondering enough to ask questions about it."

"I wouldn't want to argue against what you're saying, Jim," Patrick Henderson responded politely, "but I don't know if that is really *science*. It's certainly great to have a religious feeling, but that's not science. And let's face it, with all that I already have to get through in my chemistry courses, there's no time left for all the frills. I think a Christian scientist is first and foremost a good scientist. We're going to have good scientists only if we prepare them well for science programs in college and if we are able to send some on from there to graduate school."

Patrick doesn't want to say it out loud, but to him, Jim's and Ted's approach is just a recipe for mediocrity. What constitutes science is perfectly clear: it's in the textbooks, and what teachers have to do is to get this material across as effectively as possible. Patrick has been doing it this way for years, and although some of his students might complain of the tedium, he always sends a healthy cohort on to college science courses. The school's reputation for academic excellence depends on teachers like Patrick.

Geoff Schmidt is one of Patrick's high school colleagues; Geoff teaches physics. This is his thirteenth year at Mountain City, and his dedication to Christian teaching in large part persuaded his wife, Sue, to "pack up her Ph.D. and toddle off for teacher training," as she would explain to the curious. Geoff has become a little tired over the last few years, finding that the pressure to cover the material often gets in the way of what he most enjoys about teaching—relationships with his students. Also, he really gets little scope to deal explicitly with a Christian perspective on his discipline. Now that Sue is on staff with him, however, he's gained something of a new lease of life. Her excitement and continual questioning have been stimulating and challenging. Although they haven't set about it in a conscious manner, Sue and Geoff have been putting together something of an agenda for change in the way science is taught at Mountain City. They're both too ingenuous to be capable of plotting, but something of a quiet revolution may yet be underway.

So here we have them, this mixed bunch of teachers with diverse experience and varied understandings of the place of science in the school curriculum. How are they to proceed? Is there any way that they can move out of their entrenched positions rather than digging themselves in deeper? Is making decisions about what and how they should teach merely an individual matter in the end, anyway, in that they can each go into their classrooms and lock their doors behind them, with no one really knowing what goes on? Or is it a group matter, with the negotiation of compromises and the hope of consensus? Or are they indeed responsible in this too to a higher authority? What about the question that Ken Heard had put to them at the outset: "How should Scripture direct you as you make decisions about curriculum?"

They had prayed together at the opening of the meeting. Most of the group were quite diligent in remembering the work of the committee in their own times of prayer at home. And the general and specific tasks facing teachers were a regular part of prayer at staff devotionals each morning.

Their prayerfulness indicated an openness to God, a willingness to have him lead them in their thinking. But how self-critical were they willing to be in subjecting the specifics of their thinking to the Word of God? How much were they relying on nonbiblical views of knowledge, the world, the learner, when they now dealt with the basic issues of the curriculum?

These were the kinds of issues that had been bothering Geoff over the summer.

"I've been doing a great deal of thinking over the last few months. I was frightened we weren't going to get far beyond merely restating our positions when we met again this year. I want to suggest an approach. I know this might sound a bit heavy, but please bear with me for a while.

"Science has long been regarded as the model of what knowledge is all about. Whether we have thought of the body of scientific knowledge or of the scientific method that has generated it, we have looked on science as the ideal to which all forms of knowledge should aspire. I want to say that I think we've been sold a bad bill of goods here. Science is one way of knowing the world alongside many others: so it is a limited, partial perspective.

"And I think we have to take more seriously what we mean when we say that human life in its entirety is religion: science is also religiously colored. It's never just a neutral, objective undertaking. It always reflects a broader perspective on life, a view of what is meaningful and valuable. In that sense, it is always biased. We have to give more thought to the way in which Scripture should direct our scientific activity. The scientific competence we seek to give our kids should be approached within this sort of framework."

Ted agrees. Ted has a great sensitivity to environmental issues. He's what's known in some circles as a "bioregionalist." He grows his own vegetables, recycles fastidiously, and stresses the biblical teaching on stewardship. He has set up a food co-op in the downtown area, and was greatly influenced by his early reading of Schumacher's *Small Is Beautiful*. He is concerned about a "holistic" approach to science teaching, though he recognizes that the use of the word can get him in trouble in a day when New Age religion is rampant. Ted and his wife, Hennie, worship with the Mission Hall congregation and are both deeply committed to ministry to the fringe people. Their two children are not yet attending Central Station; Hennie is keen to have a third, but Ted is not sure that this is ecologically responsible.

"You've just reminded me of something that I read about Robert Oppenheimer. When he was asked about the construction of the atom bomb, he said that it was of no consequence to him what was going to be done with it when it was built. He was just doing a job of physics! I think he said something like they would have made it any color or shape that the politicians wanted, as long as it was technically feasible. That makes me sick! I think if we try to teach science outside a social context, outside a concern for justice, we are implicitly teaching our kids to have this neutral, technical view of science. I think science has to be embedded in other, more complex, real-life settings if kids are going to learn that responsibility goes hand in hand with understanding. We don't just want our kids to know, we want them to be wise. They need more than to know about things, or that such and such is a fact, they need to know how to act in faithfulness to the Word of God."

Joan suggests that they take a break for coffee, so the group wanders across the hall to the Middle School staff room. When they get there, they find the members of the Literature Policy Committee waiting for the urn to come to a boil. Ted asks Cal Holbrook how their meeting has been going. Ted and Cal belong to the same church, and they also see each other socially quite often.

The Lit. Committee was formed initially in response to the concerns of a number of relatively new parents in the school. Cal was at the center of these concerns, having set up an overnight simulation activity arising out of the study of Lord of the Flies with grade eight. Some of the kids had gotten too serious— one of them chased another around a tree with an axe, accusing him of stealing. There had also been the incident in grade three, where the teacher had been reading The Lion, the Witch and the Wardrobe to the class. One of the fathers had told his daughter that this was ridiculous. "Everyone knows animals can't talk," he'd said, promptly pricking the bubble of her fascination with the tale. Another, more sophisticated, parent had complained that to represent Christ as a Lion was not only not justified by Scripture, but that the theological interpretations spun around this whole metaphor were decidedly suspect. Once people got talking in the car park, witches and centaurs and all sorts of fanciful creatures came in for their share of criticism as well, so that pretty soon there were murmurings about "New Age" ideas infiltrating the school.

"Making any progress, Cal?" Ted asked, as they moved over into a corner of the room.

"Early days, early days, Ted. We've just started talking about the kind of understandings that literature embodies. Not getting too far. I'm interested in stimulating kids' imagination and creativity, but there seems to be this notion that the truth only comes wrapped up in 'facts.' Some parents seem to equate anything from fantasy literature with the occult or some form of idolatry. I sometimes wonder how well I fit in this place. You'd think that the Bible didn't contain huge slabs of Ezekiel or Jeremiah, not to mention Balaam's ass."

"Well," Ted responded, "something Geoff just said in our group rings some bells. It's as if a scientific, intellectual way of understanding is the only model that people have of truth."

"You're right, Ted. It's like Plato saying that most people only see the shadows on the wall; they never get behind the appearance to the reality. Only the intellectuals can penetrate to the true nature of things, because they can think abstractly and form clear ideas. The rest are caught in the illusions of what they see and hear, which is always changing. The concept of a horse is the same everywhere, but every actual horse is different from every other one."

"Well," said Ted, "Plato was onto something, but I'm afraid his paganism led him to distort things quite a deal. What does it say in Hebrews? 'Faith is being certain of what we do not see.' It seems to me that the reality that we have to grasp is not first of all intellectual but religious. There is more to life than meets the eye, but truth can only be found by a response of faith to God's revelation. Not that we want to be anti-intellectual, just that the intellect is only one way of responding to the world, and reasoning can never give us the complete story."

"Okay, I can certainly buy that, but what's it got to do with teaching literature and science? I think I'm on your wavelength, but spell it out for me a bit more."

Ted didn't get a chance at this point—a fact that left him a little relieved—as the conveners were urging their groups back to work.

"See you on Thursday night, Cal."

"Sure thing, Ted—but see if you can have an answer for me by then!"

Ted and Cal are struggling with a tradition with a long history in Western education. Only what can be stated in clear and logical terms is regarded as the truth. This tradition has dominated conservative Christian thinking as well. When the two come together in the Christian school setting, the effect is multiplied. History is taught as an endless collection of facts, science is presented as a series of laws to be memorized, and theology is believed to reveal the logical skeleton undergirding biblical revelation. Then, everything is assessed through multiple-choice tests, which assume that life's questions are relatively simple, each having only one right answer.

The teachers at Mountain City have taken steps in the right direction. They have begun to talk with each other; they know that a supportive, communal environment is necessary if schools are going to change. They have committed themselves to questioning their fundamental assumptions in the light of Scripture but they're not all that sure how to go about it. They have come to the point where they are not willing to take things for granted. They recognize that being a distinctively Christian school means that they have to reflect a biblical perspective more faithfully than they have thus far.

They have agreed to work with some basic guidelines. In the first place, they start from the assumption that everything that exists is created by God and is therefore basically good. Satan can distort and pervert what God has made, but he cannot destroy it. This is the second reality that they take into account. Because of Adam and Eve's rebellion, everything suffers the consequences of human sin and God's Word of judgment holds for all things. Taken together, these two principles imply that as Christians we will always see good—and because of Christ's redemption, hope for healing—where others see only evil, and that at the same time we will look for brokenness where others see only normality (Wolters 1985).

Education as an Outworking of a Theory of Knowledge

Scripture does not give us a theory of knowledge but it sets a direction for developing such a theory. The opening proclamation of Scripture is that the world is ordered and structured by God: it is his creation. We were made to be at home in this world. Thus, we can feel comfortable with our common sense assumptions that we are in touch with the real world in our everyday experience. We recognize our limitations, however. Being creatures, we can never have more than finite understanding; being fallen, we accept that sin distorts such understanding that we do achieve. We accept all knowledge as a gift of Christ, in whom are hid all the treasures of wisdom and knowledge. Knowledge is indeed a response to God's revelation, in his world and in his Word. To truly know is to listen to that revelation and to respond aright, to hear and to do. When God speaks, he also calls us to act, because he made us to care for his world. Knowledge brings responsibility, for it is a call to obey the Word of the Lord. All knowing is thus basically religious in character.

161

Our everyday experience of God's meaning-full creation—not just of "natural things" like waterfalls and birds, but of people and social relations as well—is thus the source of genuine, comprehensive knowledge. Through creation, God speaks to us in many ways: we are called to recognize the ethical demand in the needy neighbor, the aesthetic demand in the sunset or the Sistine Chapel, the economic demand in our use of the world's resources, and so on. We do not *impose* these dimensions on the world for they are part and parcel of the richness that God has created (Lewis 1943). Not to be sensitive to these dimensions is to overlook what is of great worth, worth that comes purely from being that which God chose to make.

Thus, we are also called to respect the many-sidedness of being human, the rich variety of ways in which God enables us as image bearers to interact with the world. Though we each respond in these various ways, we also have our particular strengths. God has gifted everyone and all these differing gifts are necessary for the healthy functioning of the body—because we also each have our weaknesses.

These different ways of responding are different ways of knowing. We can therefore say that truth comes in many forms: that the truth of a bird's song, a Rembrandt painting, an amoeba under a microscope, or an act of compassion is as valid as the truths we can more easily express in sentences (Cooper 1986).

We are created in interdependence. Our knowledge is also a communal possession: we do not know as individuals in isolation from each other. From the learning of language to the enjoyment of some kinds of food and not others, we are embedded in cultural contexts and we depend on each other for understanding. That we learn to speak Chinese or English and to interpret the world through its words and structures is a gift to us from God through others. When we have seen Othello, we can never look at jealousy in the same way again—if we have eyes to see. Our everyday experience of this emotion has been transformed. When we have contemplated the notion of black holes or Einstein's theory, our view of the cosmos will have changed. When we have studied the impact of colonialism on Third World countries, our sympathy should be energized by the demands of justice.

The school is a primary site in which this interaction with others in the human community takes place. It is in part by bringing students into contact with what Matthew Arnold called "the best that has been thought and said" (much of which is organized in the academic disciplines) that they grow in understanding. We do not come to know creation as isolated individuals, but always in cultural contexts.

Classical, Romantic, and Biblical Traditions

We have said that all knowing is basically religious in character. The two major Western traditions of thinking about knowledge in various ways deny this at the same time as they exemplify it. The classical tradition, with which Ted and Cal were wrestling, does this by claiming the objectivity of theoretical and scientific understanding. The romantic tradition, on the other hand, acknowledges no reality beyond that of individual feelings. Both traditions deny a source of order and meaning beyond human experience and substitute instead a source within this experience.

It is tempting to set these traditions in opposition to each other, and then to force a choice between them. Certainly, when either one is accepted as the complete story about knowledge, they are incompatible. However, when we place them within a broader biblical framework, insights drawn from one can complement the other.

The classical tradition stresses theory and intellectual rationality. Theory uses organizing laws and concepts to interpret experience. The resulting categories allow us to talk and think about a wide range of individual things and the ways they function. In mathematics, for example, we think of the numerical and spatial functioning of things in general. We can use the same formula to calculate areas for carpeting a room as for fertilizing a field, and, in fact, we can do the same calculation without reference to any existing thing at all.

The classical tradition views rationality as *the* way to truth. In comparison, concrete experience of creation is unimportant. Only theorizing gives *real* knowledge. It was this tradition that led the French Revolutionaries to enthrone the goddess Reason in their pantheon. Human reason seemed to promise control over the forces of the natural and even the social world. This is also why today people often assume that there is a scientific or technological solution to all problems.

The essentialist perspective in education is a form of the classical tradition. It emphasizes passing on fixed knowledge and timeless truths to students, rather than engaging them in making knowledge for themselves. Educators in this tradition believe that the best way of understanding the English language is by a systematic study of grammar, that music theory is more important than learning to play an instrument, and that Madeline Hunter's formula-like steps of direct instruction exemplify successful education.

The romantic tradition is impatient with the classical reliance on theory. Instead, romanticism emphasizes experiencing the concrete

163

world in its rich individuality. It focuses on feeling rather than reason, on the particular rather than the general. It is more at home with aesthetic encounters, imagination, and intuition. In the school, romanticism bases the curriculum on student needs and interests. It favors engagement with concrete materials rather than abstract calculations. In so doing, it often rejects any kind of order that would seem to inhibit the freedom of the individual; rather, it makes individual decision making the arbiter of meaning.

The romantic tradition, with its emphasis on free human action, has done great damage to the gospel proclamation that the whole world belongs to God and that we are to serve him in every area of life. In schools, it leads to practices that make individuals a law unto themselves. The acceptance of "invented spelling" by young children is helpful if it is a starting point for learning the importance of standard spelling for communication and understanding of the language. It is a distortion of the God-given order of language, however, if it is taken to mean that children can spell words in any way they choose.

With the classical emphasis on theory and rationality and the romantic emphasis on experience and imagination, educational debates are often framed as a polarization of the disciplines of knowledge and everyday experience. The traditionalists line up against the progressives. Regrettably, while each side recognizes an important aspect of our interaction with God's world, it ignores the complementary aspect.

The biblical framework, on the other hand, recognizes this complementarity. It sees as equal realities both the law of God in creation and the creatures that are subject to it. It is concerned with how to *act wisely*, that is, with how to act in *this* particular situation in a way that is faithful to the ordinances of God. Knowing the law of God by rote is but ignorance if one does not act in love; faith without works is dead. Actions in turn are judged wise or foolish depending upon whether or not they are faithful to that law. Truth is what one does (1 John 1:6) more than what one says.

The Bible calls us to live in trust and faith. The model for knowing is a personal relationship, sometimes person to person, sometimes person to thing, but personal nonetheless. Believing *in* is prior to believing *that*, and doing, living, and abiding in the truth have primacy. We begin with the context of involvement, not spectatorship, with action and response. To know the truth is to walk in the way, to obey Christ's commandments. Rather than seeing action as an *addition* to knowledge based in experience or intellect, we recognize that our knowledge begins and ends with whole-bodied interaction with creation.

But the Wisdom Literature highlights that creation confronts us in often puzzling ways, when we have to *act* but cannot act mechanically, merely by applying some rules. A particular situation calls for a unique decision. It calls for the responsible exercise of freedom, for judgment and discernment, for wisdom. In calling us to obey his commands, God never takes this responsiveness away from us: it is at the heart of being made in his image. We are called to active engagement with God's world.

Consider the advice of the wise man (Prov. 26:4, 5):

> Do not answer a fool according to his folly,
>   or you will be like him yourself.
> Answer a fool according to his folly,
>   or he will be wise in his own eyes.

Before we know which directive to follow, we need to take into account the complex richness of a particular situation. Like a doctor making a diagnosis, we need to focus our "expert knowledge" in a judgment of what is best for this particular person. As teachers, sometimes we need to reprimand a student publicly and sometimes we need to wait for a quiet conversation: it will depend in part on who the student is and on the likely reaction.

Christian schools need to recapture the concrete and individual dimensions of experience. Here is the proving ground for wisdom; here is where faith responds to the law of God. Unfortunately, we too often see teaching that relies on information being transmitted in simplified, abstracted form, rather than active engagement with the meaning-rich creation. Even attempts to be concrete can become excuses for classification activities:

Grade seven science teacher: Okay, kids, I've got this big box of about thirty rocks here. What I want you to do is to pick them up and look at them and see how many of them you can name. You should check each rock against the list of rocks and their characteristics that I have given you. Then you should write the name of each rock you identify in your book and copy down the description.

School learning can include both experiencing and theorizing without polarizing the two. Moreover, given what we have said in chapter 6 about ways of knowing, insight into God's world comes not only in concrete experience and theorizing, but through many other avenues as well. This growth in knowledge involves a *rhythm* of *immersion* in experience, *withdrawal* and *return* (MacMurray 1969).

Normally, we are immersed in experience, playing freely and trustingly in creation. This might be in conversation with friends, a walk in the park, the reading of a book, or the eating of a meal. But at times it is necessary to stand back and analyze a situation or to struggle with, for instance, an ethical challenge. Solving a difficult mathematical problem may require abstract theoretical reflection. Making decisions about the family budget, however, though it will require calculations, will be more a matter of ethical judgment. We will have to consider which actions will be the most beneficial for those for whom we are responsible. A threatened rift with a loved one will also require focused ethical insight, which is neither the direct application of abstract principles nor a mere reliance on previous experience (because no situation simply repeats an earlier one). On such occasions, we distance ourselves from the situation in order to reflect on it. In most cases, this reflection will not be theoretical at all, because we are not looking to formulate general principles. Such reflection will more often have a concrete focus, a concern with how to act faithfully here and now. Only after deciding on a response do we act, in this sense returning to immersion in concrete experience again.

Such a rhythm, we believe, should characterize school learning, both in the classroom and outside it. We first immerse students in a situation, broadening their experience by asking them to read a novel, paint a canvas, read an article from a newspaper, conduct an experiment, explore a forest, visit an abattoir or a council office, engage in a simulation game, or hold a debate. Then we invite our students to stand back from time to time to focus on the world in various ways. This focusing might be aesthetic or ethical, or it might be analytical. The purpose of this focusing is that they might act in more informed and responsible ways, that they might respond purposefully. We seek both to broaden and to deepen our students' experience in a complementary manner.

We have structured this book to reflect this rhythm. We have used the vignettes as a way of recreating concrete experience and "immersing" you in everyday situations, with the richness of diverse personalities and perspectives. Then we have invited you to stand back for a time to reflect with us on the issues these situations raise. In this way we hope you will return to your classrooms with greater insight into how to think but, more importantly, how to act.

Different Ways of Knowing

Cal and Ted belong to a Bible study group that meets on Thursday evenings. After a light meal, they spend an hour or so studying Scripture. At the moment they're working their way through 1 John. Of particular interest has been John's linking of knowledge, obedience, and love. Knowledge of God seems to be closely connected with actions. Afterwards, while they're having coffee and a slice of pie, Cal is keen to pursue his Tuesday conversation with Ted. After a little prompting, Ted warms to the subject.

"What I am groping towards is this. The fundamental reality is religious. We confess this, we proclaim that everything is religion, that Christ's lordship extends to every square inch of creation, but we continue to teach our subjects as if they contain the whole truth, as if we can teach the facts of science and then add some biblical references to them. And I think that the problems you are having with fantasy literature relate to this issue as well. People don't look at fantasy as a God-given, created way of responding; they view it with suspicion because it doesn't seem to speak the truth. And they approach it moralistically or theologically rather than as literature, literarily. Granted, fantasy, just like any other kind of writing, can serve idols rather than the Lord, but the problem is one of religious direction rather than the fantasy form itself."

"Okay," Cal responded, "so I said that lots of people seem to have a one-dimensional view of reality. Everything is sort of 'thin,' there's no texture, no complexity. The facts, man, just the facts. Fantasy opens up different windows on reality, but people don't want to look through them. Sometimes I think they're scared of what they will see. But what's the connection you think can be made?"

"Well, in science I think we rely too much on textbooks, and the textbooks almost all have the view that knowing means having the right words, the right formulas. The view is that truth is contained in precise, logical statements and that these propositions are pretty much true by definition. Even when it's not just a matter of definition, we're content to have our kids approach things as if it were. We don't want them to do real experiments; we just give them exercises to illustrate the propositions. They already know the answer before they start, and if the 'experiment' doesn't go the way it should, it's because the kids made a mistake, no less—not that they should see what they can learn from what they did. We're scared of getting them to really hypothesize and explore. Learning is just a matter of memorizing, of following the rules so that you arrive at the answer that the teacher has predetermined."

"I'm going to make a bit of a jump, Ted, but you've just reminded me of something. When I was doing a summer course, I was talking at lunch with someone in the business department at Bethlehem College. He said that when he was meeting with representatives of the business community in his city, a common complaint they had about graduates of the college was that they were socially inept, in the sense that they didn't know how to relate to people in the broader community.

"Now it seems to me that we can generalize that observation somewhat. Our Christian schools and colleges might be very good at turning out academic achievers, people who can apply academic knowledge in academic contexts, but what sort of use are these people able to make of that knowledge? How have they learned to apply it in real-life situations? And even if they are socially adept, in terms of being able to make polite and interesting conversation, of being able to rub shoulders with 'ordinary' people, I would want to ask a further question. How willing and able are they to apply their knowledge in pursuit of social justice?"

"Listen, Cal, you're on the track of an agenda that goes beyond what either of our committees will be able to address. Do you think anyone will buy it?"

"Well, I don't know about Ken. He's more into damage control than rocking the boat. But I reckon we've got to get into some basic issues if we're going to do things any differently in our schools. I mean, what's the point of Christian schools if they just do the same things as the public schools, even if in some cases they do them a little bit better? That might just mean that we are providing an elitist education for those parents who can afford it—though I know many parents work mighty hard to pay for it. We may as well pack up and go home. It would sure make some parents happy if they didn't feel pressured or even compelled by the church and their friends to spend all that money on their kids' tuition.

"I would think," Cal continued, "that if we're going to break out of the mold of a worldly view of education, one thing we have to get really clear on is what the Bible tells us about what it means to be human. I think the Bible leads us to believe that the real core of our humanness is our relationship with God, that the meaning of human life is found not in any one of the ways in which we function in the world, nor in all these ways added together, but in who we are before the face of God. Now right through the history of people thinking about the nature of people, all sorts of answers have been given. The dominant view has been that being human rests primarily in our ability to function rationally. Everything else about being human comes from our animal nature, or some such, and so is not to be taken seriously, is certainly not to be regarded as a source of real understanding about things.

"Then you have these other stories—humans are basically emotional beings, humans are characterized by their capacity to make things, they are purely social constructions, what their society makes them to be, that it is in language that one finds the heart of humanness and so on. Now I think each of these views identifies something significant about human nature. And I think a biblical perspective frees us from having to locate the whole truth in any one of these ways of functioning at the same time as it releases us from having to deny the reality of any out of fear. We wish to acknowledge the richness, the many-sidedness of being human, and that there is more to learning than can be expressed in propositions."

"So let me see if I can sum it up, Cal. When we look at fantasy literature, for instance, we can say that it's one expression of the richness of being human, that we shouldn't be frightened of it, that Christ's redemption touches this area of life as much as any other? That the whole person is created in the image of God, that the whole world is God's world, and that everything in it is ordered by his law?"

"Yeah, something along those lines."

"All right, but I still have some problems. Suppose some book or film promotes a sinful point of view, how can that be justified? I mean, you can't just say anything goes."

"True enough, Ted, but let me push you back a bit. Every book or film—except the Bible, of course—is going to promote a sinful point of view, in one way or another. I don't think we should get into the position of saying, 'Lo! There is sin. Over there is grace.' This side of Christ's return, the wheat and the tares grow together. Sin and grace are intertwined—but where there is sin, grace abounds! No, I think the real issue is sorting out the overall religious direction of something and seeing how this distorts the bits and pieces with which it deals—and also where the true nature of things has been revealed, by God's grace. All people live in God's world and are sustained by his grace. They can't help but bump up against the reality that is God's world."

Hennie had been listening for a while, her arm slipped through Ted's. "My experience of church and Christianity has sure changed since I met Ted," she commented. "Maybe it's because he's not from North European stock, or perhaps it's his Catholic background. But our traditional Protestant way of approaching things seems often too abstract, too intellectual, as if there's no real flesh to the gospel. I think even in the way that we worship there's too much emphasis on head knowledge, and in our schools we've talked too much about world view and not enough about ways of being and doing in the world. What I want to achieve most of all with my own children is that they see God's presence in all the ordinary things of life, just like we see things of greatest significance in the bread and the wine. We commune with God through the things he has made. The creation is God's and our playground. He gives us all these wonderful gifts—food, family, and friends, the air we breathe, the music we listen to—and we have to offer each one back to him in thankfulness, in his service."

169

This sparks off an idea for Ted. "I want to relate this to the whole idea of responsive discipleship that we're working with at school. We are made to be connected with the rest of creation in fruitful ways. Sin has alienated us, but Christ brings us back. We have to learn to respond in all that we have been made to be—intellectually, but also emotionally, morally, culturally, and so on. I think too often we've thought of a faith response as assent to propositions, and not enough in Romans 12 terms of a whole-bodied response.

"I think we can come at it from the angle of our relationships. We stand at the intersection of all sorts of relationships, and to be in relation to God and neighbor—in relation in ways that are faithful to God's purposes—this is our calling. It's a calling to openness and trust, to awareness and sensitivity, to empathy and compassion. I think school is one place—only one place, but in our culture, a very important place, all the same—where this responsiveness is to be nurtured. Someone put it in terms of the fact that now that nothing created can have absolute importance, then everything is of absolute importance. Now that we are freed from the worship of things that God has made by our worship of him, we can really take everything he has made seriously, without fear of idolatry, without fear."

We have argued in this and the previous chapter that we should recognize a range of different ways of knowing and that our schools should promote students' growth in these. The problems that Cal is having with fantasy literature and in his reflections on social knowing arise in large part from the more restricted classical view of knowledge that predominates in our society. The situation is complicated by the challenge that comes from time to time from the romantic tradition, when it suggests that feeling and expressiveness are all that is important. Because the problem with fantasy literature arises more specifically from the difficulty that we often have with aesthetic imagination, we will turn our attention to aesthetic knowing. This will serve as an example of the various ways of knowing.

The aesthetic is part of our everyday experience, given in and with our experience of things. We may not always be conscious of it, but it is implicit in the choice of colors in someone's clothing, in the blight of beer cans along a highway median, and the fragrance of a magnolia blossom. The aesthetic is seen in the way we furnish and decorate our classrooms, the playful care with which we select words and structure sentences, the humor and lightness of touch with which we manage interactions with students, the music we play and the songs we sing, and the brightness of displays with which we enliven classroom life.

But in addition to this everyday experience of the aesthetic, there are moments of heightened aesthetic sensitivity that stand apart, as when someone gasps at a sunset or points excitedly to a bursting rose bloom. We may think of the artist (though such sensitivity is open to the artist in each of us) who decides to take a littered highway as a subject for a painting. The interplay of colors, when portrayed richly in oils, is perhaps also a metaphor for a wasteful society. The artist has approached the scene aesthetically, first imagining and then crafting a new aesthetic object. In the midst of crafting the painting, the artist stands back from time to time to contemplate and to ponder—what would be the appropriate color, texture, tone, patterning?—before returning to the canvas. This is the aesthetic way of knowing.

Chaim Potok seeks to portray the aesthetic way of knowing in some of his novels. In *The Gift of Asher Lev* (1990), the artist tries to explain it to a group of yeshiva students. After drawing three representations of a ram on the board—a childlike version, a "realistic" drawing (though, as the artist points out, the children have never seen a ram of that size or color) and a more abstract form—a student suggests that the third is "an inside look at the ram," a look from the *artist's* inside. He explains: "Art begins when someone who knows how to draw . . . interprets, when someone sees the world through his own eyes. Art happens when what is seen becomes mixed with the inside of the person who is seeing it. If an exciting new way of seeing an old object results, well, that's interesting, isn't it? That's the beginning of serious art" (Potok 1990, 134–35). He then goes on to draw their teacher in the style of three different artists: Matisse, Modigliani, and Picasso. It is obviously Miss Sullivan, but. . . .

We are suggesting that the nurturing of such aesthetic insight, among other ways of knowing, is an important task of the school. Teachers will help students' aesthetic insight to grow as they show they value it by the attention they give to such response, by seeking regularly both to model it for and to elicit it in their students, by broadening their experience of aesthetic responses to creation, and by challenging them to deepen their own aesthetic way of seeing the world.

We may also stand back from our everyday experience in order to form clear ideas about its aesthetic dimensions. With a theorist's concern for generalizations and patterns, the concrete instances are of interest as examples, not in and of themselves. Thus, a teacher may lead students to compare the styles of twentieth-century painters in order to be able to explain the relationships between them, the interplay between Picasso and Matisse or between Dadaism and Surrealism. The problem is that it is so often this theoretical reflection on aesthetic experience (or other modes of experience), rather than aesthetic experience itself, that is central to the school curriculum.

Schools have a special function in our culture. They set about to lead people in learning in a systematic way. Their activities are directed largely by a carefully planned curriculum. But schools should seek to lead not only in learning, but also in reflecting on and about learning. This is not such a major concern of others who help people to learn in other contexts. In the everyday world, education is largely tacit. Instructional conversation is immersed in the particular practical context, as when a driving instructor leads a learner through a series of interrelated skills and expectations. In schools, however, much more needs to be made explicit, for in schools students should be taught to understand and to reflect critically on what they are doing (Bowers 1987, 144). We want students not only to act, but to act purposefully, and for this reason we invite them to stand back and examine their ordinary experience.

The danger that arises from this emphasis on reflection is that it is often separated from its context. This happens not only with the way that areas of study are introduced but also in the failure to reintegrate vocabulary, concepts, and theory with everyday experience (Bowers 1987, 144). This is not an inevitable outcome of a school's role. Teachers err when they focus on giving reasons for actions without ensuring that students have the experience for which the reasons are an explanation: words require a supportive context. If theoretical and other kinds of understanding are to be translated into wise action, schools must enable students to integrate this understanding with concrete experience. Just as inadequate, of course, is when teachers simply ask students to *do* without any thought as to why they are doing it.

The Rhythm of Learning

We have described growth in knowledge (learning) as a threefold rhythm. The first "beat" in this rhythm is *immersion* in experience; the second is by *withdrawal* from experience, a distanced focusing on it; the third is by *return* to experience in a purposeful response.

When one finds out more about the water by splashing around in it, or more about a person just by "wasting time" with them, or more about a character by reading further in a book, one learns through a fuller, broader, richer *immersion* in experience. This is "playing around" with the world, a quality we must help to flourish. Unfortunately, schools tend to inhibit such activities, emphasizing instead what is really the last step in the chain, that of testing the answer. Elbow (1986) remarks on the foolishness of this approach, because it is limited to the refinement of what is already known rather than to the generation of anything new. Order and logic can only lead to what is already implicit in the premises; they "are useless unless you have fecundity to impose on them" (Elbow 1986, 30).

The second "beat" in the rhythm of learning is *withdrawal,* when we mentally stand back from experience in order to focus on it in a particular way. This withdrawal may be because creation poses a problem to us. Creation is dynamic and active, and demands responses. Trees grow, people are unpredictable, institutions change, and we may not just sit back and watch. Withdrawal may also come because sometimes we pose a problem to creation: we see a stewardship problem in the city's use of water, an ethical problem in the way the administrator has disciplined a student, or an analytical problem in deciding how to organize an itinerary. It will obviously be a primary responsibility of the teacher both to pose problems to students and to help them learn to pose problems themselves.

Let's think about these two kinds of problem-posing from the point of view of a teacher. The first kind occurs, for example, when I am confronted with a student who seems perpetually uninterested: I am called to respond in a pedagogically effective manner. I am responsible to search for strategies that will engage the student, or to dig down into underlying causes. I may not do so, of course, but either way I have learned something about the call to exercise my craft more faithfully, as well as about myself. Rather than being comfortably immersed in my experience, I face an "arrest" in it (Oakeshott 1966), a kind of a hiccup that intrudes in the normal flow of experience, calling me to re-evaluate and perhaps to change course. Another example might be when as a teacher I receive a number of complaints from parents about my use of fantasy literature: what was to me unproblematic has suddenly become very much so!

The second kind of problem-posing occurs when I actively pose a problem to the world. This would involve deciding to see a situation as, say, one of pedagogical concern, when this is not written on the face of it. Although I have felt quite comfortable working through the textbook and there have been few complaints from the students and none from the administration, I may decide to experiment for a time with alternatives. I decide to view a situation as a problem when others have not perceived it as such.

173

Whether or not I have correctly perceived a problem is of course a matter of wisdom and discernment. Seeing problems where there are none, or overlooking significant problems in favor of less important ones, is not going to be helpful. Problem-posing, as a way of coming to know, is governed by the laws of God. The fool is the one who does not act in conformity with God's law, does not see things in their right relationships to God and to each other; the wise person, however, is firmly rooted in the Word of the Lord. Such a person is able to discern what problems are most crucial.

The third "beat" in the rhythm of learning is that of *return* to experience in action, when we *do* something in and to the world on the basis of our standing back and focusing on it in a particular way. Our response is then purposeful and informed. We embark on a particular project, whether small or large scale. We seek to carry through certain carefully chosen intentions. We are committed to a course of action. Our response is not merely a reaction to a stimulus, but the responsibly considered step of a personal agent, as befits one made in God's image (Oppewal 1984). This applies whether we are seeking to determine an "unknown" in an algebraic equation, deciding to purchase a product from a supermarket shelf, determining a stance on our nation's involvement in an international conflict, or evaluating the rightness or wrongness of a character's actions in a novel. Schools should be places where this attitude of careful reflection, of "thoughtfulness" in all its connotations, is nurtured, guided, and practiced.

We may think of this rhythm of learning as giving rise to two different ways in which our knowledge grows. In the first way, through immersion in experience, we learn as our encounters with the world *extend and broaden*. In the second way, our knowledge is *deepened* as we stand back from the experiential world through problem-posing and return to it in purposeful responding.

Rhythms are good to dance to, if you're so inclined. We can imagine one of those floor diagrams that marks out the steps for us. It would be in the shape of a triangle. The base of the triangle represents our immersion in experience, and we may move back and forward along the base, extending and enriching our experience. The two sides represent withdrawal and return: we step back at one point, moving along one side to pause at the apex, but return to the base at a different point, to act with deepened insight. We have developed a new way of seeing and being in the world, which may now be incorporated in our everyday experience.

The broadening of knowledge is relatively straightforward: the cognitive structures are already established, and new experiences slot readily into place, enriching understanding gained previously. Solving a long division problem when I have mastered the process is no great challenge, though it might well consolidate that understanding and increase my confidence. Even writing a haiku might become second nature for some. The teacher will seek to enrich and solidify student experience, without promoting monotony.

Lest the preceding be misunderstood, we should make it clear that we are referring to the learner's own cognitive structures, and not to the structures of knowledge that secular scholarship often holds to be objectively established and religiously neutral. As Christians, when we confront the "truths" of the disciplines, we should always be aware of the challenge implicit in them. They reflect religious commitments that are in conflict with the gospel. They therefore pose problems to which we should respond with a critical stance. This need for spiritual discernment will be central as we seek to deepen our knowledge in faithfulness to the Lord.

Obviously, then, the deepening of knowledge is more complex than its broadening. It involves the development of new knowing structures, the construction of new categories of insight. When we face a mathematical problem that we do not have the resources to solve, we need to develop new strategies. Or we come to view aesthetically something that we previously did not, much as Wordsworth discovered the joy of lakes and mountains, or our students (we hope!) discover the joy of Wordsworth. What was previously *just there*, perhaps even "boring," is perceived in a fresh light. We have learned, because we have seen connections that we previously did not see.

Much of teaching involves challenging students with a new way of looking at things and helping them to make connections they would not otherwise think of making. The challenge is to invite them to make connections that are neither so remote as to promote disinterest nor so threatening as to arouse anxiety. The teacher must evoke just the right amount of tension that students will want to take the step into the new and hitherto unknown, so that they are eager to make connections between previous and proffered understanding. Piaget describes this necessary step in learning as "disequilibrium"; Dewey says that the most important question to ask about any proposed educational experience concerns the quality of problem it involves. We are saying that we want students to be open to God's presence in his world, so that they are able to hear him speaking and will respond in active obedience.

"When I asked you to read this book," Cal Holbrook explained to the grade sevens, "I said that the first thing I wanted you to do was to enjoy it. Authors don't write their books so that they'll be studied in schools: they write them so that people will enjoy them. In a sense, when we start to analyze a book, we kill it. But I hope I'll be able to give you a deeper enjoyment of the book than you originally had, and if not, sometimes schools have to sacrifice some books for the sake of your deeper appreciation and understanding of other books.

"Okay, I know already that some of you have had problems with this book because it's fantasy; and I know that some of you enjoyed the book but your parents had problems with it. So I think we're going to have to do some talking about that. But first, I want you to work in pairs, telling each other what it was that you most liked about the book. After you've done that, I want you to try to find two words that best seem to sum up the theme of the book. I want you to try to find two words that are opposites."

After the students had talked with each other for fifteen minutes, Cal drew their attention back to the front of the classroom.

"I want you to give me your pairs of words so that I can write them up on the board. Thanks, Sara, what do you have?"

Cal compiled a list of terms, which he called "compressed conflicts" or "binary opposites." "Hopeless hope," "courage and cowardice," "vice and virtue," "black and white," "suffering joy," "sacrificial salvation," "love and hate," "anger and compassion"—the students had done a good job, some of them making suggestions that were perceptive and also creative, some of them sticking with more conventional categories. But Cal was pleased that all of them had stood back from the novel far enough to be able to articulate at least some themes.

"Thanks, Grade Seven, you've done a splendid job. Now, I want you to choose a couple of terms—not your own, but someone else's—and I want you to draw two columns, with one word at the head of each column. Then I want you to list characters or incidents in the novel that best illustrate the particular term."

After the class has been working for some time, Jo raised her hand. "What's your problem, Jo?"

"Well, Mr. Holbrook, sometimes I want to put a character under both columns. They just don't seem to fit neatly in one or the other. Like, sometimes Hadrach does things that are really courageous and sometimes he runs away from things he should do."

"Good question, Jo. What do the rest of you think of that? Have you had the same difficulty, or is it always straightforward? I tell you what, given the time we have left, we won't talk about it further now, but for homework I want you to do one of two things. I want you either to work out a two-minute drama-tization of an event from the point of view of one the characters, or I want you to write a one-page perspective on an incident as if you were one of the char-acters. We'll start tomorrow's class with some drama and some readings.

"I want you to make sure you've got the whole list from the board copied down, and then you can go."

Cal's goals were fairly simple. He wanted his students to enjoy the book first of all. Through his classes, he wanted them to develop a love of literature and reading. He knew that good books bring students into contact with situ-ations that most of them will never actually face in real life, but that are close enough to what life is about to make them more sensitive and better equipped to handle such situations when they arise. He knew that imaginative literature can give a way of seeing ordinary events that heightens students' perceptions of the real issues at stake, particularly the issues of what values should be adhered to, what views of life best promote justice and shalom, and which lead to evil and destruction.

Cal didn't draw sharp lines between kinds of truth. He knew that nonfic-tion is not just a reporting of the facts but involves interpretations, that fiction in general is a reshaping of experiences that people have actually had, and that fantasy literature is just at one end of the spectrum of an imaginative response to human experience. He had also lived long enough to know that "truth is often stranger than fiction," and that some things that really happened to people would not be believed if they were included in a novel. Sometimes, fic-tion can be the best way of preparing people to be realistic.

Of course, he also knew the problems that some parents had with fantasy literature. At one point, his job had been on the line, and he and Ted Pakula had talked at length about the issue. But for Cal, literature is a main avenue by which the school can sensitize students to the ways that religious vision shaped people's decisions. His primary goal was to challenge his students to think about the perspective that was driving the actions of characters. With older students, he also concentrated on the perspective that led the author to build the imaginary world that he did. He knew this kind of standing back from the experience of a novel, to reflect critically on the author's presuppositions, is most difficult—but also most crucial. Schools had to help students not take things for granted, in all sorts of ways.

Many years ago, Cal heard Francis Schaeffer say that reading a modern novel or going to a movie was like going to war. Schaeffer had said that this kind of experience was necessary if Christians were to be equipped for spiri-tual warfare, and Cal agreed. He was somewhat more positive than Schaeffer, however, accepting that no one could escape from the envelope of God's grace. He knew that Christians could learn important things from non-Christians—

not just how to fight them. He had a deep-down assurance that the whole world belongs to God, that idols have no ultimate power, and that to the pure, all things are pure. He also believed—he remembered Augustine saying something similar—that the gold and silver of the pagans, all their cultural and intellectual achievements, belonged in the end to God's people, and that they would find their place of praise to God in the new heavens and the new earth. From time to time, fantasy, with its recurrent picture of the victory of Good, gave Cal glimpses of the new creation. He knew the risks involved, when human (or pseudo-human) actions seemed to bring salvation, but he also knew the gospel. There were some risks he felt warranted to take.

Safe Risks

A biblical perspective on knowing differs from any secular perspective because it assumes that we are at home in creation: we know the One who built the house. As Christians, we do not start from a position of doubt. We confess that the fear of the Lord is the beginning of wisdom. Standing in a personal relationship with the Creator of all things, we know we were made for this relationship and for a special relationship of dominion with creation. When God brings the animals to Adam so that he might name them, he witnesses that humankind has the calling to participate actively in both discerning and shaping meaning. The animals *may be* distinguished and named, and Adam is fully *capable of doing* the distinguishing and the naming. He is called to be imaginative and creative in responding to creation.

And when Adam does this—when we do this!—we identify the nature of something, not in and of itself, but as God's gift, and in relation to him. "To name a thing is to manifest the meaning and value God gave it, to know it as coming from God and to know its place and function within the cosmos created by God. To name a thing, in other words, is to bless God for it and in it. . . . [This] is not a 'religious' or a 'cultic' act, but the very *way* of life" (Schmemann 1973, 15).

To *know* is thus to stand—indeed, to walk—in the right relation to God and to what he has created. It is to treat things with integrity, according to their God-given character.

Things are always known relationally, never in isolation. There is no such thing as a "brute fact." If we respect the rich interconnectedness of all things as we learn, our understanding will not only be deeper, as we described in the previous chapter. We will also be confronted with the rootedness of all things in Christ. Such wonderful coherence has to have a source, and Scripture reveals that this is in the Creator and Sustainer of all things.

This confession that we may trust our knowledge and truly serve God in our knowing of his world is not a justification of arrogance. Creation was made as our home, but we are now pilgrims on our way to a new earth and new heavens. We do know only in part, as through a glass darkly. One root cause of this failure to understand is the fall, with its consequences for all our ways of relating to the world. We are alienated from it—strangers by nature we are not, but a rift exists that needs to be healed. Consciously and unconsciously, we distort our knowledge of the world. Most radically, we do this as we orient our lives to an idol, seeking in this a point of coherence for our experience. Networks of explanation that allow no place for the Creator of all meaning, which explain order in life by reference to human reason, language, historical forces, or emotional drives, will lead ultimately to ignorance rather than knowledge.

As well as being limited by our fallenness, we are limited by our finiteness. We are not God, we are his creatures. We should not be dismayed: with Job, we will acknowledge that at the heart of the universe is a mystery, that what we may understand is determined by what God chooses to reveal to us. For all knowledge is also a response to God's revelation: He is an active partner in our coming to know the world.

Thus, we should give up all pretensions to complete and certain knowledge, apart from the certitude of faith, by which we acknowledge God's revelation to us. We should accept that our knowledge is always partial and tentative, emphasizing that it is a response to a world that is already pregnant with meaning by the power of God's Word. In our weakness of understanding, God's grace is perfected: here as elsewhere our lives should be characterized by trust, not in our own capacities but in the faithfulness of God. Knowing involves risking, trying out, conjecturing—and then risking again. But our risk-taking is founded in the security we have in Christ, and in the biblical revelation that all things find their coherence in him.

God's dynamic creation does not allow us to sit back as spectators. It calls for our commitment and trust; it calls for our response. It is in this responding that we express our life as image bearers: we are response-*able*, responsive creatures. Creation in all its richness invites us to respond wherever we turn. Our ultimate response must be one of praise to God who also reveals himself to us in creation: the world challenges us to glorify God and give him thanks (Rom. 1:18–21).

We are thus invited to take risks. God did not create us as machines, to perform the one range of operations over and over again. He made us persons in his image, designed to grow from childhood to maturity in responsive interaction with our environment. He made us to grow in understanding, in love, and in faith. Just as God was willing to take a risk with Adam in inviting him to name the animals, rather than merely telling him what they should be called, we should be willing to take risks for ourselves and with others. If our lives are to be lives of service, we need to be as open and vulnerable as God was willing to make himself in Christ. Reaching out in love to those around us will always entail risk.

Reading fantasy literature—or literature of any kind—means taking risks, because there are spirits at work here, as everywhere. But in this vicarious experience, our spiritual discernment can be sharpened. And it means taking risks because our ordinary experience, our ordinary ways of viewing the world, are challenged. We are confronted with the power of evil when the valiant adventurers are vanquished; we face the possibilities of virtuous courage as our heroes battle the monster in its lair; we feel the stimulus of hope as the quest continues through the darkest and longest of nights.

But if we walk truly in faith, these are *safe risks*, for God is the sovereign Lord of every square inch of creation. He is also our Father.

The Integral Curriculum

We have already used the term *integral* in this book, without explaining why, in stressing the importance of making connections in learning, we did not prefer more conventional terms such as *integrated* or *integrative*. The reason is that the latter terms suggest that coherence is something that is constructed only in and by the process of learning. Rather, whatever world picture the learner constructs can only be a response to the coherence that already exists in creation by the Word of God. An *integral curriculum* is one that seeks to respect this given integrality of creation, the wholeness of life lived before the face of God (Blomberg 1980b; 1991).

The coherence that all things have in Christ is ultimately the interconnectedness of service. All things were made to serve each other. The soil serves humans by sustaining life, yet humans serve the soil by tilling it so that it flourishes. The God who is Love made a world at the heart of which love was to beat.

Serving, loving, and knowing are thus three facets of the one gem. Each in its own way proclaims that standing and walking in right relationships is God's purpose for his creatures. When the reign of the Prince of Peace is truly recognized on earth, then it will be characterized by that dynamic harmony that is shalom.

The Christian school can be a signpost to God's kingdom in part by providing young people with "a sense of coherence in their studies; that is a sense of purpose, meaning, and interconnectedness in what they learn. At present, a typical modern school curriculum reflects, far too much, the fragmentation one finds in television's weekly schedule" (Postman 1979, 131–32). The Christian school, of all places, ought to be able to point students to this coherence and purpose.

Thus, we are using the term *integral curriculum* to emphasize the wholeness of life along five dimensions, which draw together the themes of this book:

Religion: the whole of life is religion, and the curriculum should be organized in a way that makes this apparent (*responsive discipleship*);

Creation: the whole world, both "natural" and "cultural," is God's creation, rich in meaning and finding its coherence in Christ, and the curriculum should lead students to experience this structured many-sidedness and meaningful unity (*seeking shalom*);

Person: the whole person is of importance in schooling, and the curriculum should guide the development of the student's various ways of knowing (*unwrapping gifts*);

Knowing: knowledge is not fragmented but a meaningful whole, being rooted in everyday experience which is concrete (i.e., whole) in character, ranging across all the ways in which we relate to the world and growing by both broadening and deepening (*a rhythm of immersion, withdrawal, and return*);

Community: the whole of life is communal in character, and this ought to be reflected in the way we structure schools (*sharing joys and bearing burdens*).

"Hi, Mrs. Fisher!" Jody called out as she went to her desk in the science room. "Did you have a good weekend?"

"Thanks, Jody, I did. I managed to get in a couple of hours kayaking on Saturday afternoon. I really enjoy it when spring finally comes around again. I hope it's here to stay, now."

Joan Fisher turns to address the class. "All right, Grade Eight, today we're going to start your projects on the chemical and physical properties of the products you've been researching for your investigative journalism projects. Remem-

181

ber, the science room is just a place where we have some special equipment and we ask certain kinds of questions. The research that you've done in the library and in your interviews with business people and shopkeepers is just as important in understanding the products you're investigating. And of course, your actual use and enjoyment of the things you are investigating should not be forgotten. What we're really hoping to do is to focus on the different aspects that go to make up your total experience of the product.

"What Mr. Holbrook and I want you to concentrate on in science is whether the claims that are made in the advertising of your product are matched by the physical properties of the product. Let's get an overview of what we're all researching."

As students began to describe their products, Mrs. Fisher listed them on the board. There was quite a range of items, from canned drinks to exercise equipment. The initial selection of products had been on the basis of advertisements that students had collected, as their English project concerned the reliability of advertising claims. This in turn was linked with their broader class study of the manufacturing and distribution process. The whole unit had been planned and was now being taught by a team of four teachers, each making a special contribution to the students' growing understanding.

"Mrs. Fisher, Becky and I are looking at licorice. We went to the store and got a whole lot of different types. We thought it would be interesting to compare them, so that we get an idea why they taste different from each other. What sort of tests should we do?"

"Well, Helen, don't you think it's interesting that some people like the salted licorice and some people don't? Why do you think that is? When I think of salted licorice, I think of Dutch people. Do you think that taste might be more than a matter of a chemical reaction?"

"Do you think we should test people's taste buds too, Mrs. Fisher?" Helen asked.

"Well," Mrs. Fisher replied, "I think it would be very interesting to look at the way in which people's cultural background might affect their response to chemicals."

"Mrs. Fisher, Jack and I are interested in seeing some of the waste products that come from making processed cheese. You know how we joke about its being like plastic—we'd like to know what they do with all the flavor they take out. But we thought we should also look at what goes into the packaging of it, the stuff they wrap each slice in. We were also wondering about its nutritional value."

The way this unit is structured guides students to see that information is important for the ways in which it helps them to make responsible decisions, decisions that will serve God, other people, and the rest of creation. Conducting scientific research, or any kind of research, is not seen as being for its own sake, but for the sake of responsive discipleship. In the science room, Joan Fisher helps students pose certain kinds of problems, complementing the other kinds of problems that they are exploring with other teachers. Because the products they are investigating are ones they already use or may decide to use in the future, their focused study will inform their present and future action.

Questions for Discussion

1. What evidence do you see in your school of the classical and romantic traditions? Does either one predominate?

2. How might viewing learning as a rhythm of immersion, withdrawal, and return help to break through the classical/romantic polarity? Outline three approaches to the same area of study that exemplify the differences between the classical, romantic, and biblical views of knowledge.

3. "Immersion, withdrawal, and return" can obviously characterize learning in schools of all kinds, whether Christian or not. How might this rhythm be employed to implement a biblical view of knowledge, not only in terms of structure but also in terms of religious direction? In what ways might it be used to promote a more spiritually critical stance toward understandings that are normally taken for granted?

4. The following is a tentative list of ways of knowing: analytical, techno-cultural, lingual, social, economic, aesthetic, jural, ethical, and confessional. The chapter briefly describes the aesthetic way of knowing, in distinction from the aesthetic dimension of concrete experience and theoretical reflection on the aesthetic dimension. Develop similar descriptions for the other ways of knowing listed.

5. Stress has been placed on "knowing as relating rightly," not merely conceptually but primarily in terms of acting. In attempting to reform our thinking and acting so that it is more righteous, how should Scripture guide our interpretation of the relationships between different aspects of creation?

6. In the last section, we describe the implications for curriculum under five headings and give a snapshot from a unit based on

this model. Select a specific area of the curriculum and develop your own example.

7. What are the implications of what is said about coherence and the integral curriculum for the curriculum framework of your school? How would an approach that relied on the divisions between the disciplines achieve the same goals (assuming that you accept that they are biblical).

Recommended Reading

1. Blomberg, D. G. 1980a. "Toward a Christian theory of knowledge."
   Eisner, E. W., ed. 1985. *Learning and teaching the ways of knowing.*
   Two discussions of the "ways of knowing" that suggest differing frameworks but support the value of a curriculum catering for a diversity of gifts or "intelligences."
   Lewis, C. S. 1943. *The abolition of man,* chapter 1.
   Explores closely related ideas about the normativity of aesthetic and other value judgments.
2. Wolters, A. 1985. *Creation regained.*
   Walsh, B. J., and Middleton, J. R. 1984. *The transforming vision.*
   Lucid explanations of a Christian world view. Both books are helpful starting points for thinking about biblical reformation of the disciplines and of knowledge generally.
   Wolterstorff, N. 1976. *Reason within the bounds of religion.*
   Runner, H. E. 1970. *The relation of the Bible to learning.*
   Seerveld, C. 1980. *Rainbows for a fallen world.*
   All contribute much to this discussion.
3. Oppewal, D. 1985. *Biblical knowing and teaching.*
   Groome, T. 1980. *Christian religious education.*
   Palmer, P. 1983. *To know as we are known.*
   Valuable for their broader consideration of the nature of knowledge.

8

How Do We Think
about Curriculum?

It is not necessary to discard the subjects that are now taught in the schools, for educational improvement is incremental. What we need to guide incremental change is a forceful idea, an attractive conception, an image of [people] and the conditions that foster [their] development. And then we need a small place to begin. (Eisner 1982, 72)

A Curriculum Team at Work

It is 3:15 in the afternoon. The teachers have just said their last good-byes for the day to students and inquiring parents; some have made a phone call, others had to run down to the office to sort some things out with the secretary. Four of the five Middle School teachers expected for the meeting have gathered in Matthew's room with their cups of coffee or glasses of water. Dennis is also hoping to stop by. Cal is the Curriculum Team Leader; he is eager to begin but there's the usual banter about various of the day's incidents and Matthew and Joan are trying to finalize the details of a field trip that they have arranged for next week.

"Well, are we ready to begin?" Cal said. "I've got to leave a little early this afternoon to pick up Sharon, so I'd like to get going."

"All right, Cal," Matthew responded. "I've got copies of the Teaching/Learning Activities for the last two weeks, if we can take a quick look at those. Most

185

of you were here when we were planning them last time, but you'll see that we made some changes along the way. I think I started to lose the kids a bit last week, so I introduced a couple of new activities to try to sharpen the focus. I also sat them down yesterday and gave them a talk on how they're handling the research process, because I think some of them are still a bit disorganized."

"Thanks, Matthew. I think that last point you made is very important. Just because we're committed to documenting our curriculum now, doesn't mean that it has to become hard and fast, inflexible. We have to keep monitoring how the kids are responding, and we have to fine-tune our plans as we go along. Anyway, let's take a couple of minutes to look over this material and then we can talk about it for a while. Then I want to go on to reflect more on the biblical perspective, and how successfully this is coming through. I'm not sure that we've found the 'golden thread' for this unit yet, the biblical orientation that makes the whole thing hang together for the students. I've still got some questions about whether we're not being too dualistic in our approach— you know, still working with so-called objective facts to which we're then trying to add Christian values."

The meetings of which this is a sample are part of an ongoing curriculum development project that has been initiated at Mountain City Christian. Together, team members are reviewing previous weeks' teaching and planning for the future. Their planning had begun at the end of the preceding semester, and built on the resources and programs that had been compiled over the earlier years of the school. They are trying to move gradually from a discipline-based approach, in which teachers take responsibility for planning and teaching their own subjects in isolation from each other, to a more integral model, in which they select an area of creation to study in common and do their planning as a team. They naturally contribute to this planning on the basis of their specialized insights, but they are also consciously trying to think of themselves as teachers of whole persons first, and as teachers of subject areas second.

Curriculum planning is coming to be seen as central to the life of the school. As they work individually and communally, teachers try out ideas of what is going to be an effective learning experience for their students. They are continually making and testing suggestions, trying to get a picture of how kids will respond, and how they might more readily encourage fruitful responses. They have a territory they wish to explore, but their focus is less on covering all the possible content than it is on leading their students through the more significant elements of it. And their decisions concerning significance will be guided overall by their main goal, which is to promote biblically-informed discernment and servanthood.

"Let's look ahead a bit to our week's stay in the city," Cal said. "As I see it, we've got a number of objectives. First, we want to broaden the kids' experience. Most of them have been to the city quite a few times now, but usually they go shopping or to the movies or maybe to a football game. We want to open them up to some of the other possibilities the city has to offer. We want to immerse them in some of its riches, so that they come to enjoy some things that are new to them. Why don't we get as many of those ideas as we can on paper first."

The group brainstorms noisily, compiling a list of all the opportunities they can think of. Ballet, the symphony orchestra, art galleries, the architecture, the stock exchange, the produce market, the city and state offices, the university, theater, shelters for the homeless, the newspaper, hospitals, business offices, banks, clubs, the museum, cathedrals, gas and electricity, water supply and sewerage, the various forms of transport people use to get to and around the city . . . the city in its rich variety. Of course, many of these resources have been used previously by the school, and others provide a focus for activities to come later. What kind of focus will these teachers adopt for this particular unit?

"I think we should try to give kids a sense of the diversity of this place," said Anna, "but that it's still a place with its own identity. What makes Mountain City, Mountain City? Is there a spiritual force that drives the life of the city, or are there competing forces? We want them to see the city as a place where they can meet God, where they can experience his creation, and where they can serve him responsibly. Some of them still have a romantic notion that one can only meet God in the countryside or on a mountain top. I think they need to see that the city can really be a fulfillment of God's purposes, even with the potential for sin that it brings."

Joan suggests that if they divide the class into teams, they could have each team looking at a distinct way in which the city functions. "We could start them off with a number of questions to investigate, and then we could lead them to come up with their own questions. Getting students to pose their own questions is vitally important it they're to develop higher level thinking skills."

"Yes, good idea," Cal said, "but let's not have too narrow a view of the kinds of questions they might ask. Let's not have just fact-finding questions, statistics and budgets and so on. Let's get them to identify the smells of the city, its colors and its sounds. Let's have some of them see what it's like to get around in a wheelchair for a day, or live on thirty cents, or with their eyes covered as if they're blind. We want them to think of ways in which the burdens of city living can be relieved and shalom can be promoted."

"One way we could give them a sense of the diversity of the city would be to start with an architectural tour," Dennis suggests. "The city has buildings representing a number of different periods and styles. It also has accommodation of the very poorest kind to the most salubrious. We could put the kids in a bus and take them from place to place."

"I also think that most of these kids are limited in their musical and dramatic experiences," said Cindy. "I think if we took them to a symphony concert, they would have to sit up and take notice of things they don't normally confront."

"I agree," said Cal, "but I think we should also have some input from the students about what would be worth doing before we fill up the whole week with activities that we think are going to be stimulating and challenging."

"And I think we have to make sure we don't just give them a good time," said Joan. "Our purposes are educational, so we have to make sure that we get them to respond in meaningful ways, ways that will really deepen their understanding of how the city works. What kinds of responses to these activities are we going to want from students?"

What Is "Curriculum"?

There are many different conceptions of curriculum and it is impossible to give a definition without taking a stand on the values that are considered most important in schooling. The overall understanding that we have of curriculum—the way we practice curriculum—will be crucial in determining the kind of school that we have.

We have seen in the work of the Mountain City curriculum team, that when teachers are planning curriculum, their focus is on what students will do as much as it is on what they themselves will do. This is necessarily so, because teachers and learners stand in a complementary, reciprocal relationship to each other. (Although you can have learners without teachers, you can't have teachers without learners.) Even if teachers have in mind that students will sit quietly and write down everything the teacher says, the focus on the student in the context of this relationship remains central.

The plan that teachers make for the conduct of this relationship is what we take to be the *curriculum*. We think of it as the *instructional program* or *program of instruction*. It has these two main elements— *what* will be taught and *how* it will be taught—but they are in constant conjunction with each other. The curriculum is thus at the heart of the school; as a systematic approach to teaching and learning, the curriculum distinguishes the school from all the other contexts in which teaching and learning take place, in the family, the church, businesses, and so on. Everything in the school has to be justified according to its educational mission, whereas in other institutions, the educational function is under the lead of other purposes. In the family, the learning of language or of standards of behavior happens incidentally, in the context of a relationship in which people are committed to each other's full human flourishing. In a business, learning is designed to enhance economic productivity. In the church, learning is focused on the biblical revelation and the growth of a strong worshiping, witnessing community. None of these goals is foreign to the task of the school, but each is secondary to the focus on learning itself. Where these other institutions have purposes that learning is intended to serve, the school is a community intentionally organized for the purpose of learning.

The curriculum should not be thought of as a static, fixed possession, encapsulated in a document in the administrator's office. Rather, it is to be a *dynamic plan for teaching and learning* (Fowler 1987); it is always in the context of *an organically developing relationship* between teacher and learner(s). Situated as it is in the interaction between particular people, with all their idiosyncracies, the curriculum is concerned with establishing the boundaries and setting the direction for this relationship. As such, it should be ever responsive to the free-flowing interactions between people.

In this "dynamic plan," we cannot in practice *separate* the "what" from the "how." We can certainly *distinguish* between the *program* and *instruction* when we think and talk about curriculum, but in the head and in the actions of the teacher, *what* is taught and *how* it is taught are two sides of the one coin (Walker and Soltis 1986).

The student experiences this integration even more forcefully. What students learn is determined not only by the content that has been selected but also by the way in which it is taught. For students, what they are explicitly and implicitly expected to do becomes part of the content of their learning. Authoritarian teaching and passive learning, rigidly segmented blocks of learning, testing and grading, the completion of worksheets and homework, the linkage between grading and attendance: practices such as these—or the alternatives to them—demonstrate the merging of content and method. "The distinction between the two . . . will not hold once it is seen that the means one employs itself defines the covert structure that embodies a significant part of what it is that students learn" (Eisner 1982, 12).

The way we think about curriculum has an important impact on the way in which we practice curriculum development and delivery. If we think in terms of the specification of content, what remains is the best way of "packaging" the content for delivery; we are caught from the beginning in an inert view of knowing and a transmission model of education. But if we react against an orientation to content by advocating child-centeredness, we will arrive at a relativistic and individualistic curriculum. Neither a focus on content alone nor on instruction alone will suffice. A curriculum that promotes growth in understanding for responsive discipleship will effectively merge the two.

In the school, we approach teaching and learning systematically. In planning for learning, we *select and organize experience for educational purposes.* What transforms "experience" from a vague and indeterminate encounter with the world (or "knowledge" from a mere summary of content) into *curriculum* is this structuring. Curriculum is a selection of learning experiences; the "content" emerges in the very process of planning for teaching. The shape of the curriculum will be determined by the criteria for selecting and organizing experience and the kind of knowledge that it seeks to promote. A fundamental question therefore concerns the nature of these criteria.

Curriculum as Religious Vision

Administrator, K–8: A key issue for me as we think about the future of Christian schools has to do with instruction. What is it that makes Christian schooling worth the time, effort, and resources? What is it that makes them specifically Christian? What is left when we throw out chapel and devotions and singing? We have to focus on what happens in the classroom, day by day. Teachers are the key element in this.

We should be asking, "What is distinctive about what we are doing?" We have to look at schools as a whole: at what point and in what ways do we provide leadership? What is really important in what we do? It's not as simple as algebra and sentence parts. Rather, we should be asking, "What are the key concepts of Christian education?" and we should be building our curriculum around these. For example, "Who is my neighbor? What is justice? What is our responsibility as citizens—not just of the country, but of the kingdom?"

The structuring of curriculum is a whole school concern, to be determined in the light of the school's vision and objectives. It is in the overarching curricular framework that we will detect the religious vision of the school, for it is in such a context that the various details of schooling—which, when considered in isolation from each other, will be similar in many different school settings—find their meaning. All schools teach reading, writing, and arithmetic, but it is the relationships between the various elements of the curriculum that are of greatest significance in expressing the school's religious direction. The Christian character of a school cannot be determined by analyzing the percentage of "sacred activities" in which it engages (Wagner 1990) but only by an investigation of the ways in which Scripture directs all the school's activities.

An integrally Christian curriculum cannot be developed by adding a spiritual veneer to so-called factual subject matter. The curriculum must find its coherence throughout as responsiveness to God speaking to us in Christ, creation, and Scripture; even in the study of physics, we need to acknowledge that the regularities we perceive are because of the faithfulness of God and in response to his Word, and not because of some independently-functioning law of gravity.

"I think Joan's right," Dennis said. "We need to give students some context or framework within which they can compare and contrast the various things they see. That's going to require some analyzing and critical thinking. I think we should have them meet with some of our parents and other contacts who work in the city, and interview them about what pressures face Christians in business and other areas. Homes and churches can be pretty safe places, but it's in the city that the really tough issues of serving God come into focus."

"Okay, so we don't want them to take everything for granted, we want to put some distance between what they experience and how they respond."

"How about having them put together a portfolio, containing a whole range of responses. They might do some straight data collection, tape an interview, draw or paint a city scene. . . ."

"Yes, and they could write a fictional piece from the point of view of a homeless person," said Cindy, who was becoming unusually excited about the direction things were taking. "Or we could have them work in groups to put together a twenty minute radio show."

"What if we integrated this with a media study?" Cal suggested. "We could look at how the news is reported in different papers and on the TV and radio. We could examine the emphases that are given to different kinds of events and activities, and why things are reported in this way. We could perhaps have them put together their own newspaper, with all the different sections—news, finance, entertainment, lifestyle, ads, and so on—but get them to think about what the really important items would be within a kingdom perspective. I would think there would be greater attention to Third World news and to the implications of economic competition between the industrialized nations for a fairer distribution of resources throughout the world, for example, rather than just a focus on how our country might end up with less."

Cindy had another idea. "Do you think we could arrange to have them shadow someone for a day, to find out what a day in the life of an accountant or an architect or a police officer is really like? We could draw up a list of questions for them to investigate, which would help them to look at the ways in

191

which people in various occupations are able to serve others and also at the temptations that people face to use their jobs merely for their own advantage."

"I'm sure that that would help them to think more concretely about what it means to be a responsive disciple," Cal said. "But I think we've enough here to keep us busy for months—I'm very pleased with the progress we've made. Perhaps what I should do for our next meeting is to map out a rough idea of the activities to include and the kind of sequence that might be appropriate. I'm really excited about the possibilities."

Curriculum Decision-Making: On What Basis?

Obviously we cannot convey everything at once to students. We make choices. But the choices we make will be limited by the options we see before us. If the supermarket shelves do not stock a certain range of products or a particular brand of that product, then our choices are that much constrained. But a critical approach to shopping (as to curriculum selection) will want to know why it is these choices and no others that are available. More frequently, we take for granted that the world is structured in a certain way, without acknowledging the extent to which it is constructed by prior human decisions. If there are no biodegradable products on the shelves, we are forced to buy products that are harmful to the environment—or to make no purchase at all. If all the banks have investments in nuclear energy or in companies co-operating with repressive regimes, where do we put our savings? As Christians, we should recognize the importance of structural alternatives, for our battle is with powers and principalities. Individual decisions can achieve little when the alternatives that are offered are equally repugnant.

So it is for teachers making decisions about how to organize learning experiences. Our choices are limited by the range of decisions that we think possible in the first place. For many educators, the disciplines are assumed to represent the array from which knowledge is to be selected. For others, the needs or interests of the child are considered paramount, for knowledge is for them, when all is said and done, an individual construction and possession. And there are of course other options.

A Christian conception of the "supermarket" is as broad as creation itself. It is God who sets the boundaries to our experience, and it is these boundaries we must respect and cherish as we make our curricular decisions. The world is meaningfully structured by the Creator himself. The disciplines are not the source of this meaning, but only one kind of response to creation, alongside of which are aesthetic, economic, ethical, linguistic, and other nontheoretical but essential responses. The disciplines are thus not the necessary starting point for curriculum. Further, we are not content to see either the disciplines or other kinds of responses as the endpoint of the knowing process. We will seek the reintegration of insights gained in these various ways in everyday experience and concrete action, because God's revelation calls us to respond in loving service.

Play, Problem-Posing, Purposeful Response

Teachers generally do not follow rational-linear models in curriculum planning, even such well-known models as the one proposed by Tyler (1949). Unfortunately, some will be linear in their approach without being terribly rational—they will just teach according to the text. For more responsible teachers, there is likely to be a free-flowing connection between all the design elements, with teachers looking for a catalyst to bring together resources, content, goals, and activities in an engaging and helpful way. They will be oriented to these points of reference and driven by certain values as they make curricular decisions, but these decisions are of the nature of creative judgments about what meaningful unit or task will best incorporate these referents (Earl 1987; Glatthorn 1987; Shavelson and Stern 1981; Smith 1986). Curriculum design is more an art or a craft than it is a science or a technology.

So what points of reference and values ought we to keep in view in planning curriculum for the Christian school? In an important sense, the themes of the previous chapters converge here. We are looking for a simple but not simplistic idea with sufficient force to give us a small place to begin. It will not of course be a blueprint for the design process; as we have said, designing curriculum is not merely a matter of the deductive application of principles, but also of creativity and imagination.

The model we are suggesting may be thought of as a cycle with three points of reference: *play, problem-posing,* and *purposeful responding.* The cycle can be entered at any point and we can move in any direction between these points. So we are not suggesting a lockstep approach, but a helpful orientation to the curriculum planning process. Such an approach seems to us to be in harmony with a biblical view of knowing, as a rhythm of immersion, withdrawal, and return. It incorporates an understanding of learning as requiring active engagement and encompassing a variety of styles and responses. It serves the overall purpose of the Christian school as a place in which we seek to promote responsive discipleship, in which gifts are unwrapped, burdens are borne and joys are shared, and shalom is continually sought.

An Analogy

An analogy that helps us to understand some of the features of such a curriculum is that of a game—let's say a game of football. There is a theoretical justification for such a comparison. Both a game and a curriculum are paradigms, in the sense that they define boundaries and tell you what to do to solve problems within these boundaries (Barker 1991; Kuhn 1970).

And having mentioned paradigms, we might invite you to consider a paradigm *shift*, a different way of thinking about curriculum, but a way that incorporates the best of what teachers already do in their classrooms. It is a paradigm designed to challenge the "text, teach, test" model that is still so powerful, with its emphasis on *exposing* students to knowledge and *covering* the content (Sizer 1985). It is a paradigm that advocates active engagement in learning as an exciting exploration of God's creation and calls for response to creation as revelation of God and his purposes.

As in games, the curriculum will make provision for practice. Obviously, learning will require practice if it is to be consolidated. Talk about the importance of play could readily be misunderstood to oppose the hard work of repeating understandings and behaviors until they become second nature. Learning is learning only if it is remembered and repeatable, if it leads to changes in the way we act. As we shall explain, we in fact see play as a significant way in which this consolidation can occur. Play is not opposed to work, but is at the heart of work as joyful service of the Lord. But at the same time, merely remembering is the lowest level of understanding that we have to deal with. Remembering in itself is a trivial pursuit—what is important is what we do with what we are able to remember. A computer can win a quiz game and can beat many of us at chess—but a computer cannot appreciate, understand, or worship.

Games, like schools, are serious business. One has to play the game as if it were real life. Even the games of young children demonstrate this seriousness—one faces their wrath in breaking the circle of their suspended disbelief. If only we could encourage all our students to regard school with such earnestness.

Yet at the same time, "it's only a game," a safe haven marked out for a time within the wider world. Schools too are designed to allow children to play around with things without risking the serious consequences that mistakes would incur in the real world. If students are to feel this freedom to grow and to explore, schools must be places in which the framework provides support for making mistakes, where being wrong is no crime. They ought to be secure environments for exploration and experimentation; being "wrong" ought to be seen as a significant step in the process of learning, which should be thought of as a process of identifying and correcting errors as much as if not more than as a process of assimilating truths. (It is worse to think you are right when you are in fact wrong than it is to be wrong and to know it: at least the latter condition allows for growth.) Schools should encourage this attitude of humility in learning.

This description of schools as safe havens for play is not a denial of the call for realism in schools, that they accurately reflect what the world is really like. They ought to be *structured*—organized purposefully for exploratory learning—without being *artificial* and abstracted, such that the school world and the world beyond are worlds apart. They should treat the present lives of students with great seriousness, while maintaining an orientation to the future challenges that these students will face.

The late nineteenth century saw the rationalization and regulation of many sports. Rules started to get written down, rule-making bodies were formed, so that one didn't depend on local customs when playing a game. One could appeal to a rule book. The spontaneous development of so many sports—baseball, cricket, different kinds of football, hockey—gave way to a rule-governed stage. Games had evolved to this point, but now their further development was to be regulated. Parents and governments did the same when they set up schools to systematically promote learning, rather than letting it happen "naturally." The curriculum is intended to set the boundaries for learning, so that what happens naturally but somewhat haphazardly is now guided and regulated so that specific goals can be achieved with greater efficiency and effectiveness.

The rule-governed structure of a game sets the boundaries for the players' creative responses, determines in outline what will and what will not count toward their goal. But the rules as written in the rule book are only an abstract structure for the game, an analysis and refining of the messiness that is the real game. The coach's game plan provides some specific suggestions for how to play within this structure, when facing particular opponents. But it is up to the players, individually and cooperatively, to provide the pace, to kick, catch, pass, and sidestep, and to bring the crowd to their feet. Each game develops its own character as the players respond within the context of the rules to each other: each is a unique instance of the "Game."

Analogously, the curriculum charts a course for what will count as meaningful learning and the teacher comes with various ideas as to how this will be achieved. But it is in the classroom, in the dynamic interaction between teacher and students, that learning comes to life; the teacher is the captain-coach, who is part of the rough and tumble but who is there to lead and guide. Teachers have to be sensitive to the opportunities of the moment. In a sense they play both with and against their students, much as captain-coaches stand a little outside, over against, as motivators and goads. They have a special office or calling.

The game requires the application of wisdom. It is not merely a matter of having the skills, of being technically competent. Nor is it merely a matter of knowing the rules, so that one knows what will count as success. One has to translate both into wise and competent action, action that will at this point serve the goals of the team. While the arena is the context for the display of certain skills, this is not in isolation, but always in the context of trying to reach some goal or overcome an impediment. Similarly in schooling: we do not seek merely the *display* of skills and abstract understanding; we seek that children will be able to use these skills and understandings in insightful service of God and neighbor, bringing justice where there is unrighteousness and peace where there is discord.

Each game is a series of problem-posing segments. Attempting to catch the ball in football is a discrete problem to which a player responds with purpose, as in deciding when to kick, when to pass, and when to run. The creative responses, the moments of greatest excitement and jubilation in sports are the spontaneous, seemingly non-rule governed responses to the problem, when technical excellence is submerged in creative flair.

Each player has a position, a role, but within these roles players have the greatest possible freedom, freedom both to make mistakes and to grasp opportunities. Split-second decisions are made, to kick or to run, to go left or right, to cover this opponent or that.

In the classroom, twenty or thirty children are careening this way and that, mentally and emotionally if not physically, and the teacher is trying to lead the way. Teachers judiciously pose problems to students but more importantly, students are encouraged and guided to do the same, to take the initiative in directing their own learning. They are the players, and the teacher has succeeded when they freely and actively take on the curriculum's goals for learning. Then, the excitement of the class is evident as they strive toward a common goal. Together, the class looks for those moments of creative insight and discovery, of understanding suddenly as well as painstakingly achieved, of application of skills and understandings acquired in new and startling and incredibly rewarding ways. In an attitude of dogged perseverance, all will be on the lookout for those moments when the unexpected occurrence provides an opportunity to be grasped.

There is an overriding purposefulness to players' responses. They are goal-oriented, but there are many different ways in which the goals can be achieved. The ends are common, though the means of achieving them are virtually limitless—within the rules. And so it ought to be within schools, where the curriculum sets the goals yet teachers allow and indeed seek for many paths to their achievement.

No two games are ever the same, but the most unsatisfying games are those that are the most predictable. The interest of a game depends upon the interplay between form and freedom: too much form, and the game becomes mechanical and dull; too much freedom and chaos reigns, and nobody is able to carry anything through to resolution. The same conditions apply in the classroom, where the teacher's careful guidance through the curriculum depends upon a responsive sensitivity to the nuances of student learning.

A team sport depends obviously on cooperation and understanding between the various players: the "stars" who seek only their own glory might well shine for the moment, but will in the long run defeat the team's purposes; or to put it differently, stars will in fact depend for their virtuoso performances on the solid preparatory work and support of their teammates. Similarly, the most effectively functioning classroom will be one in which the students are encouraged to be team players, cooperative learners, with gains both for those who are weak and those who are strong in particular abilities.

A Problem with "Problems"?

Sam Freeland is the Resource Teacher at Central Station. Somewhat of a paradoxical figure, he is perceived as a warm and loving person who can yet be pushy and insensitive. He sees an objective to be achieved and then goes all-out for it. "I like the emphasis on problem-posing," Sam said. "It gives a way of thinking about active engagement in learning, certainly. But I don't think everything in a school can be thought of in terms of problem-posing. What if I just want to read a poem or a section from a book to kids, so that they just enjoy the experience? There's no problem posed in that, nor should there be. I want them to think into the poem, to feel it, to play with the images. I certainly don't want them to think of it as a problem. In fact, one of the biggest problems we have as teachers is just that kids think things are problems when instead they should be responding positively to them. The notion of 'problem' is altogether too negative in tone."

"Well, you would still agree that how to get them to enjoy the poem presents a problem for the teacher?" asked Karla. "That in our planning, we should still maybe think in terms of posing problems?" Karla has in the back of her mind Stenhouse's (1975) notion that the curriculum is like a hypothesis, to be tested out by students and teachers together in the laboratory of the classroom. The teacher's plan is a "best guess" for what will promote learning at this point.

"Sure," Sam replied, "but you're stretching things too far to try to think of everything in terms of problems. I can agree that what we want from students is a purposive, personal response, but I really think there's a place for creativity, appreciation, enrichment that is not covered by the notion. It makes life out to be full of tension all the time; I often think that what we need to do is sit still more and pay a-ttention."

"Yes, and there's something else too," Jim contributed, somewhat excitedly. "Sometimes understanding just comes, like in a flash of insight. Sometimes things just come together in new ways, without our having consciously sought them. They come like a gift. In fact, I think all understanding is at root a gift, a gift of God's revelation by the Holy Spirit."

"Agreed—we see nothing but what God enables us to see. But the responsibility for us as teachers is to not just sit around and wait for insight, but to plan for it," Karla said. "That's the whole purpose of curriculum. Maybe we can't guarantee understanding on the part of students but we have to do all that's in our power to maximize the conditions in which this is likely to occur."

Dennis tries to draw some threads together. "Okay, we want kids to respond to what we are teaching, to be responsive in the classroom, and out of it for that matter. And we don't just want them to be responsive, we want their responding to have a certain orientation to it: we want them to be disciples of Christ, to respond in thanksgiving and service. I like the idea that one way in which we can achieve that is through play. We need to remember that God has built a rhythm of rest into his world—sleep, the sabbath, jubilee, the rest into which we will enter at last. Resting implies trusting, means recognizing that everything ultimately is God's provision for us. I think it's by giving kids the freedom to explore, to play with new ideas, to try things out—to rest, in the sense of not consciously setting out to achieve a particular goal all the time, beyond the experience itself—that we generate creativity. When we are still before the face of God, or in contemplating a painting, or just enjoying the company of another person—really deep learning can occur without us ever actually setting out to get something out of the encounter. I'm sure that's what the Westminster Confession has in mind when it talks about the calling to enjoy God."

"Well, as long as we're each putting items on the notice paper, I may as well say my piece," Patrick chimed in. "I know I probably won't get much notice taken, but I want to remind us all of the place of skill learning—and even rote learning. Sometimes we just have to focus for a time on the practice and mastery of skills. Especially at my level of the school, in the senior high school years, that's going to take up most of the time."

This gets Sam's hackles up a bit. "Sure, Pat, but even skill learning can be more interesting, more intrinsically motivating if we see it not just as repetition, not just doing the same thing over and over again. It's really trial and error-correction, where the goal is a certain sort of performance and we are continually working to correct our activity to come into line with it. It's not merely repetition, in fact, it's recognizing a problem in our performance and trying to overcome it, to bring it more in line with what we believe the performance should be. The first step then is to recognize that we do have a problem. It's really like trying to shape our activity to a predetermined design, or like a violinist trying to realize, to make real, the problem that is posed to her by a composer's score. People will put an incredible amount of energy into such learning if they recognize they are striving for a worthwhile goal. Learning to draw with perspective or to factor equations is much more significant and readily pursued if they're seen not as skills in isolation but as ways of working through problems to a solution. I don't think skill learning is as hard to explain in the problem-posing paradigm as the areas that we've talked about as play. Maybe we need to go with a 'problem plus play' paradigm."

"Well," Dennis responded, "wherever we go with that, we are all agreed that schools should be in the business of promoting 'real learning,' meaning learning that has relevance and applicability not only inside but also outside the school context, and that oftentimes we're not doing a good job of this. It's got to be learning for life. This doesn't mean that it always has to be immediately 'useful,' or even 'nonacademic' in character, it just means that the school doesn't exist in and for itself but is a preparation for life in the world."

"Right," said Sam, "we want kids to be able to apply what they have learned in school outside school as well. But I think we want them to be able not merely to apply, but also to think past and beyond what they have learned in school. We want them to be able to generate new understandings that they haven't been presented with in school. We want them to be creative and in a sense, autonomous, to be able to think for themselves."

"Well, if we want that, can we teach them the 'skills' of creativity in school—if there are such things?" Patrick finds himself somewhat surprised to be taking this tack.

A Playful Curriculum

The Christian life is one of being surprised by joy. Wherever we look, we see the miracle-working hand of our Father; whomever we see, we see the image of God. We live our lives out of gratitude to him for what he has done for us in Christ. We know that our Redeemer lives, and that he has renewed our lives, that we might live fully and abundantly in his service. The whole of our lives, in every area, has been restored, as indeed has the whole of creation. We live lives in which love has cast out all fear, and we can run now with joy, feeling God's pleasure. In Christ, we possess all spiritual blessings, the treasures of wisdom and knowledge. We can share with the stars as the children of God, singing together and shouting with joy at the wonders of his creation (Job 38:7).

This is the joy we wish to share with our children, and to do so through their schooling as through all their other experiences. The curriculum should first and foremost reflect this joy and celebration, this wonder and amazement at being alive in such a rich and vibrant world, fashioned for us as our home. We are not strangers here; we are called to rule—which means to serve—to the glory of God.

We choose the word *play* to describe this, in part because play is so often missing from the experience of our children—at least when we confront them with the "serious" things of life, such as the school curriculum. Certainly, we give them many opportunities for play at other times—perhaps too much—but we do this as a reaction to the harshness of the rest of life. Rather than a rhythmic integration of work and rest, our culture encourages an excess of joyless work and a surfeit of mindless play. We need to recover the biblical balance, in which everything we do is conceived as service to our Father, in which there is playful joy and shalom in our work done in gratitude to him and play is also part of the work we are called to do in his creation. We are to be responsive in our discipleship: there has to be a certain play in our faithfulness, as befits those made in God's image, and not a mechanical and legalistic conformism for obedience's own sake. True discipleship will be characterized not by brittleness—I have to do this because a stern and omnipotent God demands it of me—but by suppleness, a free will-ingness to please our loving Father. The yoke that we bear is light, and the life that we are saved to live is abundant.

The metaphor of play thus has for us these fundamental religious dimensions, "enjoying God and his world." But we use it to encompass a number of related dimensions as well.

From the point of view of our understanding of knowledge (chap. 7), we use it as the curricular equivalent of immersion in concrete or everyday experience. We learn as we rest in the coherence of things, as we allow ourselves to move freely (either relaxedly or intensely) among its various components. We come to know people, organizations, living rooms, dogs, language, by our ongoing exposure to them, if we are sensitively open. The curriculum should allow ample opportunities for this "playing around with creation." In educational terms, we may think of it as *broadening* experience.

Some people regard this as the aesthetic, creative, affective, imaginative domain of curriculum, one they would argue has been much neglected or denigrated in our school culture. They may see it as the realm of freedom and individuality, necessary to compensate for the overrationalization of our society. We can certainly learn much from those people who have focused their attention on these aspects of God's creation, but we must be careful to rid their observations of the distortions that enter in because they have so often—as in the romantic tradition—made these aspects the source of order and meaning.

All true understanding of God's world, and not just certain kinds of it, requires this playful engagement. This realm of play is a response to the ordinances of God, for it is in responding to these that we find blessing and joy. Would not Adam have found joy in God's revealing the animals to him, in their myriad wonderful forms? Would he not have found joy in wrapping his mouth around newly-found names for them, playing with the possibilities of language and doing his God-given work at the same time?

We have noted the charge that a curriculum according a place to the dimension of play is not a serious curriculum. On the contrary, we would argue that play is necessary if children are to make those broad connections between the various aspects of their experience that are so important to effective learning. To bring together seemingly unconnected things in playful ways—as in humor or scientific theory-building—is a productive rather than a wasteful activity, conducive to deep rather than surface learning. It encourages students to cross boundaries and to connect their learning to their everyday experience. It invites them to engage with the world in the many sides of their humanness.

Too often, in Christian schools as well, we start with material that has been cleansed of its uncertainties and ambiguities, its connection with rich real-life contexts. We "clean up" life for pedagogical purposes—perhaps too often, sterilize it. We think our task as teachers is to determine the logical structure of knowledge and then to transmit this to our students, rather than to take their hands and lead them as together we explore creation. Kuhn's (1970) account of the teaching of science applies to other areas of the curriculum as well: rather than conveying the false starts and blind alleys, the frustrations and failures, the serendipitous and surprising course of scientific discovery, we paint a picture of inexorable and tidy progress as humans apply their logical powers to unlocking the world's secrets. We might look for "applications" of this clean, conceptual structure, but we have too often lost our students at the outset.

Most distressing about this reliance on a logical structure is that we limit students' ability to experience Christ, except in terms of logical propositions, statements, or assertions, because the experience of creation in its rich many-sidedness (which would evoke a response of praise, wonder, and worship) has been transformed into a system over which we think we have control, over which we think we gain mastery.

This was the mistake of Job and his friends, or of the Preacher in Ecclesiastes. The answer comes only at the end of their texts, when their words are at an end, in the silence of standing before the face of God in awe. The answer comes also in the Song of Songs, in the enraptured immersion of the one in the life of the other, not questioning and challenging, but loving and knowing. It comes in the being, rather than the doing, because here one's dependence upon the One who gives life, rather than on one's own doing, is most pointedly underscored. It comes by annunciation, as a gift of the Holy Spirit (Taylor 1972) rather than as something to be consumed or conquered. It comes by being still before the face of God and in contemplating the works of his hands. For these works speak of him, so that in the face of them, we are without excuse, and must fall on our faces in praise, honoring him for who he is.

What this implies for curriculum design is that we include periods of play in each "lesson"—defined as any segment of teaching and learning activity with its own inner coherence, which we could remove from a sequence and replace with another segment. We might well choose to begin with such a period and to return from time to time to this playful focus. Or we might begin with a problem, posed by us or by the students, and move from there into concrete experience. In either case, we need to ensure that students have the requisite experience to enable them to be able to make sense of and meaningfully integrate the structured learning we are requiring them to do. We need either to bring their past experience into focus, or provide them with the experience—direct or vicarious—necessary as a foundation for learning.

Hamlyn (1967, 26–27) makes the point thus:

> Nothing is contributed by way of understanding when people are made to recite general propositions, even if these are fundamental to a subject. Thus, to present a very young child with, say, the general principles of number theory or algebra would be a futile business; for, he must be capable of cashing such general principles in terms which mean something to *him*, if understanding is to follow. There is in the growth of understanding of any subject an intimate connexion between principles and their applications or instances. Principles must always be seen cashed in these instances, but instances must themselves be seen as cases to which principles are relevant.

In play, we lead students in the exploration of concrete experience, of instances that will be both meaningful in themselves and significant in helping them to develop more generalized understanding. Learning involves coming to make connections in experience, so we need to ensure that there is something for students to connect. Obviously, the more mature the students, the more previous experience we have to tap into, and the more appropriate it might become to introduce learning segments with even abstract problems. But even here, if they are to integrate new with earlier learning, and theoretical insights with their everyday experience, play will be essential.

If we were developing a unit on race relations, our first step might be to draw on the students' experience by having them tell their stories about the topic. We might use a novel, short story, film, play, role play, or visiting speaker to stimulate or to follow up this exercise. We would introduce students to or remind them of the diversity of ethnic groups as part of God's post-fall creational intention. We would explore the richness that this brings to life and culture. We would use music, art, recordings, literature, film, a trip to the museum or a relevant part of town, regional cuisine, and so on to fill out their experience, to immerse them in the area in a whole-bodied way. The Mountain City teachers were pursuing such an approach. Rather than making a study of cities in general from a social science text, they were using the resource of an actual city in all its rich complexity, and were wanting their students to soak up as much of the life of the city as possible. The patterns and generalizations they gradually come to perceive would then not be abstract but content-full.

Pragmatism Revisited?

"Creativity! I think I can see where this problem-posing approach would be different from Dewey's approach. Dewey had in mind that problems could all be solved by application of the scientific method, so it was still a rationalistic model. And he also had a pragmatic understanding of knowledge, so that a solution to a problem could be determined without reference to normative principles."

The apparent similarity between a problem-posing approach and Dewey's problem-solving orientation had been bothering Cal ever since they had started to discuss the notion. He had a deep-seated conviction that a Christian school should emphasize that religion and not rationality is the defining characteristic of humanness. Talk of problems sounded too intellectual to Cal, too much like textbook math exercises that students were asked to solve, exercises that were really just analytical puzzles. His sensitivity to literature and the arts generally, to the ways of conveying truth that were not primarily analytical or theoretical, made him aware of the importance of placing the rational alongside rather than above other human faculties. Problems needed to be thought of as challenges of various kinds—aesthetic, ethical, technical, and so on—each of which was at root religious.

So, although he wanted to recognize diverse forms of truth, he was also concerned with what criteria were to be applied in determining truth. He thought that this meant always trying to take account of the fact that the world in which we live is through and through God's creation, which means that it is everywhere subject to his law. Dewey's reliance on the democratic community as the measuring stick bothered him deeply. As far as Cal was concerned, there are ways in which we ought to go and ways in which we ought not to go in every area of life, ways that are determined by God's law rather than by what merely furthers the life of the community or the satisfaction of the individual. This is why problems had always to be understood as fundamentally religious.

Patrick was beginning to get frustrated. He liked to think of himself as an eminently practical man. "Look, it's all very well to drag Dewey in and to start getting all sophisticated about this notion of what a problem is, and so on, but I have basic problems with constructing a curriculum around problems. Number one, it would be very time-consuming, much less efficient than moving through a program according to a logically determined sequence, one that takes seriously the structure of the disciplines of knowledge. It seems to me that learning is going to be much more powerful if we give kids the fundamental organizing ideas, which they can then apply in a whole range of contexts, than if we take contexts themselves as our organizing principle. What is the transfer from one problem-posing context to another going to be?"

Sue could agree with Patrick in part. She knew that the curriculum had to have a coherence and an integrity to it, so that a problem-based fragmentation did not simply replace a subject-based fragmentation. "Sure, Pat, we will want to emphasize the development of cognitive structure by kids. But we're agreed that having them merely memorize the details of the disciplines is not going to help them to do that. They can learn facts, figures, and algorithms for tests, and then promptly forget them. It happens all the time. What did that student say the other day—'Inhale it, spit it out, forget it.' What an indictment! But we are going to want them to develop rigorous and disciplined ways of approaching the world, so that they actually retain the facts, that is, know how to retrieve them and employ them when they have to. 'Knowing that' is really only a kind of 'knowing how.'"

"Well, Sue, I'm not convinced," Patrick said. "But if you take problems— let alone problems and play—as the basic organizing principle of your curriculum, what's going to provide the coherence, and the guarantee that you've actually considered all the areas that a school curriculum ought to consider? Aren't you just talking about another progressivist view of curriculum? And we know where that leads! Kids might be enjoying themselves, but will they be learning?"

"My response to that, Patrick, is that we have to come back to biblical fundamentals." Dennis has been giving the question of biblical perspective a lot of thought recently. He has begun to see his role in the school as one of calling the faculty back to this central vision. "In terms of structure, we will have to start with what Scripture says about creation. We would map out the contours of creation as we understand these in the light of a biblical world view. You know, that there are distinct structures, distinct kinds of things that God has created, like the plant and the animal kingdoms, like marriage and business, and that in each of these areas there are responses that are in conformity to God's purposes and responses that are not. Then, we would recognize that there are varying courses one can chart through experience of creation, and that we are looking largely for experiences that will promote growth in responsive discipleship."

As Dennis anticipated, Cal was in agreement. "Right on, Dennis. Our goal is not going to be Dewey's 'that which is productive of further growth' but rather, that which leads to more faithful action. Discipleship is not merely a matter of individual fancy or feelings; it's a matter of taking our place here and now in the story of God's people, in real continuity with what we know about faithfulness as this is revealed to us in Scripture and in the history of the people of God—and in the history of all people for that matter, because even Cyrus can be God's servant, or Galileo.

"If we guide students to know the world as it really is, then they will see its coherence. In the end, it's a matter of faith, a response of faith on a kid's part. The coherence of creation cannot be found within creation itself, but only in Christ. If we lead them to think the truth lies elsewhere, or if we guide them to see only fragmentation, we'd better watch out for the millstones!"

Patrick is impressed with this line of argument, but his concerns remain. "We should never forget the special nature of schools. They are places designed to promote learning, so we will want to measure everything that happens in school in terms of this goal. Not just any learning, of course, but learning that promotes discipleship. I agree, Dennis, our schools have to be places of real rigor, where students are called to the highest possible standards of which they are capable. A large part of this involves the standards that are set by the various disciplines, the languages that people have used to respond to creation."

"Sure, Pat, some of these are the languages of the disciplines, in the academic sense of subject areas," Sue said. "But some of them are disciplined in other ways, like the disciplines of musical or artistic conventions, or the disciplines of a trade, or even the discipline of loving a friend faithfully. We've agreed in our mission statement that when we talk about the promotion of learning, we have far more in mind than traditional academic learning. But you're right, everything in a school has to promote the goal of learning for discipleship. That's why we spend so much time working on the curriculum."

"Okay, Sue, but whatever the area, we have to work within the established boundaries as far as possible, or at least when we wish to diverge from these, we have to demonstrate very good grounds for doing so. There is a continuity of story in the human endeavor, a community of understanding that ought to be maintained, because we have been created to live in community. The disciplines are really just one part of this community of discourse."

Dennis is reminded of another basic component of the school's vision, and takes the opportunity to promote it. "If we are going to stress community, we need to remember that we are members of two communities, and that these can sometimes, or maybe often, function at cross-purposes. I mean, we have our solidarity with all people in Adam, but we also have our solidarity more specifically with those who are members of the body of Christ. I suppose it's really a matter of being attuned to the spiritual direction that is at work in particular contexts, so that we stand with when we should and also stand apart when we should. If we draw from the disciplines, we are going to need to give them our own peculiar twist, because they have been developed in the main in secularized contexts, and often according to explicitly secular principles. It's not a matter of being distinctive for the sake of distinctiveness. It's a matter of being faithful to the truth. Sometimes that will mean we're in agreement with the consensus in a discipline, and sometimes we'll be in disagreement. But it does mean that we can't take the disciplines at face value. We need to remember that we're not just dealing with objective knowledge. Here, like everywhere else, there are distortions at work, often quite subtly."

The Problem-Posing Curriculum

Through our playing around in God's world, our knowledge is *broadened* and enriched. But in the problems posed *to* creation by us and *by* us to creation (in a moment of *withdrawal*), our knowledge is *deepened*. As we focus on the world in a particular way—ethically, economically, theoretically, technically, and so on—we stand over against creation in ways that will actually change our experience of it. A problem-posing curriculum is one that plans for this new way of seeing and being in the world as a continuous process. A couple of examples will help to make this clearer.

The first is the ACME Crew Project, a nine-week unit for high school students integrating the academic and vocational curriculums (Beck, Copa, and Pease 1991). This began with a scenario (the period of play that in this instance provides a meaningful context) about a family furniture business that was losing its share of the market to imported furniture. In response to this problem, students and teachers from economics, wood technology, and family and consumer economics classes decided to develop, produce, and market a new line of shelves. Teachers acted in their normal roles, drawing on their expertise as specialists, and also as business consultants, helping students deal with such practical problems of work life as compensation, equity, performance review, risk-taking, and cooperation.

It is worth noting that teachers recognized the inherent challenge to their teaching philosophies. One commented, "Kids are asking real questions. It will be hard for some teachers to let go and let kids seek and discover knowledge" (Beck, Copa, and Pease 1991, 31). This is of course both the risk and the reward of teaching in a problem-posing way. Teachers can never comprehensively predict the issues that are going to be raised or the paths that will need to be explored. Teachers must be prepared to give up some of their control and power in order to empower and enable their students.

207

This is how Beck and colleagues reported the project. But we will do some further imagining about the range of problems with which students might have dealt in this context.

We have to decide what the shelves will look like. What timber will we use? What would have an interesting grain? What would be strong but relatively inexpensive? Are the shelves going to be painted? How do we go about raising capital? Are the girls going to be involved in doing the actual building? Who's going to do the drafting? How do we decide what to do with the profits? Should we distribute them evenly among the workers? How much should the investors get? What about contributions to needy people—do we have a responsibility there? Should we be allowed to play the radio while we're working? How long should our breaks be? What safety measures should be observed in the production process? What does it mean to be a faithful steward in this context? Is the timber that we are using going to last as long in the shelves as it would take to replace it by growing the necessary trees? Are we taking advantage of the unique features of the timber—its beauty, or its ability to bear stress? Are we responsible to replace the trees we have used or is that someone else's responsibility? Who should make the decisions—should we all be involved, or just the management? How do we calculate the amount of timber we need to order? How do we decide how much to order in terms of possible economy of scale—what if we buy too much because it's cheaper per unit to do so but then can't sell most of it? Should we build shelves with doors? What have been some different designs for shelves and bookcases at different times and in different places? How should we advertise the shelves—what would be an honest but still appealing way to inform people about these shelves and their strengths and weaknesses?

Clearly, the range of problems that can be explored in such a unit is both wide and rich, requiring the practice of many of the skills and understandings that might be addressed in a traditional curricular framework but in a much more "real-life," concrete way. Gifts will be unwrapped, students will have to work cooperatively, and they will be called at each step along the way to reflect on how their decisions reflect a commitment to shalom, to stewardship and justice in God's kingdom.

Another project—a joint one between applied mathematics and business management teachers—focused on the viability of a proposed Frisbee golf course; teachers thought this might be a valuable recreational resource for teenagers in the community.

The unit emphasized statistical applications and analysis. Students collected two types of data. Using a Frisbee accuracy range, they gathered data for different distances and angles for the course and effects of student characteristics such as left/right handedness, age and grade level. They also conducted market research with fellow students. Students entered the data into the database and graphing functions of Apple-Works™. With the computer at the intersection, mathematics students took the direction of learning the statistical concepts, and the business management students moved in the direction of analysis. The final products were videotaped impact statements and a decision not to build a Frisbee golf course. (Beck, Copa, and Pease 1991, 30)

We can see once again that such a unit could have a much broader application than the teachers involved chose to give it, although even so it illustrates the ways in which mathematical and accounting skills and concepts can be explored in more concrete, meaningful contexts than is usually the case. Issues of recreation, physical fitness, competition, and the aesthetic appearance of the proposed course come to mind as areas that could also be explored, all in the context of what it would mean to respond faithfully to the Lord's intentions for shalom-filled human life.

A student production of a play or the design and construction of housing for Habitat for Humanity (as already undertaken by a number of Christian schools) are another couple of examples of problem-rich contexts in which students can play around purposefully. In producing a play, for instance, there are aesthetic problems (the design of costumes and sets, the color of lighting, the choice of make-up), technical problems (set construction, lighting control, acoustics), economic problems (cost of hiring lights and other equipment, admission charges, time taken away from other activities), literary problems (interpreting the text), social problems (both those raised in the text and those that arise as a group works together for an extended period), and the central problems of drama and language. Again, in such a context, students would need to learn to work cooperatively with each other, they would unwrap their various gifts, and they would be faced time and again with the question of what is a faithful way to proceed. Teachers would help them to discern these challenges, drawing on insights from their special knowledge of the disciplines and their own life wisdom, and confronting them with the demands of Scripture.

The teacher's responsibility in such a context is to pose problems quite directly to the students, to guide them to see problems of which they might not otherwise be aware, and to help them to pose problems themselves. It is important however that the teacher's posing of problems does not degenerate into an endless routine of exercises for students to complete. The problems must be real for the students, not merely the opportunity to show off certain skills. And a teacher might well measure success in terms of the extent to which students themselves become generators of problems. When students approach a teacher and ask whether concession tickets should be available, whether the stage hands should also take a bow, whether everybody ought to have the opportunity to take an actor's role, whether a scene should really be played as the author wrote it, given what the Bible says about edifying behavior or the potential dramatic impact of a scene, the teacher has cause to be pleased. Real learning is taking place.

A powerful strategy for promoting problem-posing is "Predict, Observe, Explain (P.O.E.)," in which students are presented with a situation and have to make a written prediction, with supporting reasons, about what will happen next or when a particular action is taken (Baird and Mitchell 1987). They record what does happen, and if this differs from their prediction, they try to give a revised explanation. P.O.E. can be used equally well in reading a novel, exploring a historical event, or investigating phenomena scientifically.

A related strategy is to invite students to write their questions about a particular topic at the beginning of a lesson. These may be written on index cards, perused by the teacher, and then placed in a central location, to be collected as students think they have been answered; not only does this help to orient the teacher to student concerns and to keep students in an enquiring frame of mind during the lesson, but the cards remaining at the end can serve as a starting point for future lessons. Various strategies should be employed to train students to ask good questions, such as asking every student to write one question beginning with "Why does . . . ?" and another starting with "What if . . . ?" Teachers may set a passage for reading, and offer to explain only in response to student questions.

A playful, problem-posing curriculum is necessarily oriented to practice, but it is thoughtful rather than mindless practice. Students are not just practicing skills; they are encouraged to be reflective practitioners. The kinds of understanding that they would normally explore in a traditional curriculum—computation, use of language, historical background, qualities of natural materials and of sound and light, for example—will also be explored here, but within a richer and thus more meaningful context. Connections will be made, both across subject areas and with their own experience, and more fruitful learning, reflecting the interconnectedness of creation, will be possible.

The nature of the problems that are posed, and the time spent in exploring them, will vary from one developmental level to another. In grade one, the teacher may challenge students to form the letter *q*, or will set up a number of learning centers with various problems to solve: Will it float? How can I divide these objects into two categories? What shapes can I make from these pieces? Problems such as these are challenging to students of this age, as so much in the world is still new to them. At higher levels of schooling, the problems will be more complex: perhaps the problems of male-female relationships as presented in a novel or those of environmental degradation confronted close at hand and further afield. Problems may also become more abstract, within the limits of a subject area, but it will be best if these too emerge from and are reintegrated into concrete problem-contexts.

Teachers should employ strategies that will help students to be metacognitive. These could include asking them to identify what the main task for the lesson was, what the purpose of an activity was, and what they think should be done next. Students should be encouraged regularly to reflect on their own progress, through a journal or a weekly assignment. Monitoring questions can be inserted in tests ("Have you used the correct tense throughout this passage of translation?") and procedural checklists can be completed before submitting assignments ("I have checked that I have answered every part of the question." "I have used the required form for the references").

Purposeful Responding

Problem-posing facilitates effective learning, in a way that respects the responsible freedom of persons made in the image of God. It calls students to choose to respond, and to do so in ways that are faithful to God's intentions for his creatures. It takes seriously that the creation in all its concrete complexity is turned to us as revelation, and that we are to seek to listen to the voice of God as he speaks to us.

This problem-posing approach does not exclude direct teaching via the lecture and the chalkboard, nor will it rule out sustained attention from time to time to skill development. But its pervasive rhythm will call students to "consider, choose and commit" (Oppewal 1984). It will invite a purposeful response, challenging them to say yes to the good in creation, no to the evils that sin has wrought, and the "Amen" of Christ to the healing that can be accomplished.

Thus, curriculum planning will not be content only to *raise* problems. As responsible guides of our students, we will be concerned that they learn to *respond purposefully* to problems. This does not assume the application of a particular method to *solve* problems. There is no such guaranteed method for most complex problems and we will also be seeking to encourage a range of responses to problems in accord with the variety of students' gifts.

Scripture proclaims to us the purpose and purposefulness all of life, in a creation ordered and sustained by God. We cannot accept the view that we are adrift in a world of confusion, where nothing can be done to move toward shalom. Instead, we will lead our students to respond in hope, claiming the redemption that Christ has wrought and acting to bring healing. We cannot coerce this response, because it has to be given freely from the heart. But we trust that the Holy Spirit is working to call forth this response from his people, and that our privilege as teachers is to serve as his agents, witnessing to Christ's lordship in all things.

Knowledge drawn from the subject areas should inform teachers' decisions about the kind of responses to problems that are on target—when aesthetic or economic criteria are more significant, or when to use Pythagoras' theorem or quadratic equations. Students should not be asked to reinvent the wheel, though they will hopefully develop a greater insight into why the wheel was necessary in the first place and what purposes it can serve. The "standards of excellence" embodied in the disciplines will also be maintained, though the proving ground for academic learning is a much closer approximation to the complexity of out-of-school problem-solving than are the normal devices of tests and quizzes.

In the ACME Crew Project, students were asked to wrestle with a wide range of problems. These problems had to be considered one by one and in their complex relatedness, as students decided how to act. As teachers helped students to focus on these problems and as they guided students to act thoughtfully and carefully, with clear intentions, they called students to respond purposefully. The students were not merely required to complete a task because of an agenda established for them by the teachers, they were invited to take responsibility for their own learning and actions. They were called to respond to God's ordinances for stewardly use of resources, to the God-given properties of the timber as they worked the grain, to their God-ordained obligations to their neighbors, near and far. In all of this, they had the opportunity to learn that all of life comprises moment-by-moment decisions of how (and whether) to act in faithful response to God—that life, in its entirety, is religion. The most purposeful response that can be made is that of the disciple, responding in grateful obedience to the Lord.

Conclusion

The model presented in this chapter is suggested as one way of implementing the principles of an integral curriculum, outlined in chapter 7. The emphasis is on active engagement of students in their learning. They are not merely the passive recipients of information or the robotic reproducers of skills, but take responsibility for forming their own understanding and abilities. They are respected as persons, images of God, and not treated as animals or machines. They are called to be *responsive disciples*, and are prepared for real-life decision-making by learning in real-life contexts.

Second, there are real learning opportunities for students of all kinds of ability and interest. The slices of creation that are explored are sufficiently rich as to allow students both to be challenged in a variety of ways and to contribute in a variety of ways. There are many different kinds of problems embedded in the areas of study, not only theoretical problems, but also aesthetic and stewardship problems, ethical and technical problems. There is a host of opportunities for *unwrapping gifts*.

Third, because both students and teachers have many more opportunities to work together, they are more able to recognize their interdependence, *sharing one another's joys and bearing one another's burdens*.

Finally, the concrete and appropriately complex problems that teachers invite students to address allow for a ready consideration of religious, normative issues. They are encouraged to be *seekers of shalom*, searching out paths of action that will bring the healing power of Christ to bear, both now and in the future.

We hope that this chapter has given you a "forceful idea" that can help you to evaluate the curriculum structure of your school in biblical perspective. In the next chapter, we will address the question of determining the overall program for the school, before returning in more detail to strategies for devising units of instruction at the classroom level. We trust that in these and other chapters of the book, you will also find "a small place to begin."

Questions for Discussion

1. Do you think that the play, problem-posing, purposeful responding model reflects a biblical view of knowing and learning? What
strengths and weaknesses do you see in the model from this
perspective?

2. What opportunities do you see in the model for curriculum design
in your school? What do you see as the limitations of the model
as a guide for practice, and how would you correct these?

3. A major argument for organizing the curriculum in integral units
(the model described in this chapter being one way of doing this)
is that it enables teachers and students to confront the religious
(What is the source of order and meaning?) issues and the normative (How *should* I act?) issues more readily than a subject-
based or integrated curriculum. In what ways do you think the
model would be helpful in highlighting issues of religious perspective and faithful service?

4. In what ways could the model be adapted for use within a subject-
based curriculum structure?

5. What opportunities are there in your school for teams to work on
curriculum development? What organizational changes could
you make to facilitate this?

6. Does your school have a systematic approach to writing up curriculum? Is someone in your school responsible for oversight of
this? Are funds set aside specifically for this purpose? Does your
school have, for example, curriculum writing grants for summer
projects?

7. What mechanisms does your school have in place to ensure that
the whole school community is involved in curriculum development? In what ways are teachers accountable for their curriculum development?

Recommended Reading

1. Walker, D. F., and Soltis, J. F. 1986. *Curriculum and aims.*
A good general introduction to the influence of educational values on conceptions of curriculum.
2. Eisner, E. W. 1979. *The educational imagination.*

An important critique of traditional perspectives.

3. Freire, P. 1972. *Pedagogy of the oppressed.*
   A major source for the notion of a problem-posing pedagogy. Difficult to read but worth struggling with, in a critical frame of mind.

4. Blomberg, D. G. 1980. "Curriculum guidelines for the Christian school."
   Develops the idea of an "integral, problem-posing" curriculum for Christian schools.

5. Fowler, S., ed., Van Brummelen, H., and Van Dyk, J., 1990. *Christian schooling: Education for freedom.*
   Van Brummelen, H. 1988. *Walking with God in the classroom.*
   These books explore many ideas that are complementary to those discussed in this chapter.

9

How Do We Decide What to Teach?

Are Textbooks the Answer?

"Hi, Ted! It's sure nice to see you here!" Linda Clements spotted Ted as she stood in the lineup for lunch at a conference on the teaching of social studies at Mountain City State College. Linda is the teacher of a combined grade five/six class at a small Christian school one hour's drive from Mountain City. Linda continued, "I'm really thankful that I was given today off to attend these sessions. After teaching for a year and a half, I needed some fresh ideas. You know, I struggle to keep up with all the work, and our small staff just doesn't seem to have time to discuss anything but the nuts and bolts of who has playground duty or who will look after coffee for parent-teacher interviews."

"Let's sit at that small table at the side," Ted suggested, "and compare notes on this morning's sessions." Both Linda and Ted had attended the workshops on the use of classroom resources. Ted said, "My workshop leader showed very clearly how textbook knowledge represents messages about our present society and what those who pull the political strings want the future to look like. Do you remember how Paul Vitz a few years ago criticized American textbooks for deliberately cutting out all references to faith and religion? Well, that may be changing with California, for instance, now insisting that textbooks must address America's Christian heritage. But I'm starting to see that there are much deeper problems with textbooks that can't be solved with some additions about religion. I heard once again this morning that seventy-five percent of what happens in classrooms depends either directly or indirectly on textbooks. That means they have tremendous power in controlling teachers—and, consequently, in affecting the minds of our children. The so-called rational decisions made by textbook publishers are anything but neutral!"

Linda responded, "I remember one of my college profs emphasizing that textbook content not only influences the beliefs, values, and attitudes of students, but also the ways in which they learn. But I'm so busy just keeping up from day to day that I've given it little thought as I teach. I'd like to implement some of your approaches at Central Station, but I seem to be forced back to using the one class set of textbooks I have for each major subject. Our library is the pits, our district public library is ten miles down the road in the next town, and I don't have the time or money to provide other resources. Yet I know that the textbooks limit what I'd like to do."

Ted rejoined, "I heard this morning that the concept of text is not limited to print resources. For instance, the texts students use today include audio tapes, videos, and computer software. But the prevailing knowledge promoted in such school texts is usually based on a world view at odds with our Christian one. And that, it seems to me, is true both because of the content and the type of pedagogy implicit in them."

"But if that is so," Linda asked, "how can a teacher like myself provide effective Christ-centered education in her classroom? Parents sacrifice a great deal to send their children to our school, and I believe I guide students to look at issues from a Christian point of view, but almost all my resources are secular. Moreover, the handful of Christian textbooks we have available may have the right perspective, but they're not always well written and seldom pay attention to pedagogy. And the few software programs I have for the computer in my classroom use such flagrantly behavioristic approaches to learning that they are suitable mainly for drill reinforcement. As you can tell," she grinned, "I'm rather frustrated."

"It seems to me that the key is that we keep on analyzing resources for their basic values, for how they view the world and how they view humans and their calling—including whether they treat students as responsive images of God in the way they structure learning," Ted answered. "We can then use the text as a tool, not as a master. Even in your case, you have personal resources in the classroom and around the school—yourself, your students, your parents, your surroundings—that you can draw on in your learning activities. As you get more experience and discover how to use those resources and build up your personal bank of integral units, you'll likely find that you need the 'official' textbooks less and less."

They spent the rest of their lunch hour exploring ideas on how Linda could do this. Linda's surprise encounter with Ted became, for her, the most valuable part of the conference.

Textbooks promote conformity. Produced for a mass market, they must satisfy the lowest common denominator of expectations. Effectively, they must be able to sell in California and Texas or they will fail commercially.

Conformity is reinforced by textbook-based teaching but also by many other assumptions about what schools should look like. Sizer (1985, 5–6) found a stunning uniformity in his study of high schools:

> This big country contains numerous educational jurisdictions, with authority decentralized. Nonetheless, as one visits communities one is gradually struck by how *similar* the structure and articulated purpose of American high schools are. Rural schools, city schools; rich schools, poor schools; public schools, private schools; big schools, little schools: the *framework* of grades, schedules, calendar, courses of study, even rituals, is astonishingly uniform and has been so for at least forty years. In most schools, I visited biology and social studies classes, and I could soon predict the particular topics under study during a given month in Bio I or U.S. History, whatever the school. While the texts had different covers and authors, their commonness was stunning. . . . High school is a kind of secular church, a place of national rituals that mark stages of a young citizen's life. The value of its rites appears to depend on national consistency.

The issue of content selection is obviously closely related to that of textbooks. Are Christian schools generally successful in breaking out of the mold of North American education and in designing programs that reflect the distinctives of their faith? Or are they marked by conformism and compromise with the surrounding culture (Wagner 1990), demanding conformity from their students as well? You will have to make that judgment for your own school.

Linda's and Ted's discussion highlights two issues Christian teachers need to address with respect to curriculum resources. First, what are the common world-view-related biases in textbooks and other resources and how can Christian teachers capitalize on an awareness of this as they use them? Second, how can learning activities incorporate classroom resources to help students become thoughtful, responsive disciples rather than being uncritical assimilators? To answer the first question we will briefly consider the predominant nature of textbook content; for the second, we will give some suggestions that relate to issues we will explore further in the following chapter.

Van Brummelen (1991) analyzed the content of Canadian elementary textbooks, and most of his conclusions appear to apply to resources in the United States as well. Today's textbook authors, he claims, promote a consumer-oriented, self-reliant individualism (even in the choice of a large proportion of word problems in mathematics!). The authors assume that long-term change, rooted in technology and in our economic system, is inevitably positive.

Individualism is the view that it is individuals choosing to do things together for common social and economic advantage that leads to the formation of institutions and groups. A family, for instance, is a convenient grouping of people living together to promote self-interest—but the individuals within the family are autonomous. The theme that recurs time and again is that "everything is possible when I am me." There is no recognition, let alone encouragement, of scriptural norms for family life or of the fruit of the Spirit embodied by concepts such as humility and compassion.

While the Golden Rule as well as the need for obedience to the law are not totally disregarded, students are seldom faced with situations where they consider serious moral and social problems. Textbook authors present a superficial morality that, they feel, will not be controversial. As a result, they fail to deal with the need for making long-term commitments in life or developing dispositions on the basis of well-defined values. As long as we try to work hard to earn money, we can all fit comfortably into our current Western way of life. The serious consequences of sin such as wastefulness, injustice, discrimination, immorality, and family and social breakdown are neglected. Students are spurred to choose their own values; Christmas, for instance, means "what you make of it." Christian faith, if mentioned at all, is shown in a truncated and often negative light, and the role of religion as a way of encountering the fundamental mysteries of life is absent.

In short, textbook content contributes to the promotion of shortsighted technological, economic, and personal interests without promoting the essential shared commitments and moral and religious obligations so necessary for life.

Textbooks and other resources, therefore, need to be used critically in Christian school settings. Teachers must make selections carefully, whether that be sections in social studies or science textbooks, or the materials used for a personalized reading program. They have to help students evaluate rather than blindly accept what they read.

There are various strategies that may be employed to achieve this. As they get older, students may be asked to respond to textbook content in a textbook journal, rather than just requiring them to write summaries in their notes. Teachers should explore the underlying value perspectives in print and other resources, encouraging students to discern how these themes harmonize with or oppose a Christian world view. It is also important to identify the perspectives and questions that are not acknowledged. In short, teachers should select texts judiciously and use them in such a way that students become aware of intrinsic biases. Van Brummelen (1988, 129–30) gives a set of questions to help teachers plan effective use of classroom resources.

There is a second dimension to the use of resources. Text resources, as Ted pointed out to Linda, must be learning tools, not masters. Yet especially textbooks are surrounded by an aura: they are considered truth-giving authorities from which we passively learn flat, factual assertions. Their impersonal and objective tone encourages a feeling that they are above criticism; as Luke, de Castell, and Luke (1989, 255–56) have shown, textbooks have served as educational icons to be revered, not anthologies of challenging ideas to be played with. They are structured to convey information rather than to promote problem-posing and critical thinking.

While today's textbooks pay more attention to pedagogical concerns than in the past, perhaps suggesting a variety of learning activities, the structure of the text and the nature of the recommended activities often implicitly assume that the teacher will believe that "the textbook knows best." Fortunately, most teachers intuitively as well as purposefully emphasize and deemphasize, select and exclude (Luke, de Castell, and Luke 1989, 252). Many teachers give running commentaries and interpretations on textual content. Yet the overall configuration of the textbook too often circumscribes how teaching and learning proceed in the classroom.

Having the textbook determine the pattern of learning is a trap that teachers fall into effortlessly, particularly when, like Linda, they find it difficult to find the time to fulfill all their teaching responsibilities. But it is a trap, nevertheless. Teachers as responsive disciples are called to determine, individually and communally, the knowledge of God's world and the social issues to be studied, in the context of an evaluation of the needs of their students. Resources should be chosen to fit our intentions, rather than themselves determining these intentions. Preferably, this would involve more than just a class set of a particular textbook. Of course, sometimes we may have to alter our original plans because resources essential for some aspects of a unit are unavailable. The text-book tail, however, must not wag the curriculum dog.

In her situation, Linda's curriculum would differ from Ted's at Central Station Middle School. Nevertheless, Linda can also gradually work toward using her textbooks as only one of a number of instruments in her resource repertoire. She can adapt and develop integral, Christian units for her particular situation. She can actively collect free and inexpensive text resources, involving her students and using their own thinking and writing. She can choose learning activities that help students become discerning users of texts and that make increasing use of material and human resources other than her textbooks. In this way Linda will take ownership of her teaching and ensure that the Christian perspective she cherishes is not undermined by the biases of her texts. The teacher is a servant leader who guides; the text becomes a tool that furthers her intentions.

Programs for Diversity or Conformity?

It was nearly the end of May when Mountain City Christian School held its annual society meeting. Such events were usually not earth-shaking. Besides a devotional led by the president of the school board, reports by the principal and some of the assistants, some singing by the audience spiced with a "special number" by the choir, band, or theatrical group, and the approval of the new budget, there was usually little to discuss further—unless someone introduced something controversial.

That's exactly what happened this year. The Reverend Marshall Barton, pastor of Malachi Baptist Church, one of the fastest growing in Mountain City, was invited to lead in devotions.

Rev. Barton and his wife have three children, two of whom are in Mountain City Christian. One is in the fourth grade, and one in the fifth. They are among the few minority children enrolled. At least a dozen of the children from Rev. Barton's church do attend Central Station downtown; it's a little closer to the neighborhood where many of Malachi's members live. But most are enrolled at local public schools; none of them attends Mountain City Christian High. Rev. Barton is not happy with this, but he knows that before this would change, some things at the school would have to change.

In his devotional, Rev. Barton decided to raise some questions about the very theology that he knew his audience held dear. He referred to Matthew 19:14, Psalm 78, and Deuteronomy 6. But instead of accenting the "for us and our children" theme, Rev. Barton broadened these accents with an appeal to the missionary mandate of Matthew 28:19 and 20, "Therefore go and make disciples of all nations . . . teaching them to obey everything I have commanded you."

So this pastor of a burgeoning church tried to show, with a zeal and an intensity not often found at annual meetings, that when one links Genesis 12:3 ("all peoples on earth will be blessed through you") with Matthew 28:19, and applies them to Christian schooling, one may well be struck by the gap between the promise and the reality. "Christian schools," he said with jarring realism, "have tended to become inward directed, elitist, provincial, and separatist." Rev. Barton really created an enormous hush over his by now spell-bound audience when he proposed climactically that Christian schools ought to broaden their outreach and in fact "specialize in marginal, hard-to-reach, learning impaired, and poor children!"

Rev. Barton was not engaged in special pleading. He wasn't suggesting that the children of Malachi Baptist were educationally marginal, or underachievers, and that Mountain City should make concessions for his special learners. He was, instead, simply and earnestly pushing the unusual implications of several familiar passages of Scripture. For when, a week later, Pastor Barton was invited by Principal Ken Heard to speak to the faculty and clarify some of his remarks, Pastor Barton explained that he had a broader range of diversity in mind than first appeared.

"When I visit Mountain City Christian, and even Central Station for that matter, I see mostly white people, of middle- and upper-middle-class status, of largely similar Northern European ethnic origins, with little denominational diversity beyond subtle shades of difference within a conservative Protestantism. At the least, I think that many more denominations ought to be represented. Beyond this, I wonder whether we have a calling to serve even those students who do not yet know the Lord Jesus. And one step further: I firmly believe that the Word challenges us to ethnic and racial diversity as well. And I am quite certain that increasing diversity would also mean enrolling more students with physical, communication, and behavioral disorders and students with learning disabilities."

But he had something else in mind, too. He was convinced that somehow the total educational program, in class and out of class, ought to take account of a greater variety of gifts than was presently the case. Pastor Barton was sure that the nub of the issue had to do with defining gifts in a Christian school setting.

Ken Heard succinctly summarized Pastor Barton's remarks for the faculty: "Given diversity of such magnitude, what curricular and other organizational changes should be made at Mountain City to accommodate greater varieties of learners?" In doing so, Ken reminded his teachers of a line from the contemporary testimony "Our World Belongs to God"—that "in education we seek . . . schools and teaching where students, of whatever ability, are treated as persons who bear God's image and have a place in his plan."

The faculty had plenty to think about at the close of the school year, and Ken reminded them that he would soon appoint a committee to address some of the issues that Rev. Barton had helped raise, in the context of a broader evaluation of the school's program.

September

The committee that Ken Heard assembled began meeting in the fall of the new school year. They were given at least a year to come up with some recommendations. The members included Rob Boonstra, chair of the Education Committee, serving as co-chair with Valerie Lavigne, the assistant principal of the high school, a highly organized person known for her ability to move things along. Also serving were Rev. Greg Fouts, the high school Bible teacher; Geoff Schmidt, the veteran chemistry teacher; Cal Holbrook, a middle school English teacher; Sam Freeland, from the Central Station faculty and a member of Malachi Baptist, along with three parent representatives. Ken Heard and Karla Hubbard, the head teacher at Central Station, served ex officio.

The committee was given a mandate to advise the school board about curricular changes that might have to be made at Mountain City, not just to meet the possibility of increased student diversity, but to stimulate it.

Discussion quickly raised all sorts of issues.

"I wonder whether changing the composition of the student body, particularly in the direction that Pastor Barton suggested, would mean lowering academic standards?" one parent asked.

"Well, I'm concerned that additional attention would have to be given to remediation, and that this would detract from efforts spent on enrichment activities for the academically talented," suggested another.

Cal Holbrook asked about the meaning of the terms curriculum and program. "How extensive is our mandate as a committee? Does curriculum refer only to content of courses, and could it refer to how courses are organized in relation to each other? Does it refer to instructional methods as well as content?"

Greg Fouts, who had recently returned to his alma mater to finish a master's program in counseling, suggested that the committee's study of curriculum could get pretty "heavy" if the committee chose to dig too far into the matter. "After all, curriculum should ideally be something practical, a plan of action. But we can't avoid asking questions such as, What does it mean to be human? Who is the learner? What is education for? How should demands coming from society shape the curricular choices that we make?"

Valerie Lavigne, sensing that attempting to answer all these questions would take more time than the committee had to give, urged them to read the school's mission statement again. "It tries to answer many of the 'big questions' that Greg has raised. I think we need to look at the organizational and programmatic changes that might happen in the school, though I really have no idea what these might be."

Rob Boonstra, soon supported by Sam Freeland, suggested that, "Whatever tack the committee takes, it must think people, students. Teaching," said Rob rather eloquently, "must always face students, must answer to their needs."

Sam took up Valerie's reference to the mission statement. He reminded his listeners that their schools, both at the main campus and at Central Station, were supposed to be about the task of responsive discipleship. "I feel that Central Station faculty has taken that idea very seriously and has already instituted a number of constructive changes, but I'm not convinced that the faculty at Mountain City is too eager to do the same."

At that point, Geoff Schmidt reminded the committee of some of the handouts that Ken Heard had prepared for its meetings. "Usually, when educators want to decide what ought to be included in a school's program, they lay down certain criteria by which the choices—this goes in, this stays out—are made. I think that the focus we are looking for can definitely be found in our mission statement. We are dedicated to working out the meaning of responsive discipleship. Therefore, the committee needs to create a curricular blueprint that meets two challenges. The first is to try to increase the diversity of the student population, which I think will require us to deepen our understanding of giftedness. The second is to develop a program which will engage students more effectively with what they are learning, a program that is more in touch with the real world than the fact-based approach of most of our texts and subject outlines. Discipleship means action that is faithful to the Lord Jesus; that can't be achieved by just soaking up information."

Rob Boonstra closed with a prayer of thanks after the group decided to meet once a month until they had formulated a concrete proposal.

October

Meanwhile, in anticipation of the next meeting of the committee, Valerie Lavigne invited Karla Hubbard to prepare a report that outlined the program and accompanying structural changes that Karla had introduced at Central Station.

Karla leaped at the opportunity. She had felt all along that Mountain City faculty and some of the administrators had really paid little attention to Central Station, for whatever reason. Here was her chance to be heard.

Her report was lengthy and detailed. Some of the more unusual features of Central Station's program included these developments:

1. Since nothing important was going to happen unless teachers have time to plan together, Karla first instituted a faculty planning period every Wednesday afternoon from 2:30 to 4:00.
2. While the faculty was meeting, the students were engaged in a variety of service projects, some of which were linked to agencies in the neighborhood of the school, others of which arose from the needs at Central Station itself. For example, some students ministered to elderly people in a nearby rest home, some aided children at a day-care center, some interacted with people with mental or physical disabilities (some of whom were at a local public school, some enrolled at Central Station), or did some coaching with peers or younger children. It took some organizational skills to pull this off with approximately seventy-five students, but a parent volunteer headed the service program and a number of others provided transportation.

   Good as this system was, Karla reported that her staff thought it could be improved if these activities and the discipling perspective behind them were linked with the other courses rather than functioning as a separate component. The faculty was now working on trying to make that happen more consistently throughout the curriculum.
3. Karla went on to explain that when Central Station first began, the "explicit curriculum" was comprised of five strands: the humanities, science and mathematics, fine arts, practical arts, and biblical studies. But she and her staff had been shaping this in some unusual ways.

For example, early on the staff developed a series of exploratory courses. They could vary in size such that some might be taught once a day for two weeks, for six, or for nine; others for one class period twice a week for six weeks, and so on. Some of the courses were required, some were elective. But all of them gave the student an introduction to a wide variety of areas (like photography, furniture refinishing, aerobics, bicycling, macramé, cooking, current events, bee-keeping, outdoor education, newspaper writing, and local history) that seemed particularly appealing to young adolescents.

However, these mini-courses, like the service component, were an "add-on" to the regular, solid, "respected" curriculum. Karla and her staff saw that as another challenge and wondered what changes they could make.

Her staff also developed a theme week where for five full days the entire school would attend to a single topic. They chose "Earthkeeping" the first time, and since have tried "Christian Self-Awareness." The theme week incorporated a variety of activities that led eventually to products by all students, including creating something that had to be written, something that had to be acted out, and something that had to be constructed or drawn, thereby appealing to a variety of gifts in each learner but within a sense of commonality (Stronks 1990).

Karla indicated that, given the small size of her staff, theme weeks tended to stretch the competence and interests of the teachers to the limit. She was also beginning to wonder whether they in fact detracted from more full-scale reform of the curriculum. She had seen other schools where theme weeks not only tired teachers, but also left them with the feeling that they had done all the innovation that was required or possible.

Karla then explained that she and her staff were considering moving even more deeply into a commitment to integrality in curriculum. A couple of her teachers had proposed a unit on "Growing Old" (Stronks 1990) in which, as a team and using a large block of time several days a week, they would draw from a variety of studies. In the context of ongoing contact with elderly people, they would focus on problems that they felt young adolescents ought to know about and have some empathy for. These problems included, for example: Do you think the elderly should have the right to die when they wish? What happens to cells when they grow old? What can you find out about the effects of aging on intelligence and other mental processes? How many people now inhabit the earth? Formulate a year's budget for a person over sixty-five taking into account Social Security benefits. Study a collection of photographs of elderly people; what did the camera "see" in these people? How are the elderly portrayed in the history of art? How are older persons typically portrayed in magazines, in popular literature, in movies, on TV? What kinds of attitudes toward the elderly are being expressed in your own homes? How do you perceive the elderly?

In the exploration of these problems, teachers would guide students to purposeful responses, helping to flesh out what it meant to love these elderly neighbors as themselves. Karla suggested that such a unit would be linked to the services that an eighth-grade class could perform for the elderly—visiting them in their homes, cleaning sidewalks, cutting the grass, or washing windows; or visiting the elderly in rest homes, reading to them and playing games with them: "adopting a grandparent" in effect. This would achieve an even greater curricular coherence.

The committee was impressed, especially with Karla's explanation of how Central Station was able to use the civic resources of Mountain City. These included its library, museums, art gallery, halls of justice, jail, rescue missions, coffee houses, concert halls, and a host of others. Nonetheless, some members of the committee were stimulated to ask a few searching questions.

One of the parents wanted to know: "What happens to the fundamental skills in reading, writing, and calculating that all students must master if one takes this experiential education seriously?"

Greg Fouts asked, "If we were to play down the disciplines in favor of a more integrated curriculum, will the colleges and universities accept our students?"

Geoff Schmidt, reflecting (without sharing) faculty opinions he had recently overhead, asked, "If by the year 2000 our country is supposed to become first in the world in math and science, wouldn't such a curriculum actually work against such a goal?"

Ken Heard laid this one on the table: "We have parents who will support our school as long as the curriculum maintains a rigorous academic flavor. But if we move in this direction, I dare say some of them will be prompted to abandon the ship."

And from Rev. Fouts came this: "Look, many of us are part of a Christian tradition that has had a high regard for the intellect, for analytic rational abilities, for a systematic approach to achieving a knowledge of reality. For example, we've always demanded a highly educated clergy, and, in addition, we've always desired an educated parishioner, one alert and alive to sound doctrine. Schools and colleges and seminaries of learning are needed, we've said, to carry out the biblical command to cultivate the earth and exercise stewardship. Isn't a move in the curricular direction that Central Station is undertaking going to undercut and perhaps destroy some of the glory of that tradition?"

Sam Freeland and Karla teamed to answer some of these questions. They tried to show that the strictly sequential approaches to skill mastery apart from application, the uniform forty-minute chunks of time instead of a flexible schedule, the fragmented treatment of subject matter that could better be integrated, and other mechanisms long taken for granted did not necessarily enhance learning, particularly learning for responsive discipleship.

Valerie had her own file full of questions, but when she glanced at the clock she knew that the meeting should be adjourned. She also predicted that the committee would have to answer these nagging questions, and many others, before their work was completed.

November

Joan Fisher, a science teacher known for her devotion to academics, had recently joined the committee. She had wondered aloud in a staff meeting "whether education at Central Station wasn't just another progressive ebb in the traditionalist flow of recent events."

Joan's remark sounded ominous to Valerie. In preparation for the November meeting, Valerie had consulted with Ken Heard about Joan's probable intent.

Joan was a highly respected member of the faculty and if she dug in her heels against some of the suggestions that were flowing, chiefly, from Central Station, Valerie knew that there would be little chance for change. But if she could get Joan and some of the other "conservatives" on the faculty to see that even some hard-headed educational traditionalists have some ideas that supported the Central Station direction, maybe she could nudge Joan and others into accepting some changes. Ken wasn't sure what Valerie had in mind, but he encouraged her anyway.

She decided to try to exploit several sources. One was a book by the noted Roman Catholic philosopher Jacques Maritain, Education at the Crossroads ([1943], 1978). It was published first during the 1940s and constituted part of the attack on progressivism. When the committee reconvened, she led off with a review of the curricular framework that she found in Maritain, especially the idea that in addition to those subjects that had "knowledge" value were another set of subjects or activities (like games, sports, handicraft work, gardening, and jam-making) that had "play" value. Both, said Maritain, were essential because they helped unite "head" with "hand." As far as Maritain (1943, 45) was concerned, intelligence is not only in the head, but in the fingers too.

Valerie liked that, and quoted it often. She thought that these "play" activities could not only introduce some curricular diversity but could also help accent individual differences in an otherwise fairly seamless curricular garment. They also had a concreteness to them that clearly contrasted with the abstract nature of some of the disciplines.

Another "conserving" voice that she had read lately was Kieran Egan (1986; 1988; 1990). Maritain (1943, 60) had spoken of the educational world of the child as "the universe of imagination . . . which evolves little by little into reason." Hence the knowledge that has to be "given" to the child is "knowledge in the state of story." But beyond stating such generalities, Maritain never developed the idea.

That's why Valerie liked Egan. Convinced that the "pedagogical task is to . . . organize content about the real world in such a way as to encourage ordinary children to use their considerable intellectual abilities in learning" (1986, 63), Egan gives numerous examples of how, in elementary schools and beyond, teachers can use a "story-form model" in the serious study of history, social studies, math, language arts, and science, with the intent to convey meaning and at once appeal to the imagination of the learner. Ironically, by accenting the fantasy life of children, Egan thinks the curriculum for the elementary school can be enriched academically; he lifts up the need for leadership in the classroom by teachers becoming skilled "story" tellers who "affectively engage" the growing awareness of the pupil.

228

Valerie was even more intrigued by the work of Adler (1984). Just as conservative as Maritain, Adler expects all pupils to study language and literature, math, science, history, social studies, fine arts, and a foreign language. But Val focussed her attention on Adler's proposals that all students "irrespective of sex, career interests, or innate abilities" undertake work in crafts, mechanics, and the domestic arts! Why? Because "acquiring skill in the manual arts is as much mind-training as acquiring skill in the language arts" (Adler 1984, 154). Adler goes on to propose that all students should learn how to cook a dinner, and learn some of the mechanical functions of autos. All must be taught some plumbing and electrical skills. In this same category of manual or mechanical arts, Adler placed typing and computer skills (with age eight not too young to begin). Here was some of that same respect for concreteness that Maritain displayed. Val liked that.

In addition, Val showed how Adler advanced the ideas that history, before the seventh grade, be taught through readings in English and science; that beginning with grade seven history be taught partly through open-ended problem posing; that social studies be taught through journals, notebooks, and projects that link history, geography, social studies, and civics; and that schools henceforth and forthwith cease using present methods of educational score-keeping: testing, examining, and grading students! All this from a noted conserving educator bent on helping students acquire organized knowledge, develop intellectual skills, and enlarge their understanding of ideas and values.

At this point she looked up and to her surprise saw that the meeting had already gone beyond the hour. "I'm truly sorry to have kept you so long. There's just one more thing I want to say before we go. I think Maritain, Adler, and Egan affirm what many of us have been talking about, both here and at Central Station. They all recognize the importance of a rich, concrete experience and of engaging students with it in meaningful, whole-bodied ways. Maritain and Adler might in the end come down to saying that the disciplines are the most important, but at least they've recognized something significant about creation that an approach that is restricted to the disciplines normally overlooks. Though they're obviously very much influenced by a classical view of knowledge, I am sure that we can make use of their insights if we incorporate them within a biblical view of learning.

"Thank you for your attention today. I promise that we will stick to our schedule next time."

Highlights of the Committee's Report

The committee met on three more occasions, during which time they managed to hammer out a consensus. By March, they were ready to submit their report to the faculty:

The committee affirms that the gifts of knowing ought to be understood in broader terms than we have tended to describe them, and therefore while giving high honor to knowing as intellectual apprehension, rational analysis, or critical thinking, we must also unwrap gifts of several other kinds. Without in any way downgrading the importance of lingual and logico-mathematical knowing, for example, we must give honor in schools to spatial, musical, kinesthetic, and personal forms of knowing as well.

The committee affirms that knowledge is never for its own sake but always for a higher purpose, always as a means for cultivating whole growth and a willing attitude that leads to loving deeds. It is ultimately for growth in responsive discipleship.

Therefore, to develop our gifts of knowing, teachers will draw rigorously and critically from intellectual content and will attend to developing skills and abilities, but they will do so as far as possible in the context of concrete experience, which we have termed the realm of play. They will also extensively employ problem-posing strategies, which will call for creative and imaginative responses from students.

In this context, the committee makes the following recommendations:

1. To increase cultural and racial diversity, we affirm the necessity of promoting such diversity not only among students but also within the staff and therefore recommend that the ratio of minority faculty to the entire faculty be at least equal to the ratio of minority students to the total school population; that staff development be aimed at understanding other cultures and eliminating ethnocentric teaching styles; that cultural diversity of custom, history, and thought be integrated into the curriculum; and that criteria for tuition assistance be reviewed in order to give greater access to minority applicants.
2. The committee recommends that the school encourage the enrollment of students with physical and learning disabilities, and communication and behavior disorders. We recognize that such a program will only be possible if additional personnel are appointed. We believe however that it is time to address the injustice whereby parents of children with special education needs must bear a substantially greater cost, while children in other, equally costly special programs, can participate in these without extra tuition. We therefore recommend the appointment of a

special task force to explore the implications of this move to a more inclusive program. This committee should also investigate the alterations and additions to existing facilities that would be necessary to accommodate this more diverse student body.

3. The committee believes that little if anything will be changed unless teachers have more time together for planning. We recommend a mid-week session, similar to that at Central Station, from 2:30 to 4:00 each Wednesday afternoon. We propose that the school day on the other four days of the week be lengthened moderately to make up for the "lost" time.

4. The committee desires a more integral curriculum. We recognize that this encouragement is fairly gratuitous at the K–5 level since many teachers are already deeply committed to integral units, whether celebrating the seasons of the year, or centering on special events like Thanksgiving, Christmas, Easter, or topics like Native Americans and African-Americans. We lay down no hard and fast rules, but we are hoping that in K–5 there would be at least 50 to 80 percent of the work done in integral units, that in the middle school up to half of all the work done would be integral, and that for the high school approximately twenty-five percent would be appropriate.

5. We recommend that in the high school, to facilitate an integral approach, studies be reorganized within three groupings: arts, sciences, and foundational studies (cf. Sizer 1992).

   a. The foundational studies would include the formal study of the Bible, as well as courses such as "Living in Hope" (1992), intended to address issues like the environment, health, communication, aesthetics, economics, justice, life in community, marriage and the family, and the church, ultimately to reinforce the school's commitment to responsive discipleship, and the "world of work," conceived as a bridge between schooling and the working world, a work and study experience for those students not regularly employed that should entail no time away from class because it will be done after school, on Saturdays, or during the summer months.

   b. Within the arts and sciences divisions, the committee affirms a commitment to specialized studies, which represent a significant way in which we may come to know the world. These studies include language and literature (English and at least one other language); mathematics and science; history and social studies; the fine arts; the manual (and mechanical) arts; physical education. Although these can be taught separately, we strongly recommend that teachers, teaming together perhaps within larger blocks of time, make an effort to open

231

up creation in ways that integrate these studies, and thus challenge students to respond with a greater variety of gifts than is conventional in schools.

6. The committee recommends that the high school program, which has been divided into pre-college, commercial, and general streams, be revised in favor of an inclusive program with a required foundational section and elected specialized studies.

7. The committee recommends that the school make a special effort to overcome gender stereotyping and that both male and female students participate equally and without discrimination in math and science, manual and mechanical arts, and homemaking and parenting courses. Thus students who may be gifted lingually and logically might discover that others who are gifted mechanically are able to offer them help.

8. To get things started, the committee recommends that the high-school and middle-school staffs combined divide into small disciplinary groups and do a very simple exercise: lay out for a semester, and then for a year, just what major topics the teachers are including in their courses. After completing this task, interdisciplinary groups should be formed to undertake the same kind of curricular mapping.

9. The committee recommends that all freshmen and sophomores be required to do fifteen hours of service a year under the supervision of the teacher of Bible. We recognize that this isn't ideal, but it is a start. Some members of the committee had wanted the service component to arise out of the work in various courses but others opposed this as too radical (Stob 1989). The committee also recommends that the high-school student council be encouraged to cultivate a strong sense of social service.

10. One of the more persistent problems at Mountain City Christian High is the fact that faculty members, on any given day, will teach well over a hundred different students. The committee recommends that the entire high school student body be divided into two "houses" of up to 150 students each for the sake of literature and language, history, mathematics, science, and Bible. (Additional specialized studies and all-school activities like band and choir are to be done outside the houses.) Instructors assigned to each house will be expected to teach courses in at least two areas with the intent that each instructor would teach the same student more than once in a given day. That way faculty members would have fewer students to get to know and would presumably be better able to cultivate greater varieties of gifts (Sizer 1992).

11. The committee also recommends that, in addition to homerooms arranged by grade level, students be organized vertically in groups or clubs of not more than twenty-five, supervised by a faculty mentor, and meet with

the regularity of the old homeroom system. In such an "advisory," the social distance that often stretches between a junior or senior and a freshman would be removed. The older students or the more capable could help the younger or the less capable, thereby building caring learning communities in this more intimate setting, within the larger community of the school.

Mountain City's Response

So how did the Mountain City teachers respond to these recommendations? We have space for only a few examples but these should give you an idea.

At the fourth-grade level one of the teachers has her class engage in a "New World Expo." The children are divided into five groups, each group representing a different country. They study the history, the geography, and the social and cultural life of their nation and fulfill a range of requirements that call for a variety of gifts. They construct displays, learn to perform musical items and folk dances, prepare characteristic foods, and memorize poetry. The culminating activity is a one-day program in which parents and students from other grades are invited to visit national pavilions that the fourth-graders have set up. But what makes this expo truly special is the emphasis on how the gospel has affected each culture and how Christ's redemption might be more fully expressed: this is why it's a "New World" exposition.

As in the elementary school, the middle school teachers generally welcomed the encouragement of innovation. One sixth-grade teacher (Oosterhuis 1988), upset that her students complained that they were bored with school (she thought this expression would arise later in the eighth or ninth grades but not here in the sixth!) decided to teach "Ancient Greece" for five solid weeks by total immersion. She transformed the scheduled reading, spelling, language arts, math, science, Bible, social studies, and all the rest by having her students talk, read, write, listen, draw, dance, act and sing activities relating to Greece, with the five weeks culminating in a celebrative day-long series of activities that involved the parents and interested members of the community.

Some of the middle school teachers began planning integral units for an all-school theme week to be held the following spring, eventually deciding on the theme "Building Christian Community" after a series of events at the school strongly suggested that a pervasive meanness was an unfortunate undercurrent of school life at Mountain City.

The high school teachers were willing to accept the foundations-specialized studies framework, even though it did seem fairly complex (Goodlad 1984). For some, it seemed that the school was raising its standards for all students;

others sensed that the delicate balancing that the system would introduce represented an effort at greater diversity within some required commonalities. On the edges of a core of studies it provided the remediation that some students required at the same time that the academically able could be challenged, while avoiding the perils of tracking.

When teachers began working in teams, they were surprised by the degree of overlap in the list of topics and therefore the places where they could eliminate some of the repetition. The high-school teachers working in cross-disciplinary groups were also struck by the parallels and decided to correlate the work in several of the high school classes. This was at least a beginning.

Unlike Central Station with its weekly Wednesday afternoon service component, the Mountain City Middle teachers decided to institute a servanthood component in association with the lower grades. Middle school students were encouraged to volunteer to be a buddy to one of the lower school students. One of the more remarkable outcomes of this arrangement was the case of a sixth grader classified as seriously emotionally disturbed who was assigned to a second-grade class where he served as a tutor under the watchful eye of the second-grade teacher. Although the young man continued to present behavior challenges to his own teachers and peers, he is described by the second-grade teacher as a model of appropriate behavior and a valuable instructional asset. At Christmas, he chose to forego his own class party to attend the second-grade celebration, during which he presented gifts to the entire class and the teacher (Stainback and Stainback 1992).

The student council took up the call to service with enthusiasm. One of the first projects during the following year was to help stimulate nearly one hundred percent attendance at parent-teacher conferences, especially at the elementary levels, by serving without remuneration as sitters.

Many of the faculty liked the idea of the house structure, not realizing that behind that idea were some others. For when they became accustomed to teaching more than just their major, they eventually became more open to collaborative planning and team teaching, and moved beyond mere correlation of topics and activities toward effective integration and integrality. This illustrated a commonplace: we grow to like what we get good at.

Mountain City has developed a comprehensive plan for change which will obviously require a gradual, step-by-step implementation. We would not wish you to be discouraged by the extent of their intended reforms. They still have a great deal of work to do in working out the details. Nonetheless, although we have brought together suggestions from a number of different sources, all the proposals formulated at Mountain City have their real-life counterparts.

Mountain City has also demonstrated quite clearly that decisions about curriculum are largely decisions about how people are to be treated. They have opted for a program that will encourage diversity and thus support the unwrapping of gifts. At the same time, it respects the common humanity of all people, and the calling that we have to bear each other's burdens and share each other's joys. They have decided that the "subjects" of curriculum are in the first place the students and teachers. They have recognized that if the curriculum is to be more responsive to individuals and to God's revelation in creation, they will need to make their program decisions in terms of broad educational objectives. Only then will they turn their attention to the "textbook tail" of resource selection. But textbooks will be only one kind of resource among many that they employ.

Selecting Topics for Integral Units

The broad policy outlines for a school's program are of great significance. But the chalk meets the chalkboard at the level of unit selection and design. Now that we have discussed the broad outlines of a school program, we need to turn our attention to the specifics of unit selection. We suggest that three criteria should guide this process. These are the structure of creation, students' interests and concerns, and societal issues.

Fundamental to the idea of an integral curriculum is that creation is a meaning-rich whole, ordered and sustained by the Word of the Lord. It is the dynamic holding together of all things in Christ that constitutes shalom. Meaning in human life is founded in God's revelation to us in creation. It is creation in its integrality, rather than the disciplines as the outcome of theoretical reflection on creation, that ought to be our starting point in selecting areas for study. The disciplines help us in wonderful ways to deepen our insight into creation, and they therefore have an important place in school learning. This is especially so at the higher levels of schooling, when students have developed the capacity for sustained analytical thinking. But even there, the disciplines should take their place as analytical ways of knowing alongside the other ways of knowing. And they should always be related as much as possible to concrete experience.

Thus, the first step in unit selection is to identify an area that is rich in meaning and that has creational integrity. It is by immersion in creation, by playing around faithfully in God's world, that we first come to know. By "creational integrity," we mean that we should recognize the given structures of creation, the boundaries that God has established between various realms and between individual things. It is this ordered structure that the first chapter of Genesis points us to. Everything was made to relate to everything else in meaningful ways, and according to its own kind, within God's law order. This bounded order is reflected in the Ten Commandments, for instance, where God reveals what is faithful behavior within life's various relationships. Schools that are seeking shalom will seek the just and righteous relationships that God ordains.

We may identify four realms (physical things, plants, animals, persons) in a general map of creation. Within the human realm, we recognize distinct kinds of relationships such as the church, marriage, family, businesses and factories, artists' groups and galleries, schools and universities, the media, social clubs, the state (government and citizens) as well as activities like farming and technology. God expects us to treat our neighbors in each of these relationships in ways that are true to the particular relationship (Eph. 5:21–6:9).

These areas of creation are not static, of course. Our task as image bearers has been and is to responsively, playfully, and faithfully shape God's world so that he is glorified in the blossoming of the works of his hands. We would therefore recognize the different historical and cultural forms these have been developed. Above all, however, we would be seeking a deeper insight into the way in which varying religious visions have influenced this shaping of human life and the other parts of creation.

Thus, teachers will work to identify the significant biblical insights and responses that they will be seeking from their students. They will have clearly in mind how God intends us to act in the particular area, holding fast to that which is good. They will lead students to discern the distortions that affect our understanding and acting in this area of life. And they will work with students to discover avenues of shalom.

The area of creation selected will provide a focus for student experience. This experience will be concrete, because it will be experience of a whole, displaying creation in its many-sidedness and calling forth from students a many-sided response. A book, a film, an exploration of a period of history or of another culture may each provide this rich concrete experience, as may various out-of-classroom experiences.

In an established school seeking to move toward a more integral curriculum, the teaching staff will want to carefully examine the present curriculum and additional resources in order to determine which areas of experience, as well as skills and concepts, are significant at a given developmental level. In a discipline-based curriculum, one way to begin is with teachers listing the topics presently covered in each subject. This will help them to identify connections that are already present that could be just as adequately (we would say, more adequately) treated in an integral approach. Such a mapping of the curriculum will give confidence to teachers and also to parents that a nondisciplinary approach will still address the areas that are important.

Curriculum development that is concerned with promoting purposeful response and unwrapping gifts will also take into account those matters that are of concern to students. The curriculum will not be determined by these interests, but it will take them seriously. Students too are image bearers of God, and they should be treated with integrity.

Principal: I asked the middle school teachers in my school to identify what things the students in their classes want to know. They listed questions such as: When do we get out of here? Do we have to know this for the test? How long do we have to do this? What should I wear? Who will be there? Perhaps the teachers are correct, but now we intend to ask the same questions of the students.

One way to determine students' concerns is to ask them to write in response to the following topics: What do you think is God's purpose for human beings? What keeps you from fulfilling that purpose perfectly? What questions do you have about yourself? What do you think is wrong with the world? What questions and concerns do you have about the world?

Another approach (McDonough 1991) is to have students complete the following stems:

I wish I knew why. . .
I wish I knew how. . .
I wish I knew more about. . .
I wish I knew when. . .
Sometimes I wonder about. . .
Sometimes I daydream about. . .
Sometimes I worry about. . .
Ten years from now, this is what I see myself doing:
I like classes that. . .
I don't like classes that. . .

Whichever approach is used, the next step is to have the students, either in small groups or within the large group, present lists of responses. Ask such questions as: Where can you see any common questions or concerns about yourself or about your world? Are there any similarities or themes connecting ideas between the common questions and concerns? Identify the themes and select one theme for study. Which of our questions could we answer to help us learn about our theme? What activities could we do to answer our questions and concerns? What knowledge and skills will we need to be able to answer these questions?

In this way, students are encouraged to respond to problems posed, but also to pose problems for themselves. The same is true in the exploration of social issues.

It is appropriate for students to be involved in identifying issues that society faces but it will also be necessary that teachers bring important issues to their attention. Many societal problems overlap with the personal concerns students have. In fact, often a personal concern is simply a facet of the larger concern.

Some problems that have surfaced at the middle school and high school levels are: How should it affect our daily lives if we believe that we live in global interdependence? Does the Christian community have a special task in learning to live with cultural diversity? Can either a capitalistic society or a socialistic society be a just society? Is it possible to have a just war? What forms has discrimination taken throughout history? What are Christian schools and public schools for? How can Christians make ethical decisions concerning medical issues? What are biblical guidelines that inform political decisions? What are Christian responses to environmental issues?

Taking the information from the students' interests and concerns, societal issues, and our understanding of the structure of creation into consideration, the staff is ready to decide on specific topics for the units to be studied. At the same time they will determine which topics can be presented as problems that can be studied in integral units; they will identify relationships which can best be presented as problems in a correlated subject manner; and they will determine which areas of the curriculum can best be studied in units that are part of separate disciplines.

Having selected the topics, teachers consider how they may invite students to engage with the area concretely, in whole-bodied ways, as whole persons. The "story" of the particular unit would start with as rich as possible an immersion in the area. Certainly, there will need to be a setting of the scene if students' attention is to be engaged. And teachers will not merely throw their students in at the deep end to sink or swim; they are responsible at all points to guide their students through the terrain and they will call their students to *purposeful responses* at each point on the journey.

Examples of integral units are given in the next chapter, where we also describe a process for unit planning.

Questions for Discussion

1. This chapter assumes a broad definition of gifts in relation to the work of schools. But if "schools must be schools" (and not "churches" or "homes"), are there gifts that don't deserve recognition in a school setting? And if so, what would those gifts be? What are the priority concerns of the school as school? What kinds of gifts do you think Christian schooling should honor?

2. This chapter argues for broadening the range of students who enroll in Christian schools. The assumption is that, given rising tuition, Christian schools can be pressured toward becoming rather elitist, selective organizations. Either path has its costs. Which path can we *not* afford?

3. The chapter assumes that setting aside regular hours weekly for teachers to work and plan with each other will likely lead to a variety of educational blessings, including collaborative teaching, integral units, and the creation of a lively Christian community for learning and teaching. Is this too idealistic? Or is it the one thing desperately needed? What's your experience with this?

4. What is the structure of the curriculum in your school? Considering the possibilities outlined in this chapter, which of these might be adopted or adapted in your school? In what ways does your present curriculum structure constrain your educational endeavor? What changes other than those recommended might be possible in your school?

Recommended Reading

1. Elliott, D., and Woodward, A., eds. 1990. *Textbooks and schooling in the United States.*
   A general overview of the place of textbooks in the schools.
2. Luke, C., de Castell, S., and Luke, A. 1989. *Language, authority, and criticism.*

Apple, M., and Christian-Smith, L. 1991. *The politics of the textbook.* More critical analyses of the content, use, and production of textbooks.

3. Roques, M. 1989. *Curriculum unmasked.*
   Van Brummelen, H. 1991. "The world portrayed in texts."
   Vitz, P. 1986. *Censorship.*
   In these readings, Christian authors address textbook issues.
4. De Moor, A. 1992. *Living in hope.* Society of Christian Schools in British Columbia. *Look around* series.
   De Moor's revision of the *Man in society* materials for senior high schools includes booklets on "Perspectives," "Community," "Self," "Truth," "Government and justice," "Work and the job," and "Communication." These provide valuable examples for designing units, as does *Look around.*
5. Individual Christian schools have developed units; one example is *American culture,* available from Holland Christian High School, Holland, Mich.

10

How Do We Decide How to Teach?

"We've planned so many of these integral units that we have our procedure down pretty well, I think," Emmy Perez said as she opened the meeting of the Central Station Middle School staff with her usual optimistic flair.

"I'm glad you're chairing today, Emmy," Ted volunteered as he sat down with his cup of coffee. "Sam led our last planning session like a drill sergeant and nothing makes me more feisty than all that regimentation."

"Well, we got our work done in short order, you must admit," Sam smiled as he joined the group. "Emmy, when you chair you usually strike a note somewhere between Ted's laid-back approach and my pushing for consensus. That's not bad for a second year teacher."

Emmy got the attention of her colleagues. "Everyone's here so let's get started. This way we have of thinking of our students in grades six, seven, eight, and nine as two groups rather than as four was new to me when I came here and it certainly allows for a greater variety of possibilities in instruction. Under Sam's leadership we've completed the initial planning of the integral studies blocks for grades eight and nine this year. Our task today is to begin doing the same for grades six and seven."

"I've had some concern that, in our planning of units, we might have a potpourri effect, teaching those things that interest us rather than making certain the curriculum is informed by what truly matters," Karla Hubbard interjected. "Remember, we agreed that we will use these principles as we plan. First, our prime goal in planning is to help the students learn to unwrap their gifts, to share each other's joys and burdens, and to seek God's shalom in every area of life. Second, the topic for each unit will address three dimensions: the students' own concerns, issues that are presently of concern in society, and content that helps students experience and come to know God's world. In that respect, each topic will consist of a problem posed individually, communally, and in the broader creation.

"I know we do a good job of finding out what the students' concerns are. We also help them examine societal issues. But the part I am concerned about is helping them to come to know God's world. What part of it should be studied? We want the students to see a clear focus to their studies rather than being all over the map as far as content is concerned. And that is difficult to do since no textbook provides our focus."

"Karla, it's funny you should mention the focus that textbooks provide," said Emmy. "In preparation for this meeting I borrowed the social studies textbook being used at Mountain City in grade seven. There are twenty chapters in the book—listen while I read the topics covered. People and culture, three early civilizations, Greece and Rome, three religions, India and China, early African civilization, the Middle Ages, the rise of Europe, Europe changes the world, lands and people of western Europe, France, eastern Europe, the USSR, North Africa and the Middle East, Egypt, the Ivory Coast, Asia, Japan, Indonesia, Oceania, and Australia."

"Talk about being all over the map!" laughed Sam. "Those poor seventh graders are going to be swamped."

Ted agreed. "I happen to know that the seventh grade teachers over there do as good a job as is possible with that textbook, using cooperative learning and other interactive strategies. Still, there is far too much breadth and very little depth in trying to cover so much material—and it's depth that we want."

"The Mountain City teachers have asked me for copies of the units we have planned up to this point," Karla said. "I told them we had already agreed that anything we have done we will gladly share with them, provided they are willing to tell us ways they think our units could be improved."

Sam smiled, "I'm glad they think our work might be helpful to them. But you know, it won't really work for them to simply teach the units we have planned. It's the planning itself that really helps us understand what we are doing. Still, maybe it will give them courage to begin when they see our bungling efforts."

"We'd better get on with the work at hand," said Emmy. "I've noticed that when we plan units it seems to work well when we begin with a problem concerning people. For a possible problem or theme for this year what do you think of, 'Can there be ideal cultures?' as our guiding question?"

"How would you work that out?" asked Ted.

Emmy began to sketch a design on the chalkboard. "I've been thinking about the first question we always try to ask when we plan units. 'What is God's intention for the particular area of creation that we are studying?' In answering that we might begin with asking the students to think about what a culture would be like if it were exactly the way God wants people to be. Students might brainstorm concerning how people in such a culture would live. What would government be like? Would there be taxation? How would they care for their sick, for little children, for the elderly? What kind of transportation would they have? What kind of political system would they have? How would they educate their young? Would there be schools? What kind of recreation would they have? What kind of music would they have? Would their society be competitive?"

"This is an interesting idea," said Sam. "After they've finished describing this culture it would be nice if we could think of a book that they could read to follow the theme. Animal Farm is one possibility."

"Perhaps a short story would be appropriate at this point," suggested Karla. "But I agree that the idea has a great deal of merit."

"And after the introductory reading we could study people of specific countries and compare different aspects of their lives with our ideal community," said Emmy.

Ted shook his head. "I'm still concerned that all the students will end up with is a lot of facts that don't mean anything to them. What would happen if we were to show the kids the different large areas of the world, describe some general characteristics of each area, and have them select the area they would like to begin with? Then each group of four or five students would select a country within that area to research. They would work cooperatively and discover and then teach each other information about the people, how they live, their music, art, literature, always comparing and contrasting that culture with their original concept of an ideal society. Then a member from each group would be responsible for teaching that information to one other group. Our group discussion would focus on generalizations the students could make concerning the people of that part of the world and contrasting them with generalizations concerning the ideal society they have described. And, in keeping with our set of three questions that we always ask, they would try to determine what changes might be made if that society were to live according to the way God structured creation."

"I can help a great deal with their research concerning literature and art," said Karla, "and we have such a diverse population in this city that it might be possible to find people from these different countries to work with us. In fact, I suspect the students will be able to get information from the city hall concerning the number of people we have in Mountain City who have origins in the countries we are studying. I know the public library will also be a great source for information."

"We'll want to encourage the teams to do a lot of work with charts and graphs to keep the comparisons with different countries very visual. You know, we're all going to learn a lot from this," laughed Sam. "I can't wait to work with them on finding out about music. But how many of these topics do we hope to study during the year?"

"We're using a two-hour block every day. Why don't we begin with one geographical area and plan for a four week period," suggested Emmy. "We want to keep to our 'depth rather than breadth' policy, but they are only sixth and seventh graders and we will want to watch how long their interest is retained in an area. Let's give all of this some thought and in our next planning session decide exactly how we will begin."

As teachers plan for instruction they will want to first decide what kind of classroom environment they hope will result from the way they choose to interact with students. Palmer (1983, 70–71) describes the effect of teaching on the learning environment as follows:

> To sit in a class where the teacher stuffs our minds with information, organizes it with finality, insists on having the answers while being utterly uninterested in our views, and forces us into a grim competition for grades—to sit in such a class is to experience a lack of space for learning. But to study with a teacher who not only speaks but listens, who not only gives answers but asks questions and welcomes our insights, who provides information and theories that do not close doors but open new ones, who encourages students to help each other learn— to study with such a teacher is to know the power of a learning space.

Palmer (1983, 69) believes that to teach is "to create a space in which obedience to truth is practiced." That kind of space is not one in which the teacher is active and the student is passive. Rather, teacher and students are actively engaged together in learning and leading each other to further learning. If, as we have said, we do not know as individuals in isolation from each other, then it is also true that we do not learn as individuals either. Therefore, the classroom environment should be one in which the students are invited to learn by interacting with the world and with each other.

In some classrooms, interaction is carried on in ineffective ways. At times the questions being raised by the teacher are primarily for exposing ignorance and the questions being raised by students are designed to score points with the teacher or to help the student look more knowledgeable than the others. In fact, research suggests that overall students ask few questions in class (Kooy forthcoming). The majority of the questions they do ask are procedural, along the lines of, "How do you want us to do this?"

Palmer suggests that we must arrange instruction so that the classroom is a hospitable environment for learning. A hospitable learning environment is needed not simply because it makes students feel safe and happy or because it makes learning painless. Rather, it is needed to make the painful learnings possible. Sometimes in teaching it is necessary to expose ignorance and to challenge information that is only partially true. None of this can happen productively in an environment where people feel threatened or judged (Palmer 1983, 74).

How do teachers create a classroom with an environment hospitable to learning? In part, by arranging meaningful learning units so that what is being studied in the classroom is an important part of what is really happening in the world, thus bridging the gap between learning and living. In part, by planning instructional strategies that actively engage students with the study and with each other. And also, by ensuring that the dialogue between teacher and students and among students is as encouraging as possible (and free of sarcasm) as together they learn what it is to be obedient to truth.

Providing a Biblical Framework for Units of Learning

Having selected the area for study, teachers will want to work to identify the significant biblical insights and responses that they will be seeking from their students. How do varying religious perspectives enhance or distort our understanding and acting in this area of life? What is God's intention for this area? How can we work together to bring shalom? In what ways will the varying gifts of students be utilized and developed?

We know that teaching in a way that encourages these insights and responses is difficult for teachers. For example, in one school groups of sixth-grade students were drawing plans for an ideal recreational park. When they were asked whether they thought there were any guidelines from the Bible that might let us know how God wants people to use recreational time, they seemed puzzled. Many of them really did not seem to know what we meant when we asked them how sin had distorted or broken that part of life.

Student: It's hard for me to answer a question like that. We talk about things like that in Bible sometimes, but I don't know what it really has to do with what we're studying now.

The problem may be that teachers too often assume students transfer what they learn in Bible class to their studies in other areas. However, such transfer doesn't usually happen without help from the teacher.

Blomberg (1991, 9) suggests that one way of allowing Scripture to direct our thinking in any area of study is by encouraging students to ask the following guiding questions concerning the topic they are studying:

1. What is God's intention for the particular area of creation that we are studying? What does it mean to treat these creatures with integrity, that is, in accordance with their God-given calling in life?
2. How has this purpose been distorted by the effects of sin, as reflected in human idolatry and the outworkings of God's Word of judgment? Has this part of creation been severed from its interconnections with the rest so that it is thought to stand on its own as an absolute?
3. What are the avenues by which we may hope to bring healing and reconciliation? In what ways does the gospel impel us to action so that the Lord's shalom might be at least partially restored, on the basis of Christ's mighty work of redemption?

These three questions can be related to the biblical rhythm of knowing that we have described, a rhythm of immersion, withdrawal, and return. They can thus also be seen as one specification of the play, problem-posing, and purposeful responding model for curriculum. We need to open ourselves to the Word of God, to listen to God's voice to hear his will, in an attitude of humility and trust. We need to look critically, with spiritual discernment, to see the effects of sin. And we need to recognize that our knowledge brings with it responsibility to act as agents of reconciliation. In this way, we carry out our calling to be conservers, discerners, and transformers.

It is also important to think of the many different ways of knowing in planning, so that our curriculum planning is oriented to unwrapping students' gifts. We should also think of the many ways in which creation functions. One model that is helpful for the purpose has been developed by the authors of *Living in Hope* (De Moor 1992). They call it the "PERSIATE + G" model. This is an acronym for Political, Ethical, Religious, Social, Intellectual, Aesthetic, Technological, Economic, and Geographic. Another useful tool for keeping the diversity of creation in view is the modal model, adapted from the work of Dooyeweerd (1969) and his colleagues. This model identifies fifteen different created aspects of experience: confessional, ethical, jural, aesthetic, economic, social, lingual, techno-cultural, analytical, sensory, biotic, physical, kinematic, spatial, and numerical.

Within the context of the biblical perspective on creation, the fall into sin, and Christ's redemptive work, and respecting the rich diversity of creational functioning, teachers will plan a range of problems that can serve to deepen students' insights into the area. They must be alert as well to the problems that students might themselves pose. In fact, teachers must encourage students to pose their own problems and will arrange ways for them to seek solutions to these problems.

A curriculum for responsive discipleship will have the promotion of service as its goal. Our wisdom finds its meaning and coherence in Christ not merely intellectually (as critique of secular perspectives and promotion of biblically-informed perspectives) but as bodily service of Christ in all areas of life. This is our spiritual worship. A Christian curriculum will seek to unwrap individual gifts in order that we may bear the burdens of others as we communally seek the coming of the kingdom as shalom.

In unwrapping gifts, we will wish to take account of what is known about children's growth and development. It will be appropriate in each unit to focus on certain skills necessary for exploration of the problems posed. Sometimes it will be necessary to take time out from the problem itself to conscientiously practice such skills. We need to keep in mind, however, ways of relating these skills to the broader problem context.

Examples of Integral Units

One area that might be addressed by means of an integral unit is: How should natural resources be developed and used? In the context of broadening students' experience of the range of resources that

God has created, the first of the three questions may be explored. In this case we ask, What resources did God place in the world? What was his intention for those resources? How do we use those resources to glorify God and to serve our neighbor? How do we treat each of those resources with integrity, using it according to its unique qualities? To respond to the problem posed by this question, students will need to study Scripture and other sources.

We will want to link this exploration with students' own concerns. We can begin to do this with questions such as: What do you want to buy? What things do you wish your family would buy? What kinds of natural resources does the manufacturing and use of each of these objects require?

In addressing the second of the basic questions, the students will attempt to discover what goes wrong in the way that we use resources. Who uses most of them? At what rate are they used? Answers to these questions will require information from science, social studies, and math. Literature, art, and drama will enrich students' understanding of the issues involved.

Finally, how can we respond to Christ's work of redemption by caring for and using natural resources in keeping with God's intention? What steps can we take locally to do this? What steps could be taken in the broader community and globally? What responsibility do various agencies and groups, such as governments, businesses, and consumers, have in bringing healing to creation?

Another area that might be explored in an integral unit is: What kinds of personal and group conflicts arise from the way that people of a nation relate to each other? Student concerns can surface through questions concerning problems people have with personal relationships.

Next the focus would be on coming to understand how God wants people to relate to each other personally as well as on a national level. What are the biblical guidelines for relationships between people? When addressing how relationships are broken at the national level, the students might study events such as the American Revolution, the Civil War, or equal rights issues. Statistics will be one source of necessary information. The effects of science or technology on relationships would be an important part of the study. And the examples of literature, art, and music that might be part of the unit are numerous.

Then comes the question: How can relationships at the personal level and at the national level be restored? Students are invited to respond purposefully, and to creatively brainstorm ways this might and must occur.

A third area of creation to explore would be that of work. A primary focus could be their own world of work as students. A problem posed early on might be: Why should people work? In exploring the problem, students would discuss what types of jobs they would like to have and why. How do jobs change as society changes? What kinds of work do their parents do? What did their grandparents do? Their great-grandparents? What would life be like if no one ever had to work? Visits to different occupational sites and interviews with people of different ages concerning work would be part of their immersion in the topic. Students might read different essays on work and discuss with each other attitudes toward work.

Next, they would be directed into finding out what God's intention is for our work. Again, they would study Scripture and other related readings. Also guided by Scripture, they investigate what goes wrong with work. Why do some people find it very boring? How does greed distort work? In what ways does work sometimes lead to breakdown of relationships? Purposeful responses to the problems raised by these questions will lead groups of students into study of topics which are ordinarily thought of as part of social studies, technology and science, mathematics, literature, art, drama, and music.

Finally, as in every unit of study, the students attempt to find ways that people can work in keeping with God's intention.

Developing an Integral Unit

We are suggesting that, to as great an extent as possible, at every grade level, the curriculum should be organized around integral units. This is a way of helping students see the structure of creation and it is closest to the way they experience life. These units, then, become the centerpiece or core of instruction.

Many teachers at the lower elementary level have found this kind of organization relatively easy to do since they are responsible for teaching all subjects in large blocks of time. However, teachers in grades five through twelve have had far more difficulty. This is in part because of a long tradition of separate disciplines, which encourages teachers at the upper levels to think of themselves as "music teachers," "science teachers," "math teachers," rather than primarily as teachers.

In order to help teachers over the hurdle of team-planning their first unit, we offer the following guide for planning at any level. The steps of the guide are important but the order in which the steps occur will depend on the topic, the teacher, and the team.

Step 1. As a team of teachers, select a topic or a theme for the unit. This should arise in part from personal concerns of students. Students at the middle school and high school level would like answers to a great variety of questions. Some examples are:

> With all the different religions in the world, how do we know ours is the right one?
> Why does God allow such extremes of wealth and poverty in my community?
> What kind of job will I have when I leave school?
> Why don't girls go into puberty at the same time boys do?
> Why is it that some people are popular and others aren't?
> How can I figure out what my place is in the universe?

The topic for the unit also arises from common issues people currently face or will face in society. Examples are:

> Why are so many people getting AIDS?
> What kind of environmental problems will society face during our lifetimes?
> If God is in control, why does he allow terrible things to happen such as rapes, murders, and starvation?

Finally, the topic arises from areas of knowledge that will increase students' understanding of God's creation. Examples are:

> What makes different cultures rise and fall?
> How should natural resources be developed?

The topic should neither be so general that it is beyond the scope of a profitable investigation nor should it be so narrow that it restricts an integral study. It should allow students the space to play around in creation, without being so large an area that they feel lost or overwhelmed.

A team of teachers might select several themes for study at each grade level, the number depending on the grade level, the team, and the topics. Or, if grades are to be combined for the studies, certain topics might be studied each year, thereby ensuring that each student will encounter many different topics in the course of the school years. When you are first starting out to develop integral units, of course, you should set your sights on one topic. Later, when you are more proficient and confident, you can gradually add more.

Step 2. Have each teacher brainstorm independently for two or three minutes in order to identify learning activities that relate to the theme or problem. These learning activities may include people, topics, questions, ideas, or resources. Next the teachers will share their ideas with each other in order to help everyone see the richness of the theme. They will also identify the connections that exist between the different aspects of the theme.

As they brainstorm together the central theme or problem might be placed on a chalkboard with a circle around it. Spokes could be drawn out from this hub with aspects of creation (or subject areas when you are first making the transition from a subject-based curriculum) written on each. As each idea or suggestion is made, it could be listed with the subject area where it seems to belong. This will give the teachers a graphic illustration that will reveal areas that are not being covered and will help focus attention on areas that are being ignored. Such a diagram might look like this (Van Brummelen 1988, 125):

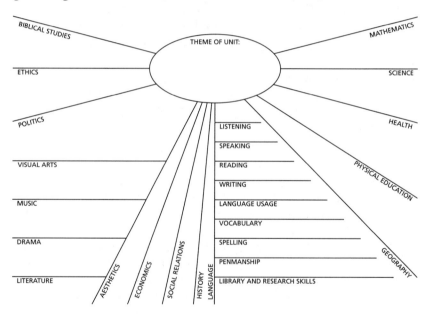

Step 3. Discuss the guiding questions concerning God's intention for this aspect of creation, how sin has distorted this purpose, and how healing and redemption may be brought about.

Step 4. Write a short description of the unit to allow parents, students, and others in the school to understand what the focus of the learning experience will be and what the experience will be like.

Describe how this topic relates to a problem or issue the students face or will face.

Step 5. Record the questions the students have already raised concerning this topic and how these questions will influence the unit. Student questions should be the point of entry into the study and are therefore a critical part of unit development. We want our students to be active problem-posers.

Step 6. List your major objectives in terms of student outcomes. Each objective should relate to the focus of the problem and to the guiding questions as well as to the questions the students have raised. A well-formed objective is clearly stated and avoids ambiguity. Each objective should tell what the students will do, what the desired outcome will be, and what criteria will be for an acceptable level of performance in terms of quality, quantity, or time. In this way, you will always have students' purposeful responses in view as you lead them through the unit.

Step 7. Identify the skills, knowledge, and content the unit is attempting to address. Specific mention should be made concerning how different subjects of the curriculum are naturally addressed in this study, so that parents, teachers, and students may be reassured that an integral approach deals adequately with areas of traditional importance.

Step 8. Describe the learning activities in detail. The activities should be identified as initial, ongoing, culminating, evaluative, or a combination of these.

Step 9. Outline plans for assessing learning. This may be in the form of student projects and it may include tests.

Step 10. Note the resources that will be needed. What literature will be available for students as part of the unit? What art forms will they encounter? What music? What people will they meet? What places will they visit?

Step 11. Draw up a time line for the unit. This should include when and where activities will occur, deadlines, responsibilities, and any other dates or times that are important to the success of the unit.

Step 12. Decide which teachers and students will be responsible for specific activities.

After teachers have become more practiced at planning integral units they will want to involve the students in many of the steps along the way. Teachers are responsible for leading the learning that occurs in classrooms, but students are ultimately responsible as image bearers for their own learning. The more students are involved in planning for their own learning and determining how they will know whether they have learned, the more effective learning becomes. The degree of student involvement in planning will of course increase with maturity, but even at the earliest levels, student input should be sought.

When planning integral units it is not necessary that all subject areas be represented in each unit. It is far better to allow an honest representation of information from subject areas that naturally flow from the central theme or problem than to have activities that are not conducive to learning simply in order to have every subject area represented. In addition, teachers should not feel compelled to plan all instruction in every subject area as part of a unit. For example, even though a particular unit might include instruction in the use of graphs or statistics, mathematics might at the same time be taught sequentially in a disciplinary framework.

Teaching Specialized Studies

Gary Wiltenberg walked to the table at the front of the library where the teachers were meeting. An expectant hush settled around the room since everyone was curious about what he would have to say concerning his attempt to use different instructional strategies. "As most of you know," he grinned as he began, "I was more than skeptical about this whole idea of using interactive instructional strategies in my classroom. In fact, I was downright against it. I'm basically a business teacher and I have always used workbooks and multiple-choice tests so that the students would know exactly what was expected of them and where they stand. That's the way I learned in my own business courses and I could get a job as a tax consultant on a full-time basis any time I decided to give up teaching." He looked embarrassed for a moment. "As a matter of fact, I almost did halfway through last semester when I was in the middle of this procedure.

"It's hard to teach an old dog new tricks and at thirty-eight I was beginning to feel like an old dog. Behind my frustration with teaching, there was still the conviction that a long time ago I believed that God had called me to it. So, I thought I would give it one last shot, and that seemed to mean giving some new ways of teaching a try. The approach I want to tell you about occurred in my grade twelve economics class. I added a unit on international business to that course last year and as part of that unit I wanted the class to learn about the European Community. I tried to plan in terms of play, problem-posing, and purposeful responding. I also thought this would be a good time to use one of the instructional strategies we studied last year. At least it would keep the committee happy if I tried.

"The procedure I chose to use is called KWL Plus (Manzo and Manzo 1990). This stands for what students know, what they want to know, and what they have learned. It's a procedure you would use before the students read, while they read, and after they have read. However, that procedure seemed a little weak for my purposes so I combined it with some ideas from the Guided Reading Procedure (Manzo 1975). The idea is that the students should learn a great deal more about the topic and relate it to what they already know as a result of the dialogue that occurs than they would if you simply lectured on the material. I should tell you that it didn't work perfectly and I really wasn't very comfortable teaching this way. But it worked a lot better than I thought it would.

"This is the way I used it. When I introduced the topic of the European Community I asked the class to brainstorm everything that they already knew about the E.C. I guess you could call this 'playing with the concept.' I thought no one would know anything but I was really surprised. Of course some had never heard of the E.C. but some students knew such things as the following: They thought it must be made up of Common Market countries. They had heard the plan was that all of the countries will have a common currency, although they thought Thatcher had been against that and they aren't sure where the present Prime Minister stands. Citizens of the countries will not need passports to travel from one country to another. The countries are going to agree on standards for products they are making. Some of the students think they will have a huge central E.C. military force and there was some argument concerning whether or not that was true. As they talked, I filled in the first column of the table. Even when I knew what they were saying was incorrect, I still put it on the board, although it almost drove me crazy to let incorrect statements appear before them. But that's the way the procedure works."

Gary shuffled through his papers while the rest of the teachers glanced around the room. Each wondered whether the others were as amazed by this demonstration as they were. Had Gary really taught this way, after all his comments about the lack of "academic rigor" when you use these strategies?

"The next thing we did," Gary continued, "was to make the problem as personal as possible. I asked the students what they thought they needed to learn about the E.C. Things got a little rough at this point because there are a couple of kids in there that clearly don't really want to learn anything. But the majority of the students carried the day and we came up with a list. As they talked I listed their ideas in the second column. Their list included such questions as: How will they keep the Germans from dominating the E.C., given their size and strength? What will all of this mean for trade with Canada and the United States? Will the Japanese still be allowed to have holdings in Western Europe? How will they figure out how each country's present currency is val-

254

ued in relation to the common currency? Will they try to have a common language? Will they try to have common political systems?"

"At that point the KWL table on the board looked like table 3.

Table 3		
Know	Want to Know	Learned
Made of CM countries	Which countries exactly?	
Use common currency	How to evaluate curr.?	
Thatcher against	Prevent German domination?	
No passports between	Imp. for Can. & U.S.?	
Standards for products	Japanese holdings?	
Central military force	Same political systems?	

"Next I wanted the class to read about the European Community. That topic isn't covered in our textbook, but I found excellent articles in news magazines and newspapers. I told them each to read one article and to try to remember all that they could because after they had read I intended to record on the board whatever they remembered. The class read silently for about fifteen minutes. At that point I had them turn the articles over and tell me the details of what they had read. As they talked, I recorded all the information in the third column. In addition, when they corrected some of their earlier misinformation, I changed it on the board. Sometimes they disagreed about the accuracy of certain points so we made a list of questions along the side. All of this was a means to purposeful responding.

"At this point, I had them reread their articles to help them self-correct their inaccuracies and to try to recall additional details. They closed their books and we made corrections and additions on the board.

"I then asked them how they thought all of that information could be structured for note-taking. They had found details concerning:

a. the composition of the European Community;
b. reasons for the E.C.;
c. citizen's rights in the E.C.;
d. setting standards for currencies and products;
e. implications for other countries.

"At that point I divided the class into four groups. I had twenty-eight students in the class and so there were seven students in each group. I assigned the students to the groups, making sure that each group had one or two of the best students and no more than one who was a behavior problem. Each group picked one of the four categories and was responsible to find and organize information on that topic.

"The next day was spent in the library doing group work. I walked around most of the time watching the groups work but there were some problems, I could tell. In one group, one girl seemed to be doing all the work. In another group, the students really weren't focused on what I considered was the most important information. I tried to correct both of those situations but didn't really know how. I could use some suggestions for what to do in those cases.

"After two library sessions, we met back in class. Seven new groups were formed with one member from each category in each of the seven groups. It was the responsibility of each class member to tell his or her group what their category group had learned. Notes were taken at this point. At the end of the period I collected one notebook from an average student in each of the seven groups. I looked through the notes taken that day to see whether they were as complete as I wanted.

"The next day I began the class with filling in the gaps that I had found in their notebooks. That took only a little while. Then we had a discussion of how countries would interact if they were being guided by biblical teachings. We talked about how that compared with the European Community, the strengths and weaknesses of the design for the European Community, and implications it holds for the future. The discussion was really great and, for the first time that year, I felt that every student was interested and involved. In addition, I gave a pretty stiff test and after grading it I felt satisfied that the students had learned a great deal."

"I don't get it," said Cal. "What you did sounds great to me. If the students were involved, if they did well on the test, and if you were satisfied that they had learned, why are you so uncomfortable with what you did?"

Gary looked around the room. "For most of my students, this will be the only time they ever study economics from a Christian perspective," he said. "While it is true that they learned a great deal about the European Community with this style of instruction, I feel sick when I think of all the topics we could have covered in the days that we spent on this one. When I shared that concern with the committee on instruction they assured me that it is far more important for students to really be involved in learning a few things than to quickly go over and memorize a great deal of information. They reminded me that business courses are being effectively taught with the case-study method and these approaches would work well with case studies. They said it is far better for students to learn how to think about new concepts than for them to cover a lot of information. But frankly, how do they know? I'm the only business and econ. teacher in this school. There is no one I can talk to about my discipline.

"And some other things concern me," he went on. "The students that sat back and did very little in the small groups did fairly well on the final test. But that's because someone else did their work for them. Do I grade them on what they learned or do I grade them on how well they collaborated? Also, the committee thought I should have given a group grade on how well the group covered the appropriate information for their topic. I absolutely refuse to give a group grade when some individuals in the group have done nothing to earn it. I'm really confused about this.

"The committee suggested that one reason I had trouble was that my groups of seven were just too big. They said I should try groups of four and give each person in the group a specific task. Maybe I'll try that. I don't want to go back to my traditional way of teaching but I need some help."

Dennis Brouwer, the assistant principal of the middle school, smiled as he walked to the front of the room to close the meeting. "Gary, you said you don't know whether an old dog can learn new tricks, but listening to you gave me courage to try some new things in my own classes. The rest of you ought to know that Karla gave me a copy of Content Area Reading (Readence, Bean, and Baldwin 1992), and Gary and I have been going through it, seeing how we can adapt some of those instructional strategies to our own teaching. There are a number of other books on the professional shelf in the library. Thanks again, Gary. I'm sure there'll be people who would like to ask you some questions."

Whether one teaches with an integral approach or with a disciplinary approach, it is essential that instruction be as rich and involving as possible. Teachers don't have to be extraordinarily creative to teach this way. It is only essential that they are willing to search out new ways of thinking about teaching and learning and are willing to use them.

Van Dyk (1986–87) has described a Christian model of teaching as involving guiding, unfolding, and enabling. Van Brummelen (1988) has added structuring as a fourth dimension. In this book, we have described a curriculum model involving play, problem-posing, and purposeful responding. Models such as these are helpful to teachers in encouraging them to think through the components and steps of teaching. Teachers who recognize their task as helping students learn commitment and responsibility will arrange instruction so that they may interact with students in ways that are pedagogically effective. We often talk about the importance of teachers being exemplary models for students in ways that they live and think. The classroom should be an environment in which a contagious influence for learning flows back and forth between the teacher and student and among the students when they are in groups (Van Manen 1991). If all of that is to happen, instruction in the traditional as well as the nontraditional classroom must be carefully planned to allow for this influence.

There are teachers who are convinced that this kind of influence and modeling can take place when they are lecturing and, in addition, that students learn more facts when they listen to lectures than with other means of instruction. They realize that teaching is more than giving facts but to the extent that facts are important, they believe they can best be learned when presented in a lecture. Some of these teachers also insist that lecture notes dictated to the students so they can be carefully copied and organized will be an important aid to learning. However, research does not support these notions. In a review of studies comparing the effectiveness of note dictation with other teaching methods in preparing students to pass tests of factual information, McKeachie (1986) concluded the following:

1. Lectures are as effective, but not more so than other teaching methods, for presenting factual information.
2. On measures of retention of information after the end of the course, transfer of knowledge to new situations, or measures of problem-solving, thinking, attitude change, or motivation for further learning, discussion methods are more productive than lectures.

Most of these studies were conducted with college students. If lectures are so ineffective with college students, how much less effective are they in the learning of high school students?

If learning is to take on meaning, students need an opportunity to rehearse orally what they have heard and must do so immediately after hearing it. This may be done in the form of buzz groups and group problem-solving. Cooperative group interaction with the use of case studies has been found to be extremely effective in promoting meaningful learning. In fact, the class interactions that have been found the most helpful in promoting learning make a great deal of use of students' language.

We know that the effect language has on the person using it is extremely powerful. When I am able to talk about an idea or concept and am able to explain it to someone else, my own understanding of that concept is deepened. That is why it is so important that parents and students discuss at home what the student is learning in school. Teachers who understand the power of language will want to arrange learning activities that encourage a great deal of appropriate use of spoken and written language on the part of students.

We know that learning is more effective when students are immersed in complex and real experiences. Teachers who understand that will want to move away from one-way instruction of teacher to student or film to student and move toward more complex instruction that involves group discovery, individual search and reflection, or role-playing. They will want to involve students in planning for ways of learning so that it will be meaningful for them.

Involving students in learning does not mean having classrooms in which anything goes so long as the students are socially active. It means searching for group learning activities, reading strategies, and other cooperative arrangements that actively engage students in taking responsibility for their own learning and helping each other learn. These are serious, important ways of arranging instruction. Learning how to teach this way will require in-service training and an atmosphere in which teachers are encouraged to attempt new ways of teaching and to share in each other's successes and failures in these attempts.

Students arrive at flashes of understanding, moments of "aha, I get it" when they see how things are connected, at different times from each other. There is a joy in coming to understand something for the first time. When students are actively involved in their own learning the moment of understanding carries with it a particular joy. But that joy in learning is often preceded by hard work, uncertainty, risk-taking, and anxiety. There are many different ways teachers can help them along the way, but what they need more than anything else during this period is a teacher who can remember having been there, one who can remember the anxiety and uncertainty and therefore who is willing to provide encouragement during the frustrating moments.

Unfortunately, there are common teaching practices that close the learning space and that create an atmosphere of suspicion rather than of hospitality. But there is also a great variety of ways teachers can "create a space for learning in which obedience to truth is practiced" (Palmer 1983, 69). It is the task of the Christian teacher to search out those ways and to teach accordingly.

Teacher 1: I think the hardest part about teaching is to plan in ways that help the students become knowledgeable enough about a topic so that they will be eager to discover how to learn more about it.

Teacher 2: I know what you mean. A teacher has to be well-prepared with knowledge about the topic and must plan carefully for instructing in ways that will truly involve students in learning. Yet, after preparing so thoroughly the teacher must be willing to step aside as soon as the students are able and willing to learn more on their own, even when that means some lesson plans will change or be omitted.

Questions for Discussion

1. What is happening in your school that creates an environment productive or counterproductive to creating a space for learning in which obedience to truth is practiced?

2. When teachers are using cooperative group learning strategies should there be times when everyone in the group gets the same grade for the work that has been done? Is that fair? How can the learning situation be arranged so that it will be fair?

3. When you are attempting cooperative strategies and one or two students try to allow other students in the group to do their work for them, how might that be handled?

4. What would be the greatest impediments to planning and teaching with integral units in your school? How might those difficulties be overcome?

5. With a partner, choose a unit topic with which both of you are somewhat familiar. Brainstorm the implications of this chapter for teaching the topic. If implemented in this way would responsive discipleship be fostered? Why or why not?

Recommended Readings

1. Blomberg, D. G. 1991. "The integral curriculum."
A further elaboration of the integral curriculum approach in a Christian school setting.
2. Lapp, D., Flood, J., and Farnan, N. 1989. *Content area reading.*
Manzo, A., and Manzo, U. 1990. *Content area reading.*
Ways of planning interactive instructional strategies appropriate for subject area classes in middle and high schools.

11

How Do We Evaluate Student Learning?

February 25

Mountain City Christian School had just received the results of the statewide achievement tests written by fourth-, eighth-, and twelfth-grade students in November. Ken Heard posted a summary of the results on the bulletin board in the staff room. The results would be reported and briefly discussed in a staff meeting. Typically, staff room conversations have exhausted teacher interest before the meeting.

"So, Jim," Linda said, "how did your students do last November? Does it look like they are still learning the basics?" She was worried that some of the new approaches in reading and writing were not preparing students adequately for future learning. She presented her own students with a carefully structured approach.

"At first glance, it looks like my students did quite well," Jim replied. "Usually our students do very well on these tests. I believe they confirm quite nicely that we do a good job of overall teaching—as well as of preparing our students for the tests. Our parents and school board certainly want us to continue to use the tests."

Having overheard their conversation, Lynn looked for an opportunity to join in. She had recently completed her M.Ed. in evaluation, and hoped to encourage teachers to talk together more frequently about student learning, and especially about evaluating their learning. She felt the need for a review of Mountain City's report card format and of the school's student evaluation policy.

"What do you think these results really show about your students, Jim?" Lynn asked. "Do they tell you anything you didn't already know from your own classroom evaluations?"

Linda jumped in before Jim could respond. "We know that these tests are a necessary and valuable exercise. They keep teachers on a proper schedule for teaching skills and let parents know that our school continues to emphasize the basics."

Jim's own response was more cautious. "To tell you the truth, Lynn, I don't know if these tests tell us anything beyond what we know, but . . ."

He paused as the bell rang and the conversation abruptly ended. Lynn mused to herself, "It happened again, just as we get into a good discussion about learning, the bell rings and recess or lunch is over and teachers have to go back to their classrooms. We really need to develop opportunities to discuss in more depth these issues that keep popping up for a few minutes here and there and then are left unresolved."

As Jim went back to his classroom, Lynn's question made him reflect on the discussions that had been held ten years ago, before Mountain City began to use achievement tests. Was it time to examine the impact that these tests were having? It seemed that assessment and accountability were becoming important issues again.

At noon Jim and Cal found themselves eating lunch at the same table in the staff room. They both shared an interest in teaching language across the curriculum and occasionally asked each other challenging questions. Today, Jim wanted to focus on the test results.

"Well, Cal, how did your eighth graders do on the test? Do the scores give you confidence that you're doing a good job?"

"To be honest with you, Jim, I don't even look at the scores anymore. As presently designed, the achievement tests only tell us that our students are above average compared to national norms. Is that supposed to mean that our students are better than others or is it just that we draw students from a particular socioeconomic background? I believe that these scores don't help our teaching. We would be better off using the time that we now spend preparing for and taking the tests on better forms of evaluation. The only feedback that parents and students receive from these tests is that the score is below average, average, or above average. Surely we can do better than that."

Jim was surprised at Cal's reaction. "I didn't know you felt so strongly about these tests."

"My problem with the tests is part of a larger issue. What are we really doing for our students if we continue to evaluate the way we are doing it now?

262

I believe we need to sit down as a staff and talk about what we mean by our marking system. I know our report card for grades six to eight is different than yours. It's high time we reexamine how we evaluate students and how we communicate that to parents. I mean, what does a number or a letter tell you? How would you like to receive a grade for each unit you teach? Come to think of it, why do we give our students grades? Tell me, outside of school, in which occupation do adults get grades? Sure everyone gets evaluated, but who gets graded with a letter or a number?"

Jim's head was spinning. He certainly had not expected this reaction from Cal. He wondered what was behind it. Cal had developed some exciting units with his eighth graders. The students were enjoying writing in many different ways much more than before. It was true that at the beginning he had been criticized by some staff members and by some parents, but the criticism had decreased substantially as they saw how involved and interested the students were.

Pearl had been listening from the adjoining table. "Cal, you know that those tests don't mean very much to most of us. I wouldn't be too concerned if I were you. Achievement tests are here to stay. We do them because we have to. Parents want to know how their children compare statewide, so if these tests provide that comparison, why not have them?"

"I can understand why you feel this way," said Joan. "But we do need ways of assessing what our students know. The problem we face is that the tests are outdated. They need to be redesigned so that they test different levels of student thinking. Too many of the questions test recall and lower-order thinking skills. Apparently there are groups of people working on a new test design that will be piloted next year."

"A new test design?" Jim exclaimed. "Oh, that would be great! Just when we have figured out some good ways to prepare our students they change the test! I hardly think that will help any of us. Let's face it, changing the design of the test only means more headaches for teachers and more worries about how the test results will be used. Why don't we sit down and discuss whether or nor these tests really assist us in teaching and whether they really assist students in their learning? Let's come to grips with what evaluation should be like in Mountain City Christian School."

Jim's challenge was echoed by the end-of-lunch bell. Students filled the hallways. Classes would soon be starting again. Lynn had overheard most of the noon-hour discussion. She had wanted to join in with some of her own ideas but had decided to listen some more. It was important to let the teachers talk through some of these issues. Sometimes a comment by an administrator sounded too much like a statement of school policy and tended to close discussions rather than provide an atmosphere that stimulated discussion. Nevertheless, Lynn knew that she didn't have to wait any longer to decide her topic for the next staff in-service day. As Jim had said, Mountain City needed to discuss evaluation.

MARCH 1 STAFF MEMO
From: Ken, Lynn, Dennis, and Valerie
Re: April 14 In-service

In view of the energetic and involving discussions surrounding the achievement test results, we propose to have a full-day in-service to examine the way we evaluate and assess students at Mountain City Christian School. Lynn has volunteered to organize a workshop for that day. She welcomes your suggestions for ideas and issues regarding evaluation that you feel we should address on that day. Please share those ideas with her during the next two weeks.

As usual, we will have our lunch together as a staff on that day. Do we make reservations somewhere or are we going to have a potluck lunch here? Would the Social Committee please make the arrangements?

During the next two weeks, Lynn did receive several suggestions regarding issues to be included in the discussion.

Jim urged her to make sure that the staff address whether they should continue to use achievement tests. Cal met with her for a good half hour to convey his concerns about the *real* impact of grades. Joan stopped by to tell Lynn that something needed to be done in the way most teachers designed their own classroom tests. She insisted that the staff had to develop test questions that stimulated higher-level thinking skills. Margie caught Lynn during recess one morning to say that she hoped that the staff would get beyond the traditional evaluation issues and begin to address newer approaches to evaluation.

Lynn was pleasantly surprised at the number of suggestions she had received. As she began to consider the format she would use for the workshop, she had a feeling she wouldn't have to worry about doing all the talking on that day. She would present the staff with some principles to guide their thinking, set up small groups to discuss several issues, and conclude with the staff developing recommendations for initiating some improvements.

7:30 April 14
It was a cool, misty spring morning. As Lynn stepped out of the house she breathed in the freshness of budding trees and greening grass. Lynn appreciated the ten-minute walk in the crisp air each morning to get to school: it gave

her a chance to run the day's activities through her head. Today, it seemed even more necessary since she would be leading a full day in-service.

On the other side of town, Glenn Prince headed out the door at about the same time. The fifteen-minute drive gave him enough time to worry about the strange ideas that might be suggested during the in-service. It seemed that whenever the staff was given an opportunity to talk things through, too many different ideas were presented. He was sure that today's session on evaluation would be no exception. Some teachers would propose that Mountain City should abolish grades and examinations; others would propose that the school should have a second category of marks that would indicate student effort. These teachers felt that an effort mark would give students and parents a clearer indication of the course grade. Oh, well, Glenn thought, a one day meeting won't lead to much change anyway, and, besides, the teachers would have a chance to express their ideas and then they could go on with their regular routines.

As Lynn reached the front door of the school, she took a deep breath. She felt confident in her preparation and in the support she would receive from several key staff members. She also knew that Ken Heard would have arranged to have beverages and pastries available all day and that the Social Committee had organized a special lunch through the Auxiliary.

"Good morning, Lynn!" Ken greeted her as she entered the foyer. "All set for the day?" He knew that she was but it was his usual genuine greeting for any staff member who had a special responsibility that day. It was his way of finding out if he needed to do anything else before the meeting started.

"Good morning, Ken! Yes, it looks like I'm all set. I hope most of the staff is ready too. You're opening the meeting, correct?" Lynn knew that he would do so with a sensitive and stimulating devotional.

Ken welcomed everyone to the meeting by expressing his own appreciation for having a day to reflect on one of their tasks. He introduced the day's topic in relation to responsive discipleship. He read Romans 12 and shared a personal story about what the passage meant for him. In his prayer, Ken gave praise for the Lord's care over the school and asked for guiding wisdom during the day's discussions. He briefly reviewed the day's schedule and then introduced Lynn.

Lynn began her presentation with some personal reflections about the first eight months of the school year. She mentioned the active discussions that had occurred when the achievement test scores had been posted. They had reminded her of some of the seminar debates that had occurred during her year in graduate school; but the discussions at Mountain City had seemed much more realistic, rooted in teacher's own experiences and less "academic" than the ones at the university. She assured the staff that today's presentation and discussion would focus on their day-to-day practices and would also be intellectually stimulating. Lynn began her presentation with a few open-ended questions.

Why do we evaluate?

As teachers suggested responses, Lynn wrote them on a large sheet of paper.

We evaluate:

> to find out what students know
> to discover if students need assistance
> to tell parents how their children are doing
> to determine a mark for the report card
> to improve student learning
> to report student standing to the government
> to find out if students understood a particular unit
> to give students an opportunity to indicate what they know
> to determine if I reached my objectives as teacher
> to give students feedback on what they know

How do we evaluate?

"Before we make a list, I would like us to take a few minutes to read a piece of writing by a seventh-grade student. Read the paragraph and think about how you would evaluate this student's work."

As the teachers read, a nervous quietness filled the room. For most of the teachers, marking was their least favored activity. Giving students a mark for the work they completed, or worse yet, a mark for work they had not completed, was a difficult job. For most of them, teacher education programs had emphasized classroom management and knowing their subject matter well. There was very little emphasis on evaluating students. Many of them remembered their first experiences with calculating marks. Some had benefitted from the advice of experienced and sensitive colleagues; some had been appalled by the suggestion that the best way to calculate a report card mark was to consider all of the marks achieved during the term without looking at whose marks they were. Would some of these feelings and experiences emerge during the day?

"Let's share some of the ways in which we would evaluate this piece of writing."

John felt that this student has some good ideas about the topic. "However, he isn't able to express them very clearly."

Pearl, not unexpectedly, hoped that this didn't represent the way most of the grade seven students wrote.

"I had a difficult time evaluating this piece of work because I don't know the purpose of the original assignment," Susan said. "Why did the student write this? Is it a personal response to a discussion topic? Is it part of an essay assignment? I need to know that before I can say much more about what this student has written."

After a few more responses, Lynn felt that teachers were ready to consider some of the principles on which their evaluation should be based. She began by referring to the Bible passage that Ken had read for devotions. "If we want our students to be and become responsive disciples, to be able to discover and develop their gifts in service to the Lord, others, and creation in general, we need to evaluate in ways that enable students to do that. The following principles, adapted from Van Brummelen (1988), should be central to evaluation in a Christian school:

"First, evaluation must allow students and teachers to function as images of God, which means that they must be actively and responsibly involved in their own learning and hence in the evaluation of that learning. Teachers must make learning activities purposeful by sharing expectations with students and helping them to reflect on their own learning. Classroom evaluation should be primarily concerned with enabling learners to become more responsive in their learning.

"Second, evaluation must contribute to the development of knowledge, biblically understood. Because response is integral to knowing, an important aspect of evaluation becomes the appraisal of the ways in which students respond to and go beyond what has been taught. Because our knowledge is partial and tentative, evaluation ought to allow for open-ended and searching discussions rather than focusing primarily on short, definite answers. Because knowledge involves taking risks, evaluation encourages exploratory inquiries and considers what students are trying to do as well as assessing explicit answers. Because people come to know in many different ways, evaluation needs to go beyond assessing analytical development.

"Third, evaluation must contribute to the classroom covenant community, by affirming each student's involvement and contribution to the community. If evaluation is used primarily to rank students, then students tend to compete with each other for the sake of being better than their classmates. Evaluation must be done in a loving, upbuilding, and patient manner, accompanied by instruction that leads to further growth; students must sense that teachers are encouraging their learning and not judging their worth.

"Fourth, evaluation is a valuing activity. The ways in which teachers publicly recognize student accomplishments and failures will demonstrate to students what is really valued. In their evaluation of students, teachers must show those factors in learning and knowledge that they consider important, that we value them for who they are as persons and that our appraisal of their learning is intended to help them develop their own gifts.

"Fifth, evaluation must communicate meaningful information to students and parents about student learning. Parents are vitally concerned about their children's progress and want to know how they are doing on a regular basis. Teachers must communicate in a variety of ways with parents so that they become aware of the interests of parents and parents become aware of the school's and the teacher's goals for learning."

Lynn concluded her presentation of basic principles by saying that teachers evaluate their students by affirming their worth as people, by recognizing their accomplishments, and by encouraging and challenging their efforts toward further development and growth.

It was 10:00 and time for a break. As teachers stood up to get some coffee, conversations quickly began. The staff had listened intently to Lynn's presentation: to talk about evaluation in this way was different from their usual focus. If they accepted these principles, their present methods of evaluation would obviously have to change.

While munching on a doughnut, Cal wandered over to where Jim and Glenn were engaged in an animated conversation about some of the things that Lynn had said. As he reached them he heard Glenn saying, "Of course we can't do away with marks. Students won't do any work without marks. If I suggested to my students that from now on I wouldn't be putting a mark on their assignments but instead would only make comments about their work, many of them would immediately reduce their effort by half."

"You might be correct in saying that students would initially react that way," Jim responded. "However, I believe that is a result of what we have told them by the way we have evaluated them for so many years. They need to be weaned off marks and shown better ways to judge their own learning."

Cal was also interested. "Glenn, if we were honest, wouldn't we admit that the grades we give are not a very accurate representation of what our students know? Don't we grade primarily because we have to put a grade on the report card for parents and other authorities?"

Glenn disagreed with both of them. "Grades are necessary in school. They are a fairly accurate measurement of what students know about the material covered and, if done well, provide parents with a sense of where their children stand in relation to others in the class. Grades are a way . . ."

"It's time to get started again," Ken's booming voice could be heard above lively conversations and insistent voices. "Bring your beverage along."

In the room, Lynn was ready to explain the next part of the session. It was evident during the break that her presentation had stimulated discussion. She hoped that it would continue into the small group activity that had been planned.

"In order for each of us to be able to contribute our ideas and to ensure that our questions have been heard, we need to spend some time in small groups exploring some of our areas of concern. In February many of you expressed several concerns about the way we evaluate students at Mountain City. Three areas that stood out were the purpose of grades, the role of standardized tests, and the function and format of report cards. We will spend about thirty minutes in our groups for an initial discussion of one of the topics. Each group should first of all brainstorm ideas and questions on their topic concerning what we do now and what we could do in view of the basic principles that were outlined this morning. Secondly, each group should report back to the rest of us in the form of a proposal regarding what Mountain City should consider doing about this issue. These are the topics for the groups:

"Group One, the purpose of grades, will meet in Dennis's room. Group Two, the role of standardized tests, will meet in Susan's room. Group Three, the function and format of report cards, will meet in Jacqui's room.

"Please meet back here at 11:15 so that each group can present its proposal before lunch."

Each of the groups made their way to the designated rooms and were soon engaged in lively debate. Lynn had tried to make up the groups so that they represented some of the differences of opinion that existed on staff. She hoped that the principles she had presented might provide a way for the groups to develop some initial agreement about evaluation.

The Purpose of Grades

In Dennis's room, Joan, Cal, Glenn, and Dennis had not taken long to get embroiled in a debate about the pros and cons of grades.

"If we really practiced our belief that students are image bearers," Cal said, "then we would not grade students in the way that we presently do. We should be able to find a better way to evaluate their work. I believe that it is wrong to compare one student's intellectual ability with another student's ability."

Not surprisingly, Glenn disagreed. "I believe that marks can be used to communicate to parents what their children have achieved. Parents and students want to know how they measure up compared with others in their class, and more importantly, how they compare with other students their age at the end of high school."

"Do you really believe," Joan asked, "that a grade tells the parent or the student anything more than where they stand compared to others? I think that the strong emphasis on grades in our community and in our society is distracting us from the real purpose of learning. With our present focus on grades, we encourage students to work for the grade rather than working for understanding and wisdom. High marks have become the overriding goal. We try to emphasize service for God and others but so many students seem to see that as a tolerable add-on, and some even consider our service projects to be a distraction from their real goal for school. Dennis, what do you think?"

Dennis had been listening quite intently to the three of them arguing back and forth. He agreed with some of the arguments on both sides of the issue and hesitated to commit himself. Nevertheless, he knew that Mountain City had to come to grips with its grading practices. After a lot of heated discussion they had revised their K–4 report card five years ago. At that time the primary teachers had tried to involve the whole staff in a thorough discussion of evaluation, but the middle and high school teachers had balked at any change. Initially, a few parents had objected quite strongly, but as parents, teachers, and students became familiar with the new format the objections had changed to expressions of appreciation. Teachers had been given more time to prepare evaluations that provided a good deal of descriptive information about student achievement. What had seemed to be a major change at the time was now an accepted and expected part of student evaluation.

So Dennis was persuaded to comment. "In many ways our present practice of emphasizing grades that recognize intellectual achievement provide honor for those who have intellectual gifts. Parents, students, colleges, and universities, indeed our whole society gives high status to those who achieve the highest G.P.A. Celebrating the development of intellectual gifts is appropriate in a Christian school. But, what does such an emphasis on grades say to those who have different kinds of gifts? We say we believe that people have received different gifts, but in school, and in society, our practice shows that we give greater recognition to some gifts than others. If our school's task is to enable students to discover and develop all of their gifts, why do we continue to place so much emphasis on grading primarily intellectual gifts? Should we not be more distinctive?"

"Well," said Glenn, "I have to admit that your arguments sound quite good. However, the real world, which we are part of and our students have to live in, is a world of grades and classes. We must grade so that students are challenged in ways that will enable them to succeed out there. They shouldn't be sheltered from the real world."

"I don't believe that we intend to shelter our students," Joan reacted. "As a matter of fact, few employers actually grade their employees in the way that we grade our students. If we want to evaluate students realistically we should be evaluating them on the basis of what they themselves are able to do. That's quite different than giving them a grade that compares them to their classmates."

270

Just as Cal was about to push Joan's idea a little further, Lynn appeared at the door and indicated that they had five minutes to wrap up their discussion and come with their proposal to the larger staff.

Dennis took the initiative. "What shall we propose? Suggesting that we change our way of grading won't go over too well with many of us. We have developed routine practices that work for us and appear to work for most of our students. We would have to allow a good deal of time for discussion and time for teachers to reflect before any decision is made."

Joan suggested they propose that Mountain City examine its use of grades in terms of the principles that Lynn outlined. "It seems to me that they provide a good basis for stating the purposes of evaluation. We believe that people have a diversity of gifts. We are trying to provide more varied ways of recognizing those gifts. We need to find better ways of recognizing and evaluating student learning in response to the gifts that they have."

As they left Dennis's room to join the other teachers, Glenn couldn't help but wonder whether their proposal would last longer than today. He had seen and read many alternate ways of evaluating students, even at the high-school level. Yet in his heart he felt that whatever happened to the proposal, grades would continue to be at least a part of any school's system of evaluation.

Standardized Tests

In Susan's room the discussion about standardized achievement tests was just as spirited. Linda, Jim, John, and Susan had barely made it back from their break when John began: "It's high time that these tests recognize that some things have changed in school curriculum. You'd think that with all the literature out there about developing thinking skills the test makers would have improved test questions. They place too much emphasis on basic skills and lower-order questions. Our students will never develop their thinking in the way they should. Also, there is reason to think that the tests may be gender-biased."

"Do you think that the tests will be improved?" Susan asked. "I believe that they will continue to test basic competencies. They're designed to serve the needs of a very broad population. It isn't likely that they will change much."

"We need to do more than hope that the tests will change," said Jim. "Look at how the test results influence how parents, administrators, and teachers feel about how our school is doing. It seems that the test results have become the yardstick by which we measure everything we do. The fact that our scores are generally at or above average is taken as an indication that what we are doing is worthwhile, and a confirmation of the quality of the education that our students are receiving. We take for granted that these tests measure what we consider to be the purpose of our school."

"Come on, Jim, we know that these tests don't measure everything that we consider important," Linda said. "None of us pretends to believe that the scores our students achieve represent all that they have learned or not learned."

"That's exactly the problem, Linda. We don't pretend to believe it. But take a look at our practices. Each of the teachers that teach students who will be writing these tests has files full of old test questions so that students can practice weeks in advance on a regular basis. I'll bet if you looked at the types of teacher-prepared tests for other parts of the curriculum you would see many questions that are similar to the questions on the achievement tests. We, and by that I mean parents, teachers, and students, perceive the test results to be important and I think they affect everything that we do."

"The charge of teaching to the tests is a serious one," John said. "I think that we try to do our best in assisting students to be reasonably well prepared. It could be that some of us are too zealous in our preparation. But if you consider how important the results are to many people in our society today, it doesn't surprise me that they are also considered to be important in our school. The real problem we face is the way in which we use the test results. We should educate ourselves and our parents regarding the purposes and limitations of different types of standardized tests. Some diagnostic tests can be used to provide information about particular levels of ability and skills so that we can design our program to meet those needs. Some tests can be used to diagnose strengths and weaknesses of specific subject areas in a school's curriculum. I would hope that we work toward evaluating students on the basis of school-established criteria and move away from using norm-referenced tests that compare students to each other. Standardized tests cannot and should not be the predominant measure of our programs."

Susan agreed, but she said the issue involved more than tests. "We have to carefully examine the ways we evaluate our students in our school. We need to come to grips with the fact that as teachers we haven't discussed what our goals for evaluation are. Each of us tries to evaluate our own students as fairly as possible. What messages do our students receive in the way we mark? Do they receive similar messages from different teachers? Are there contradictions in the way we mark?"

Just as Linda was about to respond, Lynn came into the room and said that they had four minutes to conclude their discussion and come with their proposal to the whole staff.

Linda was taken aback. "Do we actually have anything to propose to the staff? It appears to me that we haven't resolved our own differences yet."

"Let's try something like this," Jim suggested. "Let's propose that Mountain City take a look at its curriculum priorities and develop plans and processes for evaluation to fit with those priorities. While we are doing that we should clarify the purposes of the tests being used now and communicate those purposes to parents. We should explain the limitations of the tests and involve them in our discussions about better ways of evaluating student learning. Our discussions should include the negative consequences for student learning of an overemphasis on the results of these tests. Hopefully, we'll end up with an evaluation process that encourages students to show the things they are good at and discourages the current negative comparisons that occur on the basis of narrowly focused tests."

Report Cards

In Jacqui's room the discussion was more subdued, although Geoff, Pearl, Ken, and Jacqui were able to focus on several key questions. Jacqui wanted to begin by showing the others the report card that was being used for K–4. Five years earlier she had been instrumental in leading the primary teachers to review the old format. They had successfully introduced a report card that described student learning by means of anecdotal comments, supported by examples to show what and how well students were doing in each area of study.

Initial opposition from some parents had mellowed as they experienced the more detailed description about their own children's learning. The primary teachers had hoped that eventually the report cards in the higher grades would change as well. However, with the perceived need for greater accountability and more emphasis on student marks, ideas of review had died away. Before Jacqui could suggest that they look at the primary report card, Pearl tried to downplay a need for major change.

"Why don't we write a letter to accompany our present report card," Pearl said, "explaining what the grades mean and asking parents to put less emphasis on the grade when they talk with their kids about the report card?"

"I doubt if that would be enough, Pearl," Geoff replied. "The grade is a prominent feature and as far as most of our parents are concerned, the most important part. They look at the grade first and then at the class average. Many of my students tell me they are more concerned about being above or below the class average. I think it would be better if we eliminated the class average on the report card and added comments to explain the grade a student received."

Jacqui wanted to go even further. "How can you summarize all that a student has done into a grade? I don't see how one mark can adequately indicate to parents what a student knows or doesn't know, has done or hasn't done. I believe that it is important to use a number of different ways to describe student learning. By using anecdotal records, observation checklists, samples of student work, and conferences with students, we can provide a fuller description of learning than one grade will ever show."

"Report cards," said Ken, "are only one vehicle, even if they're the primary vehicle, that we use to communicate to parents how our students are doing. The report card is only an indication, a summary, of what the student has learned at a particular point in the year. We should not pretend that it tells the whole story."

"My students take home numerous papers and handouts that they have completed and I have marked," said Pearl. "If they would keep them together and show them to their parents more often everyone would have a much better idea of their grade on an ongoing basis. The report card grade simply represents an accumulated calculation that most students could do on their own. I'm always surprised when they say they didn't know that their grade was so low."

Jacqui agreed with the importance of gathering a sample of student work. "But what are we communicating to students and to parents when a mark, and maybe a brief comment, is the only thing on the report card?"

Ken knew the policy on this one. "Our report card explains our intent." He read from the form in front of him. "'We believe that the true value of this report is realized when it is used to motivate your child to learn for the sake of learning and not just for the sake of the grade. Therefore be positive when you discuss this report with your child. Give praise for work well done and the effort put into it.' I believe that a comment such as that provides some ideas about what we consider important."

"Now that you mention that comment," said Geoff, "I am reminded of a conversation that Susan and I had the other day. We both found it quite striking that we suggest that parents urge their children to consider learning to be more than achieving good grades yet as teachers the only information we give parents is a grade. Aren't we sending conflicting messages? Aren't we contradicting what we say by what we do?"

"Ideally," said Ken, "we want our report cards to show parents what and how students are learning. Maybe we need to find out from parents whether they are receiving the information that they need."

Jacqui realized it was getting near time to wrap things up. "Let's try to formulate a proposal for the rest of the staff," she said. "Shall we use the principle that Lynn gave as a starting point? She stated that 'evaluation must communicate meaningful information to students and to parents.' Let's suggest that we reexamine the way in which we hold parent-teacher interviews. How meaningful can interviews be if parents are invited to come to a school gym to stand in line and, at best, meet for a few minutes with three of the seven teachers that their children have? Surely, we could improve how we communicate with parents."

"Yes," Geoff agreed, "that principle is a good starting point. We'll propose that Mountain City review the way it communicates information about learning. The review includes examining the report cards now used in grades five to twelve to find out if they communicate what we believe and value about our students and about learning. Does our report card help us to encourage student learning? Does it recognize student accomplishments? Do parents experience them as just one of the means of dialogue available?"

Jacqui had the last word. "Don't limit the review to grades five to twelve. We could also use another look at the K to four report card."

The Purpose of Evaluation

Christian schools face pressures similar to those in society at large. On the one hand, there are moves to increase the use of tests to measure student learning and to hold teachers more accountable for what students learn. On the other hand, alternative forms of evaluation are being developed (Archbald and Newmann 1988).

It is our conviction that Christian schooling for responsive discipleship must evaluate in ways that enable students to unfold their gifts, to share the burden of difficulties in learning, and to celebrate the joys of accomplishments. The purpose of evaluation is, first of all, to encourage and improve student learning. Evaluation should enable teachers and students to assess the extent to which they have met the learning goals they have established. Students must be given opportunities to be directly involved in describing how they see their own achievements and difficulties. They will be guided by an evaluation process that recognizes achievement and assists in diagnosing difficulties according to each student's level of ability and development intellectually, aesthetically, spiritually, physically, emotionally, and socially.

Second, evaluation must provide guidance for improving instruction. Teachers need information about student learning to help identify strengths and weaknesses in order to design their teaching in ways that best meet those needs. Instead of teaching to the test, teachers should be concerned with assessing student learning and on that basis evaluating their teaching.

Third, evaluation is necessary to account for the learning that occurs in schools to those responsible for the operation of the school. Appropriate authorities such as parents, school boards, and governments need information regarding the extent to which a school meets the goals and standards which they have set.

Fundamentally, however, Christian schools must evaluate in ways that encourage students to actively respond to the many different aspects of the curriculum. Learning is not for its own sake, but for the sake of being more effective servants of the Lord Jesus Christ. We will seek means of assessment that promote humble service rather than self-glorifying achievement, and a positive account of abilities rather than a low estimate of self.

The Process of Evaluation

These purposes imply that teachers should develop the processes of evaluation as an integral part of the curriculum. If students have been actively engaged in learning by being provided with opportunities to develop different kinds of abilities and interests, if they have been able to integrate their learning within their own broader experiences and have been challenged to grow in wisdom and faithfulness, if the learning activities in which they have been involved have enabled them to develop their gifts in service of God and others, then the process of evaluation must support this rich learning.

Such a process must involve students, teachers, and parents in establishing the purpose of evaluation, determining the type of information necessary, and deciding meaningful ways of communicating about teaching and learning. The whole school community decides who will be involved and what methods will be used to evaluate learning, although teachers will have the major responsibility for initiating discussion with parents and students.

A major task involves determining the information that is required to provide meaningful descriptions of student learning. Teachers and parents can collect information through watching students in action, examining samples and collections of students' work, and talking with and listening to students. A wide variety of work should be collected to provide examples of what a student is able to do and to show students and parents the growth that has occurred over a period. By observing students interacting with peers, adults, and learning materials in a wide variety of activities, teachers will be able to attain a clearer idea of the things that students are able to do and the things they should be encouraged to develop further. Regular conversations and conferences with students will provide deeper insight into the learning that has occurred and will enable students to express ideas and feelings about their learning experiences in their own language.

Describing and interpreting what students are able to do and should be encouraged to do can best be accomplished on the basis of a rich collection of information. Have the students attained the goals of specific parts of the curriculum? Are they meeting the learning objectives that are considered important for their level of development? Description should always be in the context of previous and current knowledge about each student's situation.

The most difficult and the most important aspect of evaluation involves interpreting the information that has been collected. What does the information reveal about the student's learning? What does the teacher consider to be the learning that the student has achieved? How does the student interpret the things that have been done?

Communication about student learning should occur in many different ways. Throughout the school year, teachers must provide opportunities for sharing and conversing about information that invites students and parents to be involved in the learning process. Parent-teacher-student conferences three times a year are one appropriate way to do that. In preparation for each conference, students take home a collection of the learning activities and assignments they have completed, teachers send home a brief overview of the units that have been the focus of student learning, students evaluate their own learning, and parents prepare their responses to the work that they have seen. The focus of the conference can more clearly be a dialogue about learning, rather than parents guessing what the assigned grade means.

The entire process of evaluation must be part of the ongoing teaching and learning experiences and reflect the regular conditions of the classroom.

Multiple Avenues for Evaluation

Christian schools must provide students with numerous opportunities for developing their gifts in interdependent and individual ways and with multiple avenues for students to show what they are able to do. We suggest five ways in which present methods of evaluation can be broadened: authentic tests, portfolios, self-evaluation, projects, and exhibitions.

Authentic Tests

Although changes are occurring in some schools, many studies report that teacher-made tests continue to emphasize short-answer questions which sample knowledge of facts, terms, and concepts, and contain predominantly lower-order questions (Stiggins et al. 1986, 6) This type of test reveals only a narrow part of what students learn and often restricts their responses to one predetermined answer.

Authentic tests would require the performance of exemplary tasks that replicate the standards of performance that people face in real life and are responsive to individual students and school communities (Wiggins 1989a, 703–4). Having decided what we want students to be good at, we must design tests that present students with the full array of tasks involved in challenges that lead to quality learning: writing, revising and discussing papers; engaging in oral analysis of recent political events; conducting research; and collaborating with others on a debate (Wiggins 1990, 1).

An authentic test enables us to watch students pose, tackle, and solve real challenges and problems. Newmann (1991, 460) states that tests should provide students with opportunities to produce original conversation and writing, to repair and build physical objects, and to be involved in artistic and musical performance.

Central Station Christian School Oral History Project

As part of a unit on "Searching for Our Roots," Emmy has the ninth graders design and complete an oral history project. Students are required to write a history based on interviews and written sources and to present their findings orally to the class. Students choose their own topics, create several workable hypotheses, and develop four questions that they will ask to test each hypothesis. Completing the project requires demonstrating background research, interviewing at least four appropriate people as sources, using the evidence to support the choice of the best hypothesis, and organizing the writing and class presentation (Wiggins 1989, 707).

Science Class Performance Task

Ted has developed numerous problem tasks to challenge students to show what they are able to do. One of these tasks involves determining the density of fluids:

(a) The student is given four unknown liquids and a commercial hydrometer, and asked to solve the following problem:

Farmer Smith is having problems with his new tractor. He has decided to try the old Model A, his first tractor. The Model A has had all the oil drained out of her for storage. But Farmer Smith cannot recall which vat contains the right oil—the oil with the highest possible density. You have been given a sample of the four vats of oil. Determine which one is for the Model A.

(b) Using the equipment provided, construct and calibrate a hydrometer: You should have:

straws	plasticine	lead shot
wax pencil	ziplock bags	ruler
cylinder of water	cylinder of glycol	masking tape
(density = 1g/ml)	(density = 1.3g/ml)	

After completing the task, students must write a description of what they have done to reach the conclusion they did.

Portfolios

A second avenue for expanding evaluation in Christian schools involves the use of portfolios. At the elementary level, a number of schools have begun to develop collections of student work which they make available from time to time during conferences with students and use as an integral part of discussions with parents. A portfolio is a purposeful collection of student work that exhibits to the student and others the student's efforts, progress, or achievement in a given area. This collection must include: student participation in selection of content; the criteria for selection and for judging merit; and evidence of student self-evaluation (Arter 1990, 2). Using portfolios to evaluate student learning provides a way of increasing student responsibility for their own work, enlarging teachers' and students' views of what has been learned, and showing the development that occurs over a longer period (Wolf 1989, 37–38).

Students' portfolios will become showcases for a great variety of student work, and will document learning throughout the school year.

Central Station Christian School Middle School Writing Portfolio

As part of her language arts program, Karla requires students to read at least a half-hour per day and to produce no fewer than six rough draft pages of writing a week. At regular intervals students are asked to rank their work from most effective to least effective and to evaluate it by considering the following questions:

1. What makes this your best piece?
2. How did you go about writing it?
3. What problems did you encounter? How did you solve them?
4. What makes your most effective piece different from your least effective piece?
5. What goals did you set for yourself? How well did you accomplish them?
6. What are your goals for the next four weeks?

Over time, Karla began to see more diversity and depth to student writing, their reading, and their responses to literature. She discovered that students knew themselves better as learners, set goals for themselves, and judged how well they had reached those goals. Reflecting on her experiences, Karla agreed that "as teachers we have to believe in the possibilities of our students by trusting them to show us what they know and valuing what they are able to do with that knowledge" (Rief 1990, 25).

Mountain City Christian School
Grade Four Reading Assessment Portfolio

During the last two years, Jim has initiated portfolios as a way of broadening his evaluation of student reading. He had experienced a number of frustrations in his teaching. It seemed that students weren't becoming responsible for their own reading; he was making most of the choices about what they would read. He began to use portfolios as a way of developing their responsibility. Four principles had guided his approach: evaluation would be based on their reading of a variety of books, would examine student reading over an extended period, would include multidimensional responses, and would involve collaborative reflection by student and teacher.

The portfolio that Jim designed was an expandable file folder that held (a) samples of a student's work, (b) teacher's observational notes, (c) student's periodic self-evaluation, and (d) progress notes contributed by the student and teacher collaboratively. Portfolios came to include a broad range of items, such as written responses to reading, reading logs, selected daily work, pieces of work at various stages of completion, classroom tests, checklists, and unit projects (Valencia 1990, 338).

Jim considered one of the major benefits of portfolios to be their value in teacher-student and parent-teacher-student conferences: they were a basis for discussion of progress in reading and for the setting of future goals, an excellent way to focus on the learning that students had accomplished, and the basis for a mutual exchange about what should be done next.

Self-Evaluation

> ### Mountain City Christian School
> ### Major Assignment in Science—Student Self-Evaluation

In her eleventh-grade science class, Susan has incorporated student self-evaluation as an important part of her evaluation of the two major assignments that students complete during the year. After the assignments have been written she has students answer six questions:

1. How much time did you spend on this paper?
2. Describe the process you went through to create this paper by addressing these questions:

   (a) Where did you get the idea for the paper?
   (b) What strategies did you use to help you explore the subject?
   (c) What problems did you have while writing the first draft?
   (d) How did you go about making revisions?

3. Group comments: First, list a point your group made about your paper. Then respond to their comments. For example, do you agree or disagree with what they said? Do this for two or three of the comments your group made.
4. What are the strengths of your paper? What parts still make you feel uneasy?
5. What do you want me to look for when I evaluate this paper? What questions do you have for me?
6. What grade would you put on this paper and why? (Thompson, in Arter 1990)

Susan has found that this process has changed the ways in which students work on the assignments. As they reflect on what they have done previously, they begin to think about what they are doing in the process of researching and writing. Also, Susan finds that the self-evaluations provide her with a much broader understanding of each student for her own evaluation of the papers.

Projects

A fourth avenue for expanding student evaluation in Christian schools is a series of projects; the topics and themes will grow out of students' interests and gifts in the context of a curriculum designed to bring about responsive discipleship. Projects should be based on real-life situations, have guidelines to give direction, have open-ended rather than predictable results, and address real needs in the broader community.

Projects should be an integral part of the curriculum and should be designed so that they require students to formulate and to ask world-view questions, to explain themselves to peers and to adults, and to develop and apply their gifts in service to God and their neighbors. Projects offer students opportunities to establish connections between their school learning and the real-life settings where they will soon be expected to perform adult roles. Christian schools should have students design projects that involve them in activities in the Christian community as well as in the broader community in which the school is located.

Students choose and design their own projects in consultation with a staff advisor and, outside the school, with a person who has special interest and skills in the project topic.

Table 4
Projects Requiring Challenging, Meaningful Involvement

Kind of Project	Purpose of Project	Strategy
Service	To meet an individual or communal need.	Discover a need. Develop an action plan. Carry out the plan (expecting no reward). Reflect on the xperience of bringing healing and restoration.
Critical inquiry	To solve a problem facing individuals or society.	Choose a problem or question. Research its roots. Consider its symptoms. Propose a Christian response.
Exploring vocations	To learn about a specific vocation.	Select a vocation. Observe, study, and participate in it, exploring its tendencies, abilities, and skills.
Exploring the outdoors	To explore the wonders of the world and develop survival and endu: :v ce skills.	Plan a one- or two-week experience around this activity. Carry o'·⁺·ᵇⁱs plan.

Students should have the opportunity to work on individual as well as group projects and, upon completion, to make a public presentation of their work. Projects have the potential to become an invaluable extension and fulfillment of what students have learned during their years in Christian schooling.

Exhibitions

A fifth avenue for expanding evaluation of student learning is through exhibitions. One of the goals of Christian schooling is to celebrate the accomplishments of students and to recognize the learning that has been achieved. Exhibitions provide an avenue for students to demonstrate what they have learned and a way for members of a school community to celebrate what its students have accomplished. At present, Christian schools have a variety of public celebrations involving drama, music, academic, and athletic performances. They will provide even greater encouragement for learning by requiring that all students present a public demonstration of a project that is an integral part of the curriculum and is directly related to one or more of the goals of Christian schooling. Exhibitions will enable students to study a topic or area in which they have special interests and gifts and show publicly what they have accomplished and thereby contribute to the learning of others. The following example is adapted from Sizer (1992, 23):

Human Tendencies

Select one of the following human tendencies:

joy, courage, kindness, anger, fear, faithfulness, patience, gentleness, envy, hatred, cowardice, love, greed.

In an essay, define the human tendency you choose, drawing on your own and other's experience within a biblical perspective. Render a similar definition using in turn at least three of the following forms of expression:

a drawing, painting, or sculpture; photographs, a video, or film; a written language other than English; a musical composition; a short story or play; a pantomime or dance.

Select examples from literature, journalism, the arts, and history of other people's definitions or representations of the tendency you have chosen.

Be ready in six months to present this work and answer questions about it. The exhibition will be judged on the basis of its creativity, overall coherence and development, and thoughtfulness, as well as the quality of each of the components.

Christian schools must enable teachers and students to evaluate learning in ways that stimulate the development of a diversity of gifts. Our schools must value many different ways of growing in knowledge and understanding as we learn. Christian schools must design a process in which students, teachers, and parents evaluate learning in ways that encourage individual and communal gifts, joyfully recognizing growth and accomplishments and openly addressing difficulties.

Questions for Discussion

1. What are the evaluation procedures that are used in your school and in your class? Examine these in the light of the principles of evaluation described in this chapter.

2. How can schools encourage the development of a variety of gifts? Considering the program(s) offered in your school what gifts are students presently encouraged to develop?

3. Review the process used in your school for parent-teacher-student conferences. Are conferences scheduled so that parents have adequate opportunities to meet with teachers? Are students included in the conference? Involve parents, teachers, and students in a discussion of ways in which your school can improve communication about learning.

4. In this chapter we suggest five avenues in which Christian schools can expand their approach to evaluation. Some teachers may already be using one or more of these avenues now. If so, ask them to present what they are doing as part of a staff discussion. If none of these are presently being used, explore one or more of these further and present it to your staff to stimulate thinking about evaluating student learning.

Recommended Reading

1. Perrone, V., ed. 1991. *Expanding student assessment.*
   A valuable resource for reviewing the purpose and functions of

evaluation and for considering new ways of evaluating student learning.
2. Archbald, D. S., and Newmann, F. M. 1988. *Beyond standardized testing.*
Provides strategies for improving academic achievement in high schools.
3. *Educational Leadership* 46 (April 1989).
Many excellent articles to stimulate thinking about student assessment.
4. Arter, J. 1990. *Using portfolios in instruction and assessment.*
A helpful article and bibliography for initiating staff discussion on the use of portfolios in student evaluation.

Part **3**

Taking Up the Task

12

Changing Schools
Through Staff Development

"I'm sick and tired of these professors that Don brings in every year to 'inspire' us on our in-service days," George said. "The next day I feel like I've been involved in a hit-and-run accident. They breeze in here and then just as quickly breeze out. It's the same thing at the teachers' conventions. We have these wonderfully inspirational keynotes with little relevance to what I do in the classroom, and then lots of workshops on classroom strategies. Even if I do get excited about an idea, I often don't really know how to put it into practice."

"I know what you mean," said Lisa. "I did get excited about cooperative learning several years ago, and I tried it for a few weeks, but it seemed to take so much more energy to set it up that I sort of ran out of steam. It didn't seem like anyone else was trying it, so I had no one to talk to."

"Did you really? I tried it myself and I thought I was the only one doing it. We could have talked about it together. Maybe we would still be using it!"

"Come on, George, when do we ever talk about that sort of thing around here? We rarely discuss classroom activities as a staff."

"But, Lisa, maybe we could try it again. Maybe some other teachers would be interested. Perhaps we could set up a group to talk about it, sort of like a study group. We used to have something like that about fifteen years ago. I wonder what happened to the practice?"

"Well, do you think Don would support us in this? He seems to be a bit keener lately on us trying out some new things. Maybe he would support our efforts?"

If Christian schools are to improve teachers will need to develop opportunities to engage in learning themselves. If a Christian school is to be a vital, enriching community of learning, it ought to expect and honor the growth of its teachers and principals. Certainly, the school exists not for the teachers but for the students. But the students will derive the most benefit when the working environment is not only congenial but also stimulating for the teachers. It is not possible "to create the conditions for productive learning when those conditions do not exist for education personnel" (Sarason 1990, 13).

Perhaps the principal's response to George and Lisa would be something like this:

"I've been hoping for this for some time," said Don. "I'd be happy to support you. But I'd rather see a slightly larger group working together. What about Mary Anne and Sheryl? Would they be interested in joining you? See if you can find a time in the week when two or three of you are not teaching. Then I'll cover an additional period adjoining that one by getting in substitutes, and maybe teaching one of the classes myself. I would like to get back in the classroom a bit more anyway. I think I've become out of touch in many ways. I've talked to several other principals recently who have described the benefits they've experienced in teaching classes for some of their teachers so that they could work together planning an integral unit. Why don't you get a group together and then jot down a short proposal so I can share what's happening with the board?"

Our argument throughout the book has been that *community* is central to the faithful flourishing of the Christian school as an agent of God's grace. In the professional development of teachers, we believe that personal and communal growth are essential for staff development. Teachers must continue to learn personally and communally in order for them to encourage learning in students. In this chapter, we will argue that, in addition to a teacher's personal growth, collegiality—professional communal relationships—is essential to communal staff development. Two approaches, collegial study groups and collaborative action research, are presented as avenues that schools can employ to enhance learning for teachers and consequently for students.

Personal Professional Growth

Teachers are called to a life of discipleship, to proclaim the creative and redemptive work of Jesus Christ in their teaching. As teachers allow their hearts and minds to be transformed by the Spirit of truth, they will experience a renewal that provides them with grace and courage to fulfill their calling. It is because we are sought and known and loved by Jesus Christ that we become capable of seeking and knowing and loving students and colleagues in our teaching and learning (Palmer 1983, 113).

Teachers must look for and be provided with opportunities for developing their own gifts. We do not fully know what our gifts are when we first begin to teach. In our interactions with students and colleagues we gradually become aware of our strengths and weaknesses. As we learn to teach we must continue to expand our ways of knowing about teaching. We must set goals for our own development and look for and design learning experiences that will stimulate our own professional growth.

Teachers can use various professional opportunities to develop their gifts. Participating in professional conferences in one's area of specialization (both inside and outside the Christian community) brings teachers into contact with colleagues facing similar challenges and difficulties. Visiting other schools provides teachers with different approaches to teaching particular courses or topics. Becoming involved with government or institution-sponsored task forces enriches teachers with opportunities to reflect on their own framework and deepen their convictions. Personal growth also occurs as teachers commit themselves to revising units that they currently teach or reexamining the content and approaches used in one or more courses.

The school is often conceived as a technical delivery system. Neither the teacher nor the student is expected to exercise much judgment in the process. The curriculum is seen as setting the boundaries to teachers' interest in their students, who are measured in terms "of their relative success or failure in assimilating the lesson plan" (Schön 1983, 331).

The curriculum distinguishes the school from other settings in which education occurs. It is a systematic and dynamic program of instruction, and ongoing reflection on it is crucial to the professional growth of teachers. It should not constrain teachers' relationships with their students, because it is the curriculum rather than the students that is being tested as to whether it most effectively promotes learning for responsive discipleship. It will be in this curriculum-testing that the judgment of the teacher will be realized, refined, and developed. Christian schools geared to responsive discipleship will enable teachers and principals to be actively engaged in learning for teaching as a continuous process.

Schön (1983, 39–40) suggests that teaching is often thought of as a process of problem-*solving*: decisions are made by selecting the means thought to be best suited to achieving ends that have already been established. But there is really a prior step, that of problem-*setting*, in which we define the decision to be made, the ends to be achieved, the means that may be chosen. In planning, teachers merge their varying concerns in the curriculum, deciding what will count as meaningful in teaching and learning, and what will and will not count as progress.

In the Christian school, teachers will have the primary goal of setting biblically-inspired problems. To be in the world but not of it always implies a disjunction: we continually face the question of how we should feel uncomfortable in contexts where we are most tempted to feel at home. We are called to question the accepted patterns and beliefs in the light of the Scriptures. By the very nature of teaching, teachers are called to articulate what many others may leave implicit. We are called to actively shape knowledge where others may be tempted to take it for granted. It is in this very problem-posing that Christian teachers have constant opportunities for spiritual growth, which must be at the heart of our professional growth.

Communal Staff Development

Staff development involves more than personal professional growth. The failure of individual teachers to sustain innovations verifies the need to go beyond individual growth. Similarly, the failure of curriculum dissemination models alerts us to the inadequacy of a merely structural approach. Growth will need to be both personal and communal in nature. Although often professionally isolated from one another, teachers in Christian schools differ from other teachers in one important respect: they share a common faith, they acknowledge one Lord. Their common faith provides a basis for working out goals for learning that direct their teaching. The challenge that Christian schools face is to allow a common confessional bond to grow into collegiality. The spiritual bond that unites teachers personally will then become the basis for mutually supportive collaboration in day-to-day teaching and learning. Collegiality does not imply uniformity of practice. Rather, it consists of teachers communally working out what it means to be faithful to the Lord's purposes for learning.

Research into effective professional development programs has identified a number of significant features (Fullan 1982, 286–87; Australia 1988). The focus of staff development should be on the day-to-day tasks faced by teachers. The school setting has a pivotal role in the development and application of ideas, the practice and sharpening of skills, and the critical appraisal of curriculum. Teachers need to relate new knowledge to their career and classroom experiences and to apply and critically evaluate new practices in their own contexts. They should be involved in planning and control of the program. Teachers have significant roles as resource persons at both the one-to-one level and the formal level of workshops or courses.

A program of staff development should include the following components: theory, demonstration, practice, feedback, and application with coaching (Joyce and Showers 1981). A variety of formal and informal elements should be coordinated: training workshops and sharing workshops, teacher-teacher interaction, one-to-one assistance and meetings. If staff development is to be successful, follow-through is crucial. A series of sessions, with intervals in which teachers have the chance to try things out, is much more powerful than even the most spectacular "hit-and-run" workshop. In this process, teachers should be provided with ready access to relevant internal and external support services.

Teacher commitment to staff development should be supported by creating deliberate opportunities and incentives for career-long participation in professional learning. The interest and support of principals is vital to maintaining a healthy climate for staff development. In many ways the principal is the head learner—experiencing, displaying, modelling, and celebrating what is hoped and expected of teachers and students (Barth 1990, 46).

Institutional change and professional development are closely related. Both should be part of the ongoing growth of schools. Boards, schools, principals, and teachers need to commit themselves to the pursuit of personal and collective professional learning. Because the goal of professional development is to improve student learning, the impact of the program on students (as well as on teachers and on the broader school context) should be conscientiously evaluated.

Fullan (1982, 87) suggests that two of these points are crucial. First, "the absence of follow-up work after workshops is without doubt the greatest single problem in contemporary professional development."

This is intimately connected with his second observation: professional development will require the involvement of far more than just those people responsible for organizing the program. What is required is "systems of *peer-based interaction* and feedback among teachers combined with external assistance." In other words, it is only when collegial relations between teachers become a normal part of the school culture that effective change will be possible.

Finally, *innovation-focused* and *action research* modes of professional development are complementary approaches and both should be employed in the school. *Innovation-focused* professional development is a program to facilitate the introduction of a new approach to teaching (such as cooperative learning) or a new program (such as Philosophy for Children). *Action research* staff development is an approach that takes the classroom concerns of the teacher as a starting point and focus. The former involves bringing in an idea from the outside, the latter works from the inside out. Neither one excludes the other; indeed, both would encourage two-way movement across the boundary between the school and the outside world.

If these two approaches are conceived as means of building collegiality, with a focus on concerns that teachers have about their daily practice, they can become a significant part of the school culture and a powerful force for its ongoing reformation.

We have previously discussed peer associates (chap. 4) and teacher planning teams (chaps. 8 and 10) as important practices for teachers working together in a school. Here we will first discuss collegial study groups as a way of learning about particular innovations and of becoming more reflective about classrooms. Second, we will consider ways in which a school can organize for collaborative action research.

Collegial study groups and action research will enable teachers to begin to practice collaborative procedures and to do so over an extended period. These approaches are considered as models of how teachers may work jointly in the resolution of educational problems and as incentives for more pervasive institutional change. Successful implementation of these staff development practices will provide the impetus for an ongoing revitalization of the culture of a school.

Collegial Study Groups

"Well, Lisa, how do you think our group is going? We've managed to look at quite a bit of material on cooperative learning now, and I feel much more confident about it."

"So do I, but I'm wondering whether it might not be time to go a step further. There's been the five of us involved, but I think we could do a great deal for the life of the school if we could get more people interested."

George agreed, but he remembered all too well his last few years of feeling depressed about teaching to think that there was any point in coercing teachers into a study group. He knew that the study group had been a great help to him in helping to refresh his vision, but he knew also that he had been ready to take the step. "Tell you what, Lisa, why don't we identify a few time slots before school on one or two days of the week, and see how many people would be interested in signing up to meet once a month."

As it turned out, George and Lisa were surprised by the enthusiasm of their colleagues. Within a few days, more than twenty (out of ninety) teachers had volunteered. Because time was the selecting factor, the groups were quite varied in their composition. Each contained teachers from a wide range of disciplinary backgrounds, teaching levels, and experience.

"I'm really excited about what's happening," Don said to them. "But I think we have to make sure we get off to a good start. I want us to delay until after our next professional development day, and I'd like to spend the whole day focusing on some team-building, process-oriented activities. I don't want to co-opt the study groups by any means, but I want to show that you have my full support. I'm sure that's important. I would like to see us develop a coordinated, long-term plan, but I'm willing to allow the groups themselves to take a large part of the initiative for this. Congratulations!"

The initial day was a great success, giving the teachers a sense of being supported by the administration at the same time as they had the chance to sort out some basic issues and approaches to their work as groups. Over the months that followed, each of the four groups took on its own identity, developing particular concerns about the life of the school.

These were not only study groups but also peer support groups. As well as exploring particular concepts and materials, each teacher developed a professional growth plan. But most importantly, they learned to be able to talk with each other about teaching (Paquette 1987, 39). Rather than focusing on personalities, whether teachers or students, they became accustomed to talking about their teaching practice. This was a habit that carried over into the staff room, so that over the months there was a subtle but steady shift in conversation, away from gripes, sports, and recipes.

"You know, Lisa," George commented, "how we started out talking about cooperative learning and the value of support when you're trying out a new approach? Don't you think there's something of an irony in what's happening now? People haven't just influenced each other in the way they teach and what they teach within the same subject areas, there's been a cross-fertilization across subjects. We started out trying to get the kids to work more cooperatively, and now we find we're the ones cooperating!"

Don had noticed this too. A few years ago, he had looked at the integral units being developed by some Christian schools, and thought how impossible that would be to achieve at his own school, except of course in the elementary school, where at least some teachers had developed several unit studies. But now he wondered. Perhaps the next step would be to get his teachers into interdisciplinary teams; the correlation that was becoming more apparent in their teaching could then maybe give way to some real integrated units—and who knows, maybe real integrality somewhere down the road (Meichtry 1990, 11–12).

Collaborative Action Research

Staff development can also occur through incorporating collaborative action research into one's teaching. This is an approach that is compatible with a biblical view of knowing in many respects. It has three main features. First, it is *collaborative*, a communal approach that recognizes the contribution that can be made to understanding a situation by a group of people with different gifts and insights. It involves teachers working together and provides a practical strategy for helping teachers to break out of the isolation of their classrooms. In the Christian school, such interaction about the actual task in which teachers are engaged should be a central feature.

Second, this approach incorporates *action*. Action is not an implication or an outcome of research, it is part and parcel of it. Almost the first step taken after identifying a problem is to ask, "What action will I take to remedy it?" It thus reflects the biblical view that knowledge entails responsible action, and that it grows out of concrete experience. After implementing this action step and having set in place some procedures for observing its impact, the collaborative group provides an opportunity to reflect on the effects of that action. Reflection is used not to reach a definitive conclusion but to decide what action to take next. In other words, action research is not a commitment to one act but rather to ongoing acting.

Third, this strategy is a means of *research*. This is not the abstract, theoretical, quantitative research so often found in academic journals of education, but it is research all the same. This type of research method gets teachers involved in finding out in a careful and systematic way about what is going on in their school. It asks them not to take things for granted but to look critically at the life of their school, to frame questions about the day-to-day actions of teaching and learning. It enables them to look for answers to their questions that are not mere assertions, opinions, or prejudices but are supported by evidence and argumentation. White coats are not required; calculators and computers may come in handy but are not mandatory.

Collaborative action research is an ongoing process designed and carried out by practicing teachers. It is an approach that accepts "the wisdom of practice" (Shulman 1987). It credits the teacher with a craftsperson's understanding, a knowledge gained on the job. It says that this knowledge counts for something, that it is not only the knowledge of general principles and scientific laws that is of value but also the knowledge of particular situations, of how to act appropriately in response to concrete problems.

The first meeting of a group of teachers beginning a process of collaborative action research might look something like this:

Mike: Thanks for being willing to work with me in this group. I'm not quite sure what's going to come out of it but I was at this in-service the other day and they had a group demonstrate this approach to us and I thought, why not, it looks to me as though I could learn some useful things about my teaching. And who knows, it might be good for all of us. Anyway, let's open in prayer. [He commits the time to the Lord, asking for wisdom and a readiness to be guided by the Word and the Spirit.]

Jean: Well, Mike, where do we start? Is there any specific problem you wished us to talk about?

Mike: Well, it's important that we find a theme that we feel comfortable about exploring together. Before we actually get started on the steps that are talked about on the sheet I gave you, we need to do some preplanning. Some of the material I've got gives us some clues about deciding what we should work on but I thought we might just as well start by talking about something that we've been looking at as a staff anyway and not making much progress on.

Tom: You mean grade eight? What can we do about them? It's just the stage of life they're at. The best we can do is wait until they grow out of it. I reckon school at this stage is mainly designed to keep them off the streets. Isn't there research that suggests that they're brain dead at this stage, anyway?

Sue: Very funny, Tom—that's a plateau in brain growth, which is not quite the same thing. I must say that you've got a pretty negative attitude. I know they've been giving you a rough time in math but I must say I expected a bit more of you.

Mike: There are a few boys in that class who are so powerful, they just seem to lead everyone into mischief. The peer pressure is incredible. Plus they speak a different language from normal people—I can't understand them most of the time. And the music they listen to—I don't know how any Christian kids could get away with the sort of rubbish they play. And they're just not interested in the important things in life, you know, Shakespeare and that. Sure, some of them pray in devotions and there are a few kids who are really spiritual in some areas of their lives. But wow! it certainly doesn't seem to carry over into the rest of what they do.

Sue: I think we have to challenge them more about being in the world but not of it. They have to learn that being a Christian means standing up for what you believe and not just going along with the group.

Jean: Well, that's a concrete suggestion, Sue. The sheet that Mike gave us said that the first thing we have to do is to plan an action that will improve the situation. So, what do we actually do to put Sue's idea into effect?

Frank: I think before we do that, we have to clarify the problem a bit more. There is no point in taking any action until we have decided what is the nature of the problem we are trying to address. We have to focus in, some-how. And I think we have to think carefully about any ideas or values we have here that might not reflect a biblical way of looking at the world. Otherwise we're going to be off on the wrong track right from the start.

Mike: Well, you know, I think you've got a point. I was reading a little book by Fowler (1988) the other day about the school as a community. One of the things it talks about at the start is whether our largely negative view of the peer group might not be rather mixed up. The argument is that we are too individualistic in Western culture, and so we emphasize the importance of the individual breaking away from the peer group, taking a stand. It talked about how the Bible sees community as an equally basic dimension of life as individuality, and that we should think of turning the peer group to positive ends rather than trying to dismantle it or confront it head on.

Jean: Well, it seems to me that we have reached a bit of clarity here. We're talking about peer pressure and whether we might be able to think of it in positive and not only negative terms, in terms of grace as well as of sin. It seems that now the challenge would be to plan a step of action that might begin to turn the peer group in a more positive direction. Maybe we should actually get them working more in groups instead of trying to keep them apart.

Tom: I think we need to know more about how the class actually behaves and what Mike does with them now. There's no way that I would be happy about leaving them on their own to work in groups—there'd be a riot! I've got a syllabus to get through. It might be okay in English, but there's material that just has to be covered in math.

Frank: I agree, Tom, I'd like to hold back a little before we make any decisions. But perhaps my concern is a little bit different. We really have to be sure that we're not just involved in rational problem-solving here and merely taking lots of things for granted. Are the questions we're asking biblically-informed questions? What's a Christian approach to the issues?

Tom: Yes, you're right, Frank, but there's one other thing I want to say that I think is relevant. I really do have a problem with this whole idea of groups. It seems to me that it takes insufficient account of individual responsibility. I think the Bible is quite clear on this. Changing the structure of an institution doesn't deal with changing hearts. As Jesus said, it's out of the heart that the issues of life arise.

Sue: Okay, so the questions we should be asking ought to revolve around things like our understanding of the nature of Christian community, our view of individual freedom and responsibility in Christ, the way we look at the roles of teacher and student, and the implications of believing that teenagers are also created in the image of God and that they are called to serve him here and now.

Frank: Yeah, we know that we are called to lead kids in responsive discipleship, but we need to work out how much of their teen culture is unfaithful to the gospel and how much of it we just have trouble with because our culture is different. I mean, we also know that they are going to grow out of it. I was standing on the seat screaming at the Beatles when I was thirteen and look at me now—as solemn and sober as a church mouse.

Tom (facetiously): Now, let's not get carried away, Frank. You can't be sure what long-lasting influence that nasty experience has had on you and besides, some of your behavior does tend to be a little outrageous! But I'll go along with the general point. The challenge still is how do we deal positively with these kids now, so that school isn't a complete waste of time for them and for us.

Jean: All right, so from a biblical point of view, working communally, cooperatively, is an important thing to do. And what we have is a very strong group culture that might go too far toward swallowing up the individual but which we should perhaps harness for good rather than regarding it as an enemy. I mean, we believe that Christ is able to bring "substantial healing" to all areas of life, don't we, so let's see what hope there is for sanctification of the peer group.

Mike: I'll give it to you, Jean, when you get going, there's no stopping you! But I'm ready to suggest an action step that I think might be helpful. Has anyone heard of "jigsaw groups"? It's a cooperative learning strategy. What if we did get them to work on assigned tasks in small groups? We'd be acknowledging that there is validity in the peer group but we'd be introducing them to some strategies that would minimize the negative features and accentuate the positive—how does that song go?

Tom: I'm afraid I've got to put in my two bits' worth again. I think groups are often a way of kids avoiding their individual responsibilities. They just hide in the crowd. Sometimes they're just lazy and refuse to pull their weight. Sometimes they have their own learning difficulties that need individualized attention. And sometimes—and you've got to admit this—they're just plain rebellious and need to be disciplined. I don't think we should get too rosy-eyed about any particular method—we've got to remember that we're dealing with sinners who need to be led very firmly a lot of the time. Kids need to be taught, and not just sit around in groups having a warm, fuzzy time.

Mike: I concede a lot of what you're saying, Tom. Thanks for bringing us back to that. But I certainly don't mean those groups where one or two people do all the work and the others just go along for the ride. I mean carefully planned tasks assigned so that each person in the group has a vital part to play in its completion: each one has to contribute a piece to the jigsaw if the puzzle is to be completed. Individuals are responsible for their actions but are responsible to the other members of the group—and the group as a whole has a responsibility. Teachers have to give a lot of thought to how the task is set up and that the right materials are prepared and they have to keep an eye on what goes on all the way. It can actually put a lot more pressure on teachers to set up the process and require a lot more energy to monitor and guide it along the way.

Frank: I reckon we've had enough to chew on for today. I think we should knock off now and come back to this next week—my head's spinning! Still, it's been good to get our teeth into something together. What should we do to prepare for that, Mike?

Mike: Okay, Frank, fair enough, you're probably right. Well, we need to be more precise about the action step we're going to take. And we need to think about how we're going to monitor it, what sort of observation tools we're going to use. And we need to start keeping a personal journal to help us reflect on what we do in this project—we should start that right away, it will help us clarify what we've done today. I'll give you those other materials I mentioned; they should help us get clearer about what we're doing and how we should function as a group. They're not written from a Christian perspective, so we'll want to be critical of what is being said. I'll also get together some information on cooperative learning. I don't want us to get swamped with this but it would also be good if we thought a bit more about what the Scriptures have to say about community. And thanks a lot for all your input—I think we're going to find this a valuable undertaking.

Collaborative action research would provide teachers and principals in Christian schools with an opportunity for exploring different teaching methods and addressing issues that they face in a positive and constructive manner. Instead of placing blame for a problem or weakness on one person, collaborative action research enables the staff to accept mutual responsibility for examining the underlying reasons and together to develop a solution. A Christian community for learning provides the conditions in which collaborative action research can be successful. These conditions include a forum to share findings and frustrations, opportunities to learn and grow both personally and communally, time to reexamine and renew the principles that guide their teaching, collegial support through developing one another's gifts and sharing one another's difficulties, and celebrating the joys of the shalom that comes with recognizing the growth that students and teachers experience in learning.

The following steps of action research (adapted from McKay 1992) provide Christian schools with a way of addressing some of the issues that they face.

Step 1. Identify an issue, area of interest, or idea that some or all of the staff want or need to address. Two examples would be: (*a*) What do our tests say we value? (*b*) What gifts do our present program develop in students?

Step 2. Define the problem related to this issue or area of interest. An effective way to clarify the problem is to describe the differences between the current and the desired situation. For example: (*a*) Our evaluation places too strong an emphasis on recall of information. (*b*) The program we presently offer our students does not provide sufficient encouragement for the development of a diversity of gifts.

Step 3. Locate and read related information from journal articles, books, or workshops. Using both Christian and non-Christian authors become familiar with various ways of looking at this issue. (*a*) What should we evaluate? How should we evaluate? (*b*) Which gifts should our school encourage?

Step 4. Develop the questions to be dealt with in the action research project. Making the questions quite specific helps to narrow the focus for the research. (*a*) What type of questions do I ask on my test? (*b*) What gifts are valued in each course that students take?

Step 5. Develop an action plan by which to address the questions. A plan should specify which teachers and students are involved (one grade, several classes, or whole school), how long the project will take, how and when information will be gathered, when the results will be discussed, and when these results will be shared with other teachers and parents.

Step 6. Make recommendations based on the results of the project. Make specific classroom changes, and observe what happens to teaching and learning. Discuss further improvements that should be made.

Collaborative action research helps us continually reform the way in which we view the world of teaching and learning and specifically the way in which we develop ourselves as teachers. We cannot afford to take our present understanding as free of problems. Each stage of reflection leads to the formulation of another plan for action. The process emphasizes the importance of critical questioning and reflection. The contribution of different members of a school is essential, as a manifestation of the body of Christ at work in education. Teachers have to learn to listen to and understand one another. This is an essential part of the process of community-building, in a specifically educational context. It involves defining a common purpose and developing a shared language.

Staff development has the potential of building a momentum for changing Christian schools. As principals and teachers become learners themselves, they will broaden and deepen their understanding and experience of teaching for responsive discipleship. Personal and communal staff development are significant components of developing a school's vision, strengthening a community for learning, developing integral units, and reflecting on student learning. Principals and teachers involved as learners will provide the impetus for reexamining current practices and introducing new opportunities for student learning.

Questions for Discussion

1. Initiate a discussion of the ways in which personal and communal staff development could be stimulated in your school. What are the opportunities for growth for the principal and teachers?

2. Identify issues for particular grade levels and/or subject areas in your school. Determine which of these issues is of most importance and form a collegial study group to explore ways of resolving the issue.

3. Identify issues in your school that cut across grade and/or subject boundaries. Determine which of these issues is of highest priority. Form a collaborative action research group of teachers (and include parents if possible) to investigate one or more of these issues.

4. Using the dialogue about collaborative action research discuss the following:

   a. What do you think of the way the group tackled the task? What contribution would you have made to their deliberations? Where do you think they went off the rails?

   b. How significant is biblical input in helping to define the problem? What principles and procedures were at work in the group? How would you articulate the appropriate principles and procedures?

   c. What might happen when the group's plan is implemented? How would you further refine the action step? What methods of monitoring would you suggest? What problems do you foresee?

Recommended Reading

1. Kemmis, S., and Mc Taggart, R., eds. *The action research planner.* 1988.
   Strategies for action research in school settings. A book to be read carefully because of its view of knowledge and authority.

2. Johnson, D. W., and Johnson, R. 1989. *Leading the cooperative school.*
   A valuable reference for developing collegial study groups to build a collaborative learning community.

3. Joyce, B., ed. 1990. *Changing school culture through staff development.*
   A collection of articles on recent staff development practices.

4. Louks-Horsely, S., et al. 1987. *Continuing to learn: A guidebook for teacher development.*
   A comprehensive and concise description of approaches to staff development.

13

Recommendations for Change

A Vision with a Task embraces a program of learning for responsive discipleship. To help Christian schools with that task, we have a number of recommendations to make for the implementation of this program.

We believe that Christian schools should function as covenant communities. We often use the term *schools* when indicating who should implement these recommendations. While individuals with specific tasks will work on certain aspects of a recommendation, the school community as a whole must take responsibility for its overall implementation.

We recommend:

1. That Christian schools discuss the nature and task of learning for responsive discipleship in terms of how they can encourage their students to unwrap gifts, share joys and bear each other's burdens, and seek shalom within and outside the school.

2. That, at least once every five years, Christian schools analyze the social factors affecting the school, both those in the surrounding culture and those within the supporting community.

   a. That national and regional Christian school organizations develop materials that provide local school communities with procedures and materials for such investigation and scrutiny.

b. That local schools regularly collect data on social trends within their supporting community.

c. That local schools appoint an ad hoc committee of students, parents, teachers, and education committee and board members to analyze social changes (e.g., family patterns and problems, use of leisure time, effect of media on family life) and make recommendations to the school society.

d. That Christian schools determine and implement desirable structural and program changes that take into account relevant social factors.

3. That Christian schools compose a mission statement and corresponding objectives that unpack and clarify that statement, and revise these at least once every five years.

a. That the board, principal, and teachers regularly articulate the school's mission statement and objectives so that the school's guiding vision is clear to students and parents.

b. That schools determine whether proposed policies are compatible with their mission, and set priorities for new initiatives on the basis of the school's vision as enunciated in its mission statement.

c. That the board, committees, and staff consistently use the school's mission statement and objectives as a framework for making all decisions, including those with respect to program and instruction, evaluation, and enrollment.

4. That schools, in order to realize their vision, implement one- to two-week planning sessions by teachers prior to the beginning of classes, with the agenda being set on the basis of the school's mission statement, input from graduating and other students, and end-of-year teacher grade-level or department meetings.

5. That schools implement a system of teacher peer associates whereby pairs of colleagues support each other in prayer, by active listening, through assisting and encouraging each other, and by asking questions that require the exercise of judgment and discernment. Schools would do well to provide peer associates with time to visit each other's classes to help analyze each other's teaching, and pair new teachers with experienced ones.

6. That schools encourage mutual love, compassion, and respect among students, teachers, parents, and board and committee members so that all can fulfill their respective callings.

a. That schools promote and practice honest, forthright, and respectful communication.

b. That schools regularly affirm and celebrate their vision with parents, teachers, and students.

c. That schools, recognizing that God grants leadership and authority for service, enable all involved in the school to exercise their legitimate authority to make decisions in their areas of calling.

7. That schools include learning experiences focusing on ways of knowing traditionally underemphasized in school programs, such as the spiritual, ethical, aesthetic, spatial, intrapersonal, and interpersonal.

a. That schools offer learning experiences appropriate for diverse learning styles.

b. That schools plan their program and teaching to counter gender biases in current structures and practices.

c. That schools develop collaborative group approaches involving students of different abilities and avoid grouping or streaming students by ability (except by self-selection in specialized studies in senior high school grades).

d. That schools include experiences throughout their program that help students in their journey of faith at each level of development.

8. That schools implement an integral curriculum in which knowledge entails a personal response of insight and service.

a. That schools plan learning activities that involve a rhythm of immersion in experience, withdrawal to focus on a problem or phenomena in particular ways, and return to the experiential context to apply their deepened knowledge in new ways.

b. That schools enculture students in our Christian and common human heritage and enable them to experience the awe and wonder of God's creation, by including relevant and challenging curriculum content that the students imaginatively engage with and apply.

c. That schools undertake curriculum planning in schools communally and systematically under the leadership of a school-based curriculum coordinator.

d. That schools schedule weekly periods used solely for staff curriculum planning (e.g., from 2:30–4:00 P.M. on Wednesdays).

9. That schools develop structures that facilitate implementation of the school's vision.

   a. That schools broaden their enrollment base and work toward racial, cultural, and academic diversity among students, teachers, and board members.

   b. That the curriculum rely less on one-per-student textbooks and more on a variety of resources.

   c. That student service projects become a regular and coherent part of the school curriculum.

   d. That schools organize the curriculum at the elementary level and the foundational core at the middle and high school levels using mainly integral units, gradually increasing the proportion of specialized studies as students progress through the grades.

   e. That large schools, in order to build a sense of community and belonging, structure themselves into divisions or "houses," with a team of four to six teachers being responsible for planning and implementing the curriculum for each house.

   f. That schools change their calendars to allow for increased time for student learning, and staff development and planning. Below is one possible arrangement for the 1993–94 school year that would include 187–189 instructional days (depending on local holidays) and 18 staff planning days:

Aug. 16–24	Staff development, team planning, individual preparation (7 days)
Aug. 25–Oct. 15	36 instructional days
Oct. 18–22	Student break; parent-teacher-student conferences; teachers' conventions, staff planning
Oct. 25–Dec. 17	38 instructional days
Dec. 20–Dec. 31	Christmas vacation
Jan. 3–Feb. 25	39 instructional days
Feb. 28–Mar. 4	Student break; staff work on report cards and curriculum planning
Mar. 7–Apr. 29	38 instructional days
May 2–May 6	Spring vacation
May 9–June 29	36 instructional days
June 30	Year-end staff planning and wrap-up

This calendar assumes that teachers, as part of their contract, will attend all days set aside for planning, and that boards and teachers will adjust their contracts accordingly. Courses and institutes would be scheduled during July.

10. That the integral units focus on areas that have creational integrity and are rich in meaning, and that such units include:

   a. a consideration of God's intention for the area being studied, how this purpose has been distorted by sin and the avenues by which we may hope to bring healing and reconciliation;

   b. an investigation, within the context of Christian values, of pertinent issues addressed at the appropriate level;

   c. the posing of problems (e.g., spiritual, ethical, social, stewardship, aesthetic, kinesthetic, and technological) by teachers and students that leads to the making of decisions in real-life contexts;

   d. learning experiences for students with different abilities and interests;

   e. content and activities that deal with student questions and concerns;

   f. skills that are developed as an integral part of the unit.

11. That schools use their mission statement and objectives to formulate principles for student assessment and evaluation.

   a. That schools broaden their range of assessment and evaluation procedures to include, for example, portfolios of student work, informal observation on the basis of specified criteria, performance tasks, student self-evaluation, and exhibitions.

   b. That schools, on the basis of the principles delineated, consider the extent to which they can replace standardized tests and grades with more formative and informative assessment procedures.

12. That Christian school boards require teachers to pursue regular professional development.

   a. That boards support this by providing time and finances.

   b. That schools consider using strategies such as study groups and collaborative action research as means of sustaining this program of staff development.

Bibliography

The AAUW report: How schools shortchange girls. 1991. Wellesley College Center for Research on Women. P. O. Box 251, Annapolis Junction, Md.

Adler, M. 1984. *The Paideia proposal.* New York: Macmillan.

Andersen, W. E. 1989. The outcomes of community building. *Journal of Christian Education* 95 (June): 23–31.

Apple, M., and Smith-Christian, L. 1991. *The politics of the textbook.* New York and London: Routledge.

Archbald, D. S., and Newmann, F. M. 1988. *Beyond standardized testing: Assessing authentic academic achievement in the secondary school.* Reston, Va.: National Association of Secondary School Principals.

Arter, J. A. 1990. *Using portfolios in instruction and assessment.* Portland, Ore.: Northwest Regional Educational Laboratory.

Australia, Department of Employment, Education, and Training. 1988. *Teachers learning: Improving Australian schools through inservice teacher training and development—The report of the inservice teacher education project.* Canberra: Australian Government Publishing Office.

Baird, J., and Mitchell, I., eds. 1987. *Improving the quality of teaching and learning: An Australian case study—The PEEL Project.* Melbourne: Monash University Printery.

Barker, J. A. 1991. *Paradigms.* Keynote Address. National Staff Development Council Conference. St. Louis.

Barth, R. S. 1988. School: A community of leaders. In *Building a professional culture in schools,* ed. A. Liberman, 129–47. New York: Teachers College Press.

———. 1990. *Improving schools from within: Teachers, parents, and principals can make a difference.* San Francisco: Jossey-Bass.

Beane, J. 1992. Turning the floor over: Reflections on a middle school curriculum. *Middle School Journal* 23: 34–40.

———. 1990. *From rhetoric to reality.* Columbus: National Middle School Association.

Beck, R. H., Copa, G. H., and Pease, V. H. 1991. Vocational and academic teachers work together. *Educational Leadership* 49 (2): 29–31.

Bellah, R., et al. 1985. *Habits of the heart: Individualism and commitment in American life.* Berkeley: University of California Press.

Benne, K. D. 1990. *The task of post contemporary education: Essays in behalf of a human future.* New York: Teacher College Press.

Bennett, W. 1986. *What works: Research about reading and learning.* United States Department of Education.

Berger, E. H. 1991. *Parents as partners in education: The school and home working together.* New York: Macmillan.

Berkson, W., and Wettersten, J. 1984. *Learning from error: Karl Popper's psychology of learning.* La Salle, Ill.: Open Court.

Blomberg, D. 1980a. Toward a Christian theory of knowledge. In *No icing on the cake,* ed. J. Mechielsen, 41–59. Melbourne: Brookes-Hall.

———. 1980b. Curriculum guidelines for the Christian school. In *No icing on the cake,* 111–22. Melbourne: Brookes-Hall.

———. 1991. The integral curriculum. *Christian Educators Journal* 31 (2): 6–13.

Boerman, V. 1975. Making the square a triangle. *Calvin Christian School Newsletter* 14 (3): 1, 3.

Bowers, C. A. 1987. *Elements of a post-liberal theory of education.* New York: Teachers College Press.

Brandt, Ron. 1992. On rethinking leadership: A conversation with Tom Sergiovanni. *Educational Leadership* 49 (5): 46–49.

Bricker, D. C. 1989. *Classroom life as civic education: Individual achievement and student cooperation in schools.* New York: Teachers College Press.

Caine, R. N., and Caine, G. 1991. *Teaching and the human brain.* Alexandria, Va.: Association for Supervision and Curriculum Development.

Carbo, M., Dunn, R., and Dunn, K. 1986. *Teaching students to read through their individual learning styles.* Englewood Cliffs, N.J.: Prentice-Hall.

Castro, J. 1992. The new frugality. *Time,* 6 Jan., 41.

Clark, E. 1989. *The want makers/The world of advertising: How they make you buy.* New York: Viking Penguin.

Cohen, P. A., Kulik, J. A., and Kulik, C-L. C. 1982. Educational outcomes of tutoring: A meta-analysis of findings. *American Educational Research Journal* 19 (2): 237–48.

Coles, R. 1987. *The moral life of children.* Boston: Houghton Mifflin.

———. 1988. *Times of surrender: selected literary essays.* Iowa City, Iowa: University of Iowa Press.

Coles, R., and Genevie, L. 1990. The moral life of America's school children. *Teacher* 108: 43–49.

Cooper, J. 1986. The changing face of truth. In *Orthodoxy and orthopraxis in the Reformed community today,* ed. J. Bolt, 33–58. Jordan Station, Ont.: Paideia.

Cuban, L. 1987. Constancy and change in American classrooms (1890s to the present). Paper presented at the Inaugural Conference of the Benton Center for Curriculum and Instruction, University of Chicago.

DeBoer, P. P. 1989. *The wisdom of practice: Studies of teaching in Christian elementary and middle schools.* Lanham, Md.: University Press of America.

de Moor, A. 1992. *Living in hope.* Grand Rapids: Christian Schools International.

DeWitt, Calvin B., ed. 1991. *The environment and the Christian: What can we learn from the New Testament?* Grand Rapids: Baker.

Dillon, R. F., and Sternberg, R. F., eds. 1987. *Cognition and instruction.* Orlando, Fla.: Academic Press.

Dooyeweerd, H. 1969. *A new critique of theoretical thought.* 4 vols. Trans. D. H. Freeman, W. S. Young, and H. de Jongste. Philadelphia: Presbyterian and Reformed.

Dordt College. 1979. *The educational task of Dordt College.* Sioux Center, Iowa.

Dorner, S. 1990. The traditional family as a source of distorted gender relations. Paper presented to the Calvin Center for Christian Scholarship, Grand Rapids, Mich.

Douglas, M. 1975. *Implicit Meanings.* London: Routledge and Kegan Paul.

Dunn, J. 1985. *Life at the sacred heart.* Newton, Mass.: Network of Sacred Heart Schools.

Earl, T. 1987. *The art and craft of course design.* London: Kogan Page Ltd. and New York: Nichols Publishing Company.

Egan, K. 1986. *Teaching as story telling: An alternative approach to teaching and curriculum in the elementary school.* Chicago: University of Chicago Press.

———. 1988. *Primary understanding: Education in early childhood.* New York and London: Routledge.

———. 1990. *Romantic understanding: The development of rationality and understanding.* New York and London: Routledge.

———. 1992. *Imagination in teaching and learning.* London, Ont.: The Althouse Press and Chicago: University of Chicago Press.

Eisner, E. W. 1979. *The educational imagination: On the design and evaluation of school programs.* New York: Macmillan; London: Collier Macmillan.

———. 1982. *Cognition and curriculum: A basis for deciding what to teach.* New York and London: Longman.

———, ed. 1985. *Learning and teaching the ways of knowing.* Eighty-fourth yearbook of the National Society for the Study of Education. Chicago: University of Chicago Press.

Elbow, P. 1986. *Embracing contraries: Explorations in learning and teaching.* New York/Oxford: Oxford University Press.

Elkind, D. 1983. Teenage thinking and the curriculum. *Educational horizons* 61: 163–68.

Elliott, D., and Woodward, A., eds. 1990. *Textbooks and schooling in the United States, The eighty-ninth yearbook of the National Society for the Study of Education.* Part I. Chicago: National Society for the Study of Education.

Estes, W. K. 1982. Learning, memory, and intelligence. In *Handbook of human intelligence,* ed. R. J. Sternberg, 171–75. New York: Cambridge University Press.

Evans, A. F., Evans, R. A., and Kennedy, W. B., eds. 1987. *Pedagogies for the nonpoor.* Maryknoll, N.Y.: Orbis.

Fowler, J. 1981. *Stages of faith: The psychology of human development and the quest for meaning.* San Francisco: Harper and Row.

Fowler, S. 1987. What is curriculum? In *A10 study guide: Introduction to curriculum studies I* (pp. 8–10). Melbourne: Institute for Christian Education.

———. 1988. *The school as community.* Penrith, New South Wales: St. Paul's Grammar School.

———, ed. 1990. *Christian schooling: Education for freedom.* Potchefstroom, South Africa: Potchefstroom University for Christian Higher Education.

Freire, P. 1972. *Pedagogy of the oppressed.* Trans. M. B. Ramos. New York: Continuum.

Fullan, M. G. 1992. Visions that Blind. *Educational Leadership* 49 (February): 19–20.

———. 1990. Staff development, innovation, and institutional development. In *Changing school culture through staff development.* Association for Supervision and Curriculum Development Yearbook. Ed. B. Joyce, 3–25. Alexandria, Va.: Association for Supervision and Curriculum Development.

———. 1982. *The meaning of educational change.* Toronto, Ont.: Ontario Institute for Studies in Education Press.

Fullan, M. G., et al. 1990. Linking classroom and school improvement. *Educational Leadership* 47 (May): 13–19.

Gardner, H. 1983. *Frames of mind: The theory of multiple intelligences.* New York: Basic Books.

Garmston, R. J., and Eblen, D. R. 1988. Visions, decisions, and results: Changing school culture through staff development. *Journal of Staff Development* 9 (2): 22–28.

Gesch, C., and the students of Bulkley Valley Christian High School. 1991. *Aspects of a worldview.* Smithers, British Columbia: Bulkley Valley Christian High School.

Glatthorn, A. A. 1987. *Curriculum leadership.* Glenview, Ill.: Scott Foresman.

Glenn, C. L., Jr. 1988. *The myth of the common school.* Amherst, Mass.: University of Massachusetts Press.

Good, R. 1982. How teachers' expectations affect results. *American Education* 18 (10): 25–32.

Good, R., and Smith, M. 1987. How do we make students better problem solvers? *Science Teacher* 54: 31–36.

Goodlad, J. I. 1984. *A place called school: Prospects for the future.* New York: McGraw-Hill.

Groome, T. 1980. *Christian Religious Education.* San Francisco: Harper and Collins.

Hamlyn, D. W. 1967. The logical and psychological aspects of learning. In *The Concept of Education,* ed. R. S. Peters, 24–43. London: Routledge and Kegan Paul.

Hekman, B. 1991. The Christian school, a caring community. *Christian Educators Journal* 69 (5): 22–24.

Hollaar, L. 1991. *Re-visioning and shared values: An independent school approach.* Paper presented at the School Improvement Processes: Re-thinking Our Experiences Conference, The Ontario Institute for Studies in Education.

Holmes, M., and Wynne, E. A. 1989. *Making the school an effective community: Belief, practice and theory in school administration.* New York: The Falmer Press/Ontario Institute for Studies in Education Press.

Hyde, J. S. 1981. How large are cognitive gender differences? *American Psychologist* 36: 892–901.

Institute for Christian Education. 1990. *Handbook.* Melbourne, Australia.

Johnson, D. W., and Johnson, R. 1989. *Leading the cooperative school.* Boston: Allyn and Bacon.

Joyce, B., ed. 1990. *Changing school culture through staff development.* Association for Supervision and Curriculum Development Yearbook. Alexandria, Va.: Association for Supervision and Curriculum Development.

Joyce, B., and Showers, B. 1981. The coaching of teaching: Ensuring transfer from training. Paper, Booksend Laboratories.

Joyce, B. R., Hersh, R. H., and McKibbin, M. 1983. *The structure of school improvement.* New York and London: Longman.

Joyce, B., and Weil, M. 1980. *Models of teaching.* 2d ed. Englewood Cliffs, N.J.: Prentice-Hall.

Kemmis, S., and McTaggart, R., eds. 1988. *The action research planner.* 3d ed. Waurn Ponds, Victoria: Deakin University Press.

Kidd, S. M. 1987. *God's joyful surprise: Finding yourself loved.* San Francisco: Harper and Row.

————. 1990. *When the heart waits.* San Francisco: Harper and Row.

Kirkpatrick, F. G. 1986. *Community: A trinity of models.* Washington, D.C.: Georgetown University Press.

Kohn, A. 1986. *No contest: The case against competition.* Boston: Houghton Mifflin.

Kolb, D. 1984. *Experiential learning: Experience as the source of learning and development.* Englewood Cliffs: N.J.: Prentice-Hall.

Kooy, M. A. n.d. Questioning classroom questioning. *Journal of Learning about Learning.* Forthcoming.

Korten, D. C. 1990. *Getting to the 21st Century.* West Hartford, Conn: Kumarian Press.

Kuhn, T. S. 1970. *The structure of scientific revolutions.* 2d ed. International Encyclopedia of Unified Science, vol. 2. Chicago: The University of Chicago Press.

Kulik, J. A., and Kulik, C. L. 1984. Effects of accelerated instruction on students. *Review of Educational Research* 54: 409–26.

Lapp, D., Flood, J., and Farnan, N. 1989. *Content area reading and learning: Instructional strategies.* Englewood Cliffs, N.J.: Prentice-Hall.

Levy, J. 1985. Right brain, left brain: Fact and fiction. *Psychology Today* 19 (May): 38.

Lewis, C. S. 1943. *The abolition of man.* London: Geoffrey Bles.

Lieberman, A., ed. 1990. *Schools as collaborative cultures: Creating the future now.* School development and the management of change series, vol. 3. New York, Philadelphia, and London: The Falmer Press.

Lieberman, A., and Miller, L. 1984. *Teachers, their world and their work.* Alexandria, Va.: Association for Supervision and Curriculum Development.

Lightfoot, S. L. 1978. *Worlds apart: Relationships between families and schools.* New York: Basic Books.

Little, J. W. 1982. Norms of collegiality and experimentation: Workplace conditions of school success. *American Educational Research Journal* 19 (3): 325–40.

————. 1990. The persistence of privacy: Autonomy and initiative in teachers' professional relations. *Teachers College Record* 91 (4): 509–36.

Look around. Society for Christian Schools in British Columbia. 7600 Glover Road, Langley, BC V3 6H4.

Loucks-Horsley, S., et al. 1987. *Continuing to learn: A guidebook for teacher development.* Regional Laboratory for Educational Improvement of the Northeast Islands and the National Staff Development Council.

Luke, C., de Castell, S., and Luke, A. 1989. Beyond criticism: The authority of the school textbook. In *Language, authority and criticism: Reading on the school textbook,* eds. S. de Castell, C. Luke, and A. Luke, 89–102. Philadelphia and London: The Falmer Press.

MacMurray, J. 1969. *The self as agent.* London: Faber and Faber.

MacRae-Campbell, I. 1991. How to start a revoluton at your school. *In Context* 27: 56–59.

McCarthy, B. 1981. *The 4MAT system: teaching to learning styles with right/left mode techniques.* 2d ed. Barrington, Ill.: Excel.

McCarthy, R. M., et al. 1982. *Disestablishment a second time: Genuine pluralism for American schools.* Grand Rapids: Christian University Press.

McDonald, J., and Elias, P. 1980. *Study of induction programs for teachers.* Vols. 1–4. Final report to the National Institute of Education. Princeton, N.J.: Educational Testing Service.

McDonough, L. 1991. Middle level curriculum: The search for self and social meaning. *Middle School Journal* 23 (2): 29–35.

McKay, J. A. 1992. Professional development through action research. *Journal of Staff Development* 13 (1): 18–21.

McKeachie, W. J. 1986. *Teaching and learning in the college classroom: A review of the recent literature.* Ann Arbor: University of Michigan.

McNeil, L. M. 1986. *Contradictions of control: School structure and school knowledge.* New York and London: Routledge and Kegan Paul.

Manzo, A., and Manzo, U. 1990. *Content area reading.* Columbus: Merrill.

Manzo, A. V. 1975. Guided reading procedure. *Journal of Reading* 18: 287–91.

Maritain, J. [1943] 1978. *Education at the crossroads.* Reprint. New Haven: Yale University Press.

Marty, M. E. 1991a. *Context,* 15 June.

———. 1991b. *Context.* 23, 20, November 15.

Meade, J. 1990. Introduction to Coles, R., and Genevie, L., *The moral life of America's schoolchildren. Teachers* 108 (March): 39–41.

Meichtry, Y. J. 1990. Teacher collaboration: The effects of interdisciplinary teaming on teacher interactions and classroom practices. Paper presented at the 12th Annual Meeting of the Mid-West Educational Research Association, Chicago, 19 Oct.

Miringoff, M. 1992. Quotables. *Chicago Tribune,* 14 January, 18.

Mitchell, B., and Cunningham, L. L., eds. 1990. *Educational leadership and changing contexts of families, communities, and schools.* Eighty-ninth Yearbook of the National Society for the Study of Education, part II, Chicago.

Monsma, S., ed. 1986. *Responsible technology: A Christian perspective.* Grand Rapids: Eerdmans.

Mulder, C. T. 1990. Biblical leadership in Christian organizations. *Faculty Dialogue* 13 (Winter): 79–103.

Newmann, F. M. 1991. Linking restructuring to authentic student achievement. *Phi Delta Kappan* 72 (6): 458–63.

Noddings, N. 1984. Moral Education. In *Caring: A feminine approach to ethics and moral education*, 171–201. Berkeley: University of California Press.

Nozick, R. 1989. *The examined life: Philosophical meditations.* New York: Simon and Schuster.

Oakes, J. 1985. *Keeping track: How schools structure inequality.* New Haven: Yale University Press.

———. 1991. Can tracking research influence school practice? Paper presented at the meetings of the American Educational Research Association, Chicago.

Oakeshott, M. 1966. *Experience and its modes.* Cambridge: Cambridge University Press.

Odell, S. J. 1989. Developing support programs for beginning teachers. In *Assisting the beginning teacher*, ed. L. Huling-Austin et al., 19–38. Reston, Va.: Association of Teacher Educators.

Oosterhuis, A. 1988. An experimental approach to cross-cultural education. *Christian Educators Journal* 27 (3): 24–25.

Oppewal, D. 1984. Biblical knowing and classroom methodology. In *Christian approaches to learning theory*, ed. N. de Jong, 47–67. Lanham, Md.: University Press of America.

———. 1985. *Biblical knowing and teaching.* Grand Rapids: Calvin College.

Palmer, P. J. 1983. *To know as we are known: A spirituality of education.* San Francisco: Harper and Row.

———. 1989. Learning is the thing for you: Renewing the vitality of religious education. *Weavings* 4 (5): 6–19.

———. 1990. *The active life: Wisdom for work, creativity, and caring.* New York: Harper Collins.

Paquette, M. 1987. Voluntary collegial support groups for teachers. *Educational Leadership.* 45 (3): 36–39.

Peck, M.S. 1987. *The different drum: Community-making and peace.* San Francisco: Harper and Row.

Perrone, V., ed. 1991. *Expanding student assessment.* Alexandria, Va.: Association for Supervision and Curriculum Development.

Perry, W. G. 1970. *Forms of intellectual and ethical development in the college years: A scheme.* New York: Holt, Rinehart, and Winston.

Plantinga, C., Jr. 1990. Educating for shalom. *Dialogue* (March): 24–26. Grand Rapids: Calvin College.

Postman, N. 1979. *Teaching as a conserving activity.* New York: Delacorte.

———. 1985. *Amusing ourselves to death: Public discourse in the age of show business.* New York: Viking Penguin.

Potok, C. 1990. *The gift of Asher Lev.* New York: Alfred A. Knopf.

Powell, A. G., E. Farrar, and D. K. Cohen. 1985. *The shopping mall high school: Winners and losers in the educational marketplace.* Boston: Houghton Mifflin.

Purpel, D. 1989. *The moral and spiritual crisis in education.* Granby, Mass.: Bergin and Garvey.

Ratzki, A., and Fisher, A. 1989–90. Life in a restructured school. *Educational Leadership* 47 (4): 46–51.

Readence, J. E., Bean, T. W., and Baldwin, R. S. 1992. *Content area reading: An integrated approach.* 4th ed. Dubuque, Iowa: Kendall Hunt Publishing Company.

Rief, L. 1990. Finding the value in evaluation: Self-assessment in a middle school classroom. *Educational Leadership* 47 (March): 24–29.

Roques, M. 1989. *Curriculum unmasked.* Eastbourne, Sussex: Monarch.

Rosenberg, M. B. 1968. *Diagnostic teaching.* Seattle: Special Child Publications.

Rosenthal, R. 1974. *On the social psychology of the self-fulfilling prophecy: Further evidence for pygmalion effects and their mediating mechanisms.* New York: MSS Modular Publications.

Runner, H. E. 1970. *The relation of the Bible to learning.* 3d ed. Toronto: Wedge.

Rutherford, W. L. 1985. Principals as effective leaders. *Phi Delta Kappan* 67 (1): 31–34.

Saphier, J., and King, M. 1985. Good seeds grow in strong cultures. *Educational Leadership* 42 (6): 67–74.

Sapir, E. 1949. *Culture, language and personality.* Berkeley: University of California Press.

Sarason, S. B. 1990. *The predictable failure of educational reform: Can we change course before it's too late?* San Francisco: Jossey-Bass.

Schmemann, A. 1973. *For the life of the world; sacraments and orthodoxy.* Crestwood, N.Y.: St. Vladimir's Seminary Press.

Schultze, Q., et al. 1991. *Dancing in the dark: Youth, popular culture and the electronic media.* Grand Rapids: Eerdmans.

Schön, D. A. 1983. *The reflective practitioner: How professionals think in action.* New York: Basic Books.

Seerveld, C. 1980. *Rainbows for the fallen world: Aesthetic life and aesthetic task.* Toronto: Toronto Tuppence Press.

Segovia, F. F., ed. 1985. *Discipleship in the New Testament.* Philadelphia: Fortress Press.

Sergiovanni, T. J. 1992. Why we should seek substitutes for leadership. *Educational Leadership* 49 (5): 41–45.

———. 1991. *The principalship: A reflective practice perspective.* 2d ed. Boston: Allyn and Bacon.

Shavelson, R. J., and Stern, P. 1981. Research on teachers' pedagogical thoughts, judgments, decisions, and behavior. *Review of Educational Research* 51:455–98.

Shelly, J. A. 1982. *The spiritual needs of children.* Downers Grove, Ill.: InterVarsity.

Shulman, L. S. 1987. Knowledge and teaching: Foundations of the new reform. *Harvard Educational Review* 57 (1): 1–22.

Sire, J. W. 1990. *Discipleship of the mind: Learning to love God in the ways we think.* Downers Grove, Ill.: InterVarsity.

Sizer, T. R. 1985. *Horace's compromise: The dilemma of the American high school.* Boston: Houghton Mifflin.

———. 1992. *Horace's school: Redesigning the American high school.* Boston: Houghton Mifflin.

Skrtic, T. 1987. An organizational analysis of special education reform. *Counterpoint* 8 (2): 15–19.

Smith, D. L. 1986. On the curriculum planning processes of teachers. *Curriculum Perspectives* 6 (2): 1–7.

Snyderman, M., and Rothman, S. 1987. Survey of expert opinion on intelligence and aptitude. *American Psychologist* 42: 137–44.

Stainback, S., and Stainback, W. 1992. *Curriculum considerations in inclusive classrooms: Facilitating learning for all students.* Baltimore, Md.: Paul H. Brookes.

Stauffer, R. 1969. *Directing reading maturity as a cognitive process.* New York: Harper and Row.

Stenhouse, L. 1975. *An introduction to curriculum research and development.* London: Heinemann Educational Books.

Stiggins, R. J., Conklin, N. F., and Bridgeford, N. J. 1986. Classroom assessment: A key to effective education. *Educational Measurement: Issues and Practice* 5 (2): 5–17.

Stob, J. 1989. *Educating for responsible service.* Grand Rapids: Christian Schools International.

Strike, K. A., Hailer, E. J., and Soltis, J. F. 1988. *The ethics of school administration.* New York: Teachers College Press.

Stronks, G. G. 1984. Experiential learning: Instructional theory or outmoded fad? *Pro Rege* 14 (1): 9–18.

———. 1990. *The Christian middle school.* Grand Rapids: Christian Schools International.

———. 1991. To see the church through their eyes. *Perspectives* 6 (10): 17–20.

Taylor, J. V. 1972. *The go-between God: The Holy Spirit and the Christian mission.* London: SCM.

The guiding principles of The Potter's House Christian School. 1991. The Potter's House Christian School, 810 Van Raalte Drive SW, Grand Rapids, Mich. 49509–1149.

Tiemstra, J. P., ed. 1990. *Reforming economics: Calvinist studies on methods and institution.* Lewiston: Edwin Mellen Press.

Tinder, G. 1989. Can we be good without God? *The Atlantic,* December, 69–85.

Tucker, G. 1987. *The faith-work connection: A practical application of Christian values in the workplace.* Toronto: Anglican Book Center.

Tyler, R. 1949. *Basic principles of curriculum and instruction.* Chicago: University of Chicago Press.

Valencia, S. 1990. A portfolio approach to classroom reading assessment: The whys, whats, and hows. *The Reading Teacher* 43 (4): 338–40.

Van Brummelen, H. 1988. *Walking with God in the classroom: Christian approaches to learning and teaching.* Burlington, Ont.: Welch.

———. 1991. The world portrayed in texts: An analysis of the content of elementary school textbooks. *Journal of Educational Thought* 25 (3): 202–21.

Van Brummelen, H., and Vriend, J. 1981. *For the love of your child . . . the Christian school.* Langley, British Columbia: Society of Christian Schools in British Columbia.

Van Dyk, J. 1985. *The beginning of wisdom: The nature and task of the Christian school.* Grand Rapids: Christian Schools International.

———. 1986–87. Teaching Christianly: What is it? Parts 1–4. *Christian Educators Journal* 26(1): 30–31; 26(2): 26–27; 26(3): 10–11; 26(4): 10–11.

Van Leeuwen, M. S. 1990. *Gender and grace: Love, work and parenting in a changing world.* Downers Grove, Ill.: InterVarsity.

Van Manen, M. 1991. *The tact of teaching: The meaning of pedagogical thoughtfulness.* Albany, N.Y.: The State University of New York Press.

Vanier, J. 1979. *Community and growth: Our pilgrimage together.* New York: Paulist.

Vitz, P. 1986. *Censorship: Evidence of bias in our children's textbooks.* Ann Arbor, Mich.: Servant.

Vryhof, S. 1992. Why is NELS:1988 important? *Christian Educators Journal* 32 (1): 14–18.

Vryhof, S., Brouwer, J., Ulstein, S., and Vander Ark, D. 1989. *Twelve affirmations: Reformed Christian schooling for the 21st century.* Grand Rapids: Baker.

Wagner, M. B. 1990. *God's schools: Choice and compromise in American society.* New Brunswick and London: Rutgers University Press.

Walker, D. F., and Soltis, J. F. 1986. *Curriculum and aims.* Thinking about education series. New York: Teachers College Press.

Walsh, B. S., and Middleton, J. R. 1984. *The transforming vision: Shaping a Christian world view.* Downers Grove, Ill.: InterVarsity.

Walters, J. A. 1979. *A long way from home.* Exeter: Paternoster.

West, S. 1993. *Educational values for school leadership.* London and Philadelphia: Kogan Page.

Westerhoff, J. H. 1976. *Will our children have faith?* Minnesota: Winston-Seabury.

Whitney, D. R. 1987. On practice and research: Confessions of an educational researcher. *Lifelong Learning* 10: 12–15.

Wiggins, G. 1989a. A true test: Toward more authentic and equitable assessment. *Phi Delta Kappan* 70 (9): 703–17.

———. 1989b. Teaching to the (authentic) test. *Educational Leadership* 46 (7): 41–47.

———. 1990. The case for authentic assessment. Digest of materials prepared for the California Assessment Program. Washington, D.C.: Office of Educational Research and Improvement, U.S. Department of Education.

Wolf, D. P. 1989. Portfolio assessment: Sampling student work. *Educational Leadership* 46 (7): 35–39.

Wolters, A. 1985. *Creation regained: Biblical basics for a reformational worldview.* Grand Rapids: Eerdmans.

Wolterstorff, N. 1976. *Reason within the bounds of religion.* Grand Rapids: Eerdmans.

———. 1985. Beyond 1984 in philosophy of Christian education. *Calvinist Contact,* 25 January, 8–9.

Index

320